ONE NIGHT IN JULY

ONE NIGHT
IN JULY

THE TRUE STORY OF THE
ROSENTHAL-BECKER MURDER CASE

Jonathan Root

Coward-McCann, Inc. NEW YORK

To my friend NIVEN BUSCH *who suggested it and for* LESLIE, *with love*

Acknowledgments

I am profoundly grateful to all those who helped in the writing of this book; to the patient and resourceful librarians at the New York Public Library, the San Francisco Public Library, and the libraries of the University of California at both Berkeley and Los Angeles; to the many friends who aided and encouraged me in numberless ways—Peter and Esther Joseph, Edward Kennedy, Thomas Parkinson, Eugene Goossen, Noel Busch, Col. Allen Griffin, Jan and Kim Stussy; to Phyllis Jackson for her enthusiasm, and to Richard Gilston for his criticism. I am especially indebted to Bernice Liebow who typed the manuscript under relentless pressure of a deadline and cheerfully corrected my mistakes.

Contents

ONE NIGHT IN JULY

1. Death at the Metropole

It was exactly eleven o'clock on the steaming night of July 15, 1912, when Herman Rosenthal, a gambler, left the New York Criminal Courts building after a mutually satisying five hours with the district attorney.

He was carrying his coat over his arm and the sides and back of his pink shirt, which bloused untidily over his belt, were dark with perspiration. Herman Rosenthal was fat. His tie hung askew around his short, thick neck; his high collar, which he had unbuttoned, was cracked and soiled. His round face, with its limp mouth, wore a beaten look.

Despite the heat, Rosenthal walked hurriedly through the dim and empty corridors of the Criminal Courts building; at the doorway he paused, looking up and down Center Street, before starting down the long flight of stairs. At the sidewalk he bought an early edition of the New York *World* from a newsboy. He glanced at it once but didn't read it. He knew what was in it. His name was still on the front page.

The streets of lower Manhattan were alive with people unable to sleep in the heat and Rosenthal expected both comfort

13

and anxiety in their presence. But he found no sign of either friend or enemy.

At Pearl Street, just south of the courthouse, he hailed a taxi and directed it uptown. He hunched in the rear seat, raising himself slightly to peer out the window as the cab lurched and joggled over the cobbled pavement. There were few cars on the street, and none at all behind him, and he knew with relief that he was not being followed. He was reprieved for the moment from his fears. The breeze that swept through the cab was refreshing but to Rosenthal it seemed so cold that he put on his coat, shivering as the clammy shirt pressed against his back. Twenty minutes later, at 42nd Street, he left the cab and walked north along Broadway. At 43d Street he turned east and headed for the Hotel Metropole midway down the block. The hotel was owned by Tammany Hall's Big Tim Sullivan and the famous Considine brothers and, although a popular gathering place for politicians, newspapermen, theatrical people, gamblers, and various members of the sporting set, it had mysteriously gone bankrupt. The Metropole was Rosenthal's favorite place and he knew most of the people in it. Immediately, his apprehension vanished.

It was almost midnight and the hotel was crowded. The only relief from the heat came from batteries of electric fans which whirred noisily and swept the bar and dining room with throbbing waves of sticky air. From a cluster of potted palms in the corner of the dining room a five-piece Hungarian band was struggling to play a new hit tune, "Oceana Roll."

With his shirt still open at the throat, his coat unbuttoned, still carrying the newspaper in his hand Rosenthal walked across the lobby, oblivious of the stares of the desk clerk and the torrent of sound and smoke billowing from the barroom entrance. As he paused in the dining room doorway, searching the room, people stopped talking to stare at him as one would stare at a ghost. Since the time he had entered the DA's office late that afternoon, word had inexplicably gone out. A murder had been arranged. Rosenthal was to die tonight. He

14

appeared to be one of the few people in New York who didn't know.

Embarrassed by his friends' stares, he stumbled forward self-consciously, his gaze fixed on a table against the far wall occupied by a fellow gambler, Christian Walker, who was known along Broadway as "Boob." Walker was a slender, balding young man with pale, effeminate hands, one of which was arched around a large cigar, his elbows resting on the table. Startled by Rosenthal's appearance, he beckoned furtively with the cigar. Rosenthal heaved himself into a chair opposite Walker and instantly the sounds of the room were intensified; the hovering whine of talk and laughter, the pulselike grinding of the fans, the weary orchestra, flailing at a waltz to which a dozen couples had begun to dance. Walker and Rosenthal were now isolated as though everybody in the room sought desperately to repudiate the knowledge of their presence. Through the swirl of harassed waiters and the ebb and flow to and from the dance floor, Rosenthal could be seen clutching intermittently at passing waiters, ordering first a succession of drinks, then a large steak which he ate hungrily. Walker sat staring, impassive, yet wondering. "Herman ate," he said later, "as if he could take it with him."

Abruptly, Rosenthal scrubbed at his mouth with a napkin. Pushing his plate away, he rose with effort from the table. Walker nodded, watching as Rosenthal shuffled across the room and out into the lobby where he bought copies of all the morning papers. He wanted to see if he was still on the front page. The *World*, competing with Hearst's *American* for headline dash and vigor, stated it starkly and darkly: GAMBLER CHARGES POLICE LIEUTENANT WAS HIS PARTNER.

"Oh, you beautiful doll," the band was playing, with a thumping rhythm, "You great big beautiful doll . . ."

When he returned to the dining room, Rosenthal took a table alone by the door, stacking the newspapers neatly in front of him. He ordered a cup of coffee and began to read. He took no notice when two uptown gambling house dealers, known only as Chick Beebe and Moe Brown, entered the room with an air of haste and sat down with Walker, refusing the attentions of a waiter. They talked earnestly, with animation, frequently glancing in an anxious way across the room at Rosenthal. They were obviously startled when a police detective named William J. File appeared in the doorway, gazed quickly about the room, his eyes lingering for an instant on the preoccupied Rosenthal directly in front of him.

Fifteen minutes later, Rosenthal was shocked from his reading by a slap on the back. His head reared up in a motion of panic, his expression relaxing when he saw the dark, grinning face of Louis Webber, a short, thin and dapper man of thirty-seven who was familiarly addressed as "Bridgie" by the patrons of his nearby poolroom on 44th Street. His nickname derived from a brief marriage to a 200-pound prostitute named Bridget. He and Rosenthal were not friendly but they treated each other to an exaggerated conviviality.

"Hello, Herman," said Webber loudly, pulling a long thin cigar from his mouth. "How's everything?"

Rosenthal answered in a vacant tone, his eyes searching Webber's face. "Fine, just fine," he said. "How's with you?" Still smiling, Webber patted Rosenthal on the shoulder and turned to leave. Rosenthal watched him go.

At exactly 1:50 A.M., a waiter with a tray of dirty dishes paused at Rosenthal's table. "There's a guy in the lobby wants to see you, Mr. Rosenthal," he said.

Rosenthal swiveled about, looking through the doorway. Leaning against it, his hands jammed into his pockets, was Harry Vallon, the hatchet-faced faro dealer, who was staring at him sullenly. Rosenthal gathered up his papers, tucking them under his arm, and walked over.

Vallon pushed away from the doorway and stood erect. "Can you come outside for a minute, Herman?" he asked, casually. Rosenthal nodded, following Vallon across the lobby.

As he stepped through the doorway and onto the sidewalk, he saw two other gamblers he knew, standing to one side, and beyond them, making a ragged arc into the street, four or five men Rosenthal did not know. In any case, he could not be sure for he was momentarily blinded by the hotel's canopy lights. Nor did he notice a gray Packard touring car, its canvas top in place, that was parked directly across the street. Rosenthal stopped, squinting into the night. Then he turned his head to the right, looking west up 43d Street. There were several people in sight, among them four policemen. One was walking leisurely toward him, his hands clasped behind his back. The other three stood near the corner of Broadway, under a street lamp, chatting.

Rosenthal looked back at the men in the street, then at the gamblers grouped together on his left. No one had moved. It was an eerie tableau but it seemed merely to puzzle him. He failed to sense that it concerned him personally; nor did he realize that—as Broadway understood the arrangements for the evening—he had already lived an hour and fifty-two minutes longer than planned.

Suddenly, from the street, a grating, unfamiliar voice called. "Over here, Herman."

Rosenthal stepped forward obediently. He was halfway across the sidewalk when a burst of shots erupted from the arc of men in the street. Two bullets hit him in the face. Two more crashed into his chest. A fifth shot missed him altogether and drilled into the woodwork of the hotel doorway. Rosenthal made no sound, no movement of protest or defense. The impact of the bullets stopped him in mid-step and he crumpled to the sidewalk, rolling over on his back. As he fell, the newspapers cascaded from beneath his arm and spread themselves fanlike about his feet.

One of the men standing with Vallon stepped over and leaned down, bending from the waist, his hands in his pockets, and studied Rosenthal's bloodied face. "Hello, Herman," he said, smiling. Then he straightened up. "Good-by, Herman," he said. Those who heard him later repeated his remarks delightedly. He was from that moment on awarded a niche of

Broadway adulation as the creator of a memorable bon mot.

The men in the street ran to the gray sedan which roared off toward Sixth Avenue. It was still gathering speed when it passed Charles Gallagher, an unemployed young cabaret singer. Without intending to, he read the car's rear license plate and, also without intending to, memorized it. "NY-41313."

Vallon and his two companions dashed across the street, backing into the darkened stage doorway of the Cohan Theater where they waited and watched in the manner of privileged witnesses to history.

The entire event up to this point had been a somewhat fascinating diversion for Thomas Coupe, the astute young desk clerk at the Elks Club next door to the Cohan Theater. Coupe had been standing in the club doorway, to escape the heat, for more than half an hour. When he saw Vallon and the two men running toward him, he ducked inside the Elks Club. The next day he withdrew his savings from the bank and fled to his native England.

The strolling policeman, momentarily stunned by the sound of the shots, was running toward the scene with the other cops close behind him.

Detective File, revolver in hand, pushed his way through the crowd that was pouring out of the hotel and reached the center of the street as the fleeing sedan turned south on Sixth Avenue. He raised his gun to fire but the street was suddenly thick with people, running and pushing each other toward the hotel. File lowered his useless .38 and stuffed it back into the holster on his hip. He turned and worked his way back through the crowd to the body. He beckoned to one of the patrolmen, Officer John Brady, and the two of them ran diagonally back across 43d Street toward Broadway, to the taxi stand in front of the Hotel Cadillac near the corner. In their haste they did not see Bridgie Webber, rooted to the sidewalk halfway down the block. Webber's face was frozen in fright and he did not move until the two officers, who were joined at the taxi stand by Police Lt. Edward Frye, had commandeered a cab and were moving down

43d Street in pursuit of the gray sedan. Then Webber walked quickly to Broadway and disappeared around the corner.

It was several minutes before police reinforcements arrived from the 47th Street station and the two policemen at the body were hard pressed to keep back the excited crowd.

"Break it up, break it up," they kept repeating, waving their arms and prodding at the crowd with their nightsticks. Finally a waiter came out of the hotel and gently covered Herman Rosenthal with a clean tablecloth. The cloth made a white patch on the sidewalk—the gravestone, as it were, of one epoch in the curious social history of our age and at the same time the surveyor's mark with which a new era began—an era in which was to be revealed the structure of crime as we know it today in its relationship to politics, to jurisprudence, and to ambition and betrayal and guilt.

2. The Meaning of the Squeal

THE MURDER broke the night's strange tension. The city, which seemed to have been waiting for the news, released its energy in correlated but far-flung activities. Telephones began to ring and men began to move furtively and desperately through the waning night on unknown errands. An ambulance from Flower Hospital trundled over to the Metropole and took Herman Rosenthal's body to the 47th Street Precinct station. The driver and stretcherman took him inside and put him on a table in the back room. The tablecloth had been removed, revealing that the left side of Herman's face wasn't there any more. Aside from this and two perforations in the middle and upper body, occasioned by gunfire, he looked much as he had in life—cowed and abused and inert. You could tell at a glance that he wasn't, and had never been, a person of importance. He was a nobody. Many nobodies, similar to him, had lain, similarly leached by violence, on that back room table of the Central Broadway Precinct, and their deaths had meant nothing at all.

Yet this death was to mean something. Seven men were to die for it—two, like Rosenthal, by murder; five in the electric chair. An eighth man, because of it, was to become Governor of New York and even for a while to be much talked of as a candidate for President of the United States—an office which eventually eluded him, estopped by other questions rising from the murder of this fat little nobody. But New York District Attorney Charles Seymour Whitman could not have known about them that night. He could only recognize in the assassination of Herman Rosenthal a sort of cue which fate, perhaps once in a lifetime, offers to a man in public office. Being a person of considerable ambition, shrewdness, energy and common sense, Charles Seymour Whitman responded with alacrity.

A murder had been arranged—arranged and carried out. And, as an act accomplished, it provided the reason for the drama which followed; a drama in which a great many actors were to take part. Some of them were talented and several were truly brilliant, but the key figure at that moment turned out to be the only actual professional in the group. The part was small. It was the sort of role which an actor's agent can persuade his client to take, in spite of its apparent obscurity, by pointing out its significance in the over-all story structure. The chances are that Charlie Gallagher wouldn't have needed any persuasion. He not only wanted a job, he wanted recognition. He had been looking for a booking as a café singer for more than a week (his last job had been at Rector's, Broadway and 44th) and he was on his way over to the Metropole to make another pitch at Jim Considine, the manager. As he turned onto 43d Street from Sixth Avenue he heard shots, then saw a gray touring car charge down the block toward him, making the corner with a shrieking skid that left black tire marks on the pavement. He looked after the car for a moment, then continued on to the Metropole, where he learned what had happened. Gallagher decided it wouldn't be the best time in the world to talk to Considine about a job. He edged through the mob and stared, flinchingly, at the body. He was still there when Lt. Frye returned from his futile chase in the taxi. Gallagher went up to him.

"I got the license number of that car," Gallagher said.

"We already have it," said Frye, pushing him aside.

Gallagher accepted the rebuff—you had to expect that sort of thing from cops, especially when they were excited. However, he showed up an hour later at the 47th Street station where he repeated what he had said to Frye.

"We got the number," the sergeant snarled.

"The car went past me—this far away," protested Gallagher, spreading his arms to show the distance. "I know I got it right."

The sergeant raised his head slowly, glaring down at the young man in front of him.

"Are you a witness?" he shouted.

"No sir," said Gallagher, meekly. "I just got the license number. I thought . . ."

The sergeant cut him off with an upraised hand. He beckoned to two patrolmen standing across the room.

Gallagher was seized, lifted bodily off the floor and carried to the rear of the station where he was pushed into a cell.

"What did I do?" he wailed, as the barred door clanged shut.

In the back room, a policeman and a reporter regarded the body.

"Who did it, Eddie?" the reporter asked.

The cop shrugged. "Nobody likes a squealer," he said.

"It doesn't look good for Becker," the reporter answered.

The cop shrugged again.

"If I was district attorney," the reporter said, "I'd be right here now."

The cop did not answer.

In his apartment at 28 Madison Avenue, near 25th Street, District Attorney Charles Seymour Whitman was getting dressed as fast as he could. The phone had been ringing for half an hour but he no longer bothered to answer it. All the calls would carry the same message. Herman Rosenthal had been murdered. The second phone call, from a reporter at *The New York Times*, had annoyed him. Did he believe Rosenthal's story? the reporter asked. Was it true that Rosenthal was to have appeared before the grand jury later today?

Whitman had contained his irritation. Yes, he said, it was true. Rosenthal was to have appeared before the grand jury.

"What about Becker?" the reporter persisted.

"I'm not prepared to make any comment regarding Mr. Rosenthal's accusations as they affect Lieutenant Becker," Whitman had replied.

"Maybe the cops killed Rosenthal," the reporter said, with a laugh, and Whitman hung up without replying. He waited a minute, then called for a cab. His wife, roused by the first phone call, had gone back to sleep and Whitman did not awaken her.

Whitman reached the 47th Street station shortly after 3 A.M. He walked past the desk sergeant, ignoring him, and on into the room where Rosenthal's body lay. There he confronted Capt. William Day who was in command of the precinct. Day had expected Whitman, but he tried to appear surprised.

Whitman motioned him to step outside.

"Captain," he said, "this man was my witness and in my temporal custody. I am here to investigate the circumstances surrounding his death. I assume I have your cooperation."

"Certainly," said Day.

Whitman issued a rapid series of requests; to talk to all the policemen who had been at the scene, to any witnesses the police might have in custody. Day appeared bewildered. He said he had just arrived and had not ascertained the facts for himself. Actually, he had been on the scene both at the Metropole and in the station house for nearly an hour. He lurched away from Whitman, toward the desk, bellowing for the sergeant. The reporter who had been standing by the doorway stepped through and touched Whitman's sleeve.

"A fellow came in here with the license number of that car," he whispered, looking furtively behind him, "and they threw him into a cell."

"What car?" Whitman demanded, turning on the reporter.

"The car the gunmen got away in. The gray Packard."

It was all very embarrassing. A misunderstanding. So many

people coming in the station, the sergeant explained, so much confused activity. A terrible crime and the police so busy. In any event, the license number of the car had already been turned in, by the police themselves, and they were tracing the owner of the car now. They would know any moment.

Captain Day apologized profusely to the shaken Gallagher. "How could you have made such a mistake, O'Brien?" he said to the sergeant, in almost mock solemnity.

Gallagher's license number, Whitman discovered, was different from the four turned in by the police. Captain Day promised to check them all.

Whitman asked if anybody had seen Lt. Becker. Nobody had.

Lieutenant Charles Becker, a member of the New York police department for twenty years, was attached to the staff of the police commissioner, in command of a special squad of fifty men specifically assigned to suppress gambling, vice and rowdyism, which meant to raid unprotected brothels and gambling halls and maintain order in those that had bought protection. Becker had held this position for a year and a half. He was a handsome, hulking, barrel-chested man, well over six feet tall, and was widely feared in the underworld for his brutality.

When Herman Rosenthal issued what the newspapers were calling his "exposure" of Becker, the lieutenant's response was a meager outburst of his wrath.

"I'm suing Mr. Rosenthal," he told reporters through clenched teeth, "for criminal libel."

On the night Rosenthal was slain, Becker attended the prize fights in Madison Square Garden. With him were two friends, Deacon Terry, a police reporter for the New York *American*, and Jack Sullivan, a thirty-five-year-old newspaper distributor and Broadway character who had proclaimed himself "king of the newsboys." His real name was Jacob Reich.

The three men, riding in Becker's chauffeur-driven limousine, went from the Garden to the St. George Hotel on East 28th Street for a few drinks, and then to 33d and Sixth Avenue where Terry caught the subway for his home in Jersey City. Becker dropped Sullivan off at 44th and Broadway and continued on uptown to his home on 159th Street. He had no sooner undressed and gotten into bed than the bedside phone rang. It was about 2:30 A.M. and Rosenthal had been dead for forty minutes.

Mrs. Becker was awake, squinting at her husband in the sudden glare from the bedside lamp. He was using that gruff tone of voice she had heard on other sudden occasions and it disturbed her. The call was from Fred Hawley, a police reporter on the New York *Sun*.

"Charlie," said Hawley, excitedly, "have you heard the news?"

"What news?" Becker asked.

"Herman Rosenthal has been killed, Charlie; shot and killed in front of the Metropole less than an hour ago."

"What are you trying to do, kid me?"

Hawley's voice was forced, high-pitched.

"No, Charlie, listen to me. Rosenthal is dead. I'm working on the story and I need a statement. It doesn't look good for you, Charlie, two days after that affidavit. For God's sake give me something. . . ."

Becker cut him off.

"Where are you?"

"At the Metropole," Hawley answered, "but they're taking Rosenthal over to 47th Street."

"Wait there," Becker ordered. "I'll be right down."

He slammed the phone down and began to dress. His wife asked him if he wanted something to eat and he said he did. As she left the room to go into the kitchen, the phone rang again. The conversation lasted only a minute and Mrs. Becker was too far away to hear what was said.

Becker met Hawley in front of the Metropole and they walked along the street, toward Broadway, talking. In his story next day in the *Sun*, Hawley quoted Becker as saying he knew nothing about Rosenthal's murder, that he was sorry it had happened "because I had the goods on Rosenthal and was about to show him up for good."

Hardly anybody believed him.

The lieutenant and Hawley walked up to the 47th Street station which was in the center of the gambling district. Becker had once been stationed there.

Reporters and policemen were clustered in little groups in front of the low, gray stone building. Oddly, none of them paid any attention to Becker as he wormed his way through the crowd and entered the station. Becker stopped just inside the doorway, his gaze sweeping along the wall to his right where two dirty, sweat-soaked drunks were slouched on a bench.

At the far end of the room, dwarfed by the high desk occupied by Sergeant O'Brien, stood Whitman, his back to Becker, talking to Captain Day. At Becker's entrance, the conversation stopped. Day's gaze shot beyond Whitman to the looming figure on the portal. Whitman spun about, defensively, like a trapped trespasser. Becker stood motionless, poised, a monarch waiting to be recognized. Defiant, a newspaperman said afterward. Was there a flicker of uncertainty on the lieutenant's face? He might have known Whitman would be there, but not so soon. His eyes engaged those of the district attorney for an instant, then fell away. In that instant, it is likely that both of these resolute men knew they had been catapulted by murder into a conflict that would be resolved only when one had destroyed the other. What they could not know was that their conflict would sharply alter the face and form of American politics forever, and give new dimensions to the criminal industry.

The contrast between them was misleading. The towering, bearlike Becker, adroit in the use of the nightstick and the rabbit punch, had commanded the field in many a battle merely by insinuating into it his fearsome presence. But the engagement this time was in a different arena, one in which Becker's opponent had already proven his skill.

Whitman's brilliance had been apparent ever since his days at Amherst and, after that, at New York University Law School.

The son of a Congregational minister, Whitman may not have been a noisy moralist, but he was an unwavering one and to this was attributed his phenomenal rise in law and politics. Only forty-four, two years older than Becker, Whitman had already served seven years as a judge and had been elected district attorney in 1909 on the strength of his assaults from the bench on Tammany Hall and the graft-soaked police department. Whitman's ambitions extended far beyond the district attorney's office and he counted on fulfilling them by continuing his exposures of the evil link between crime and politics. Rosenthal, ready, willing and able to incriminate dishonest policemen by the score, had come to him like a messenger from Providence. Now death had stopped these revelations and Whitman could only revive them by finding Rosenthal's killers; it was elementary that the pudgy little gambler had been slain to close his mouth.

This had been apparent to Becker ever since he heard the news, but seeing Whitman had made it all the more vivid in his mind. In fact, thousands of New Yorkers would soon be wondering, over the breakfast table: If Becker had not silenced Rosenthal, then who had?

This idea was, at that very moment, being suggested by extras hawked along Broadway. Becker had heard the cries. "Extra! Gambler Who Accused Cop Is Murdered!"

Without a word, Becker moved slowly past the still-staring Whitman and on into the crowded back room where the electric effect of their meeting had frozen the conversation. Oblivious of the taut silence and the apprehensive looks darting from a score of eyes, Becker went directly to the table. Stonily, he studied Rosenthal's body for an instant, then turned abruptly and walked out into the dawn.

Becker's air of supreme confidence grew increasingly ludicrous in the days that followed. Between them, the lieutenant and the gambler had jeopardized the welfare of powerful interests. Rosenthal had paid up. The "confession" for which he had been killed, and which he had finished dictating to a City

Hall stenographer just before he started uptown to his death at the Metropole, had been signed in front of three witnesses and was now safely locked in the district attorney's safe. It was not much different from the confession he gave to the New York *World*.

"The first time I met Charles Becker, a lieutenant of police in New York City, was at a ball given by the Order of Elks on 43d Street. We had a very good evening, drank very freely and became good friends.

"Our next meeting was by appointment on New Year's Eve 1912 at the Elks Club. Dinner was served for ten in our party, including Lieutenant Becker, Mrs. Becker and Mrs. Rosenthal, Mr. George Levy and daughter, Mr. Samuel Lewis, Mr. Louis Hyman.

"We drank a lot of champagne that night and later in the morning we were all pretty well under the weather. Lieutenant Becker put his arms around me and kissed me. He said, 'Anything in the world for you, Herman. I'll get up at three o'clock in the morning to do you a favor. You can have anything I've got.'

"And then he called over his three men, James White, Charles Foy and Charles Steinhart, and he introduced me to them, saying, 'This is my best pal and do anything he wants you to do.'

"We went along and we met pretty often. Sometimes we would meet at the Lafayette Turkish Baths. Other times we would meet at the Elks Club and many nights we would take an automobile ride and he told me then that he wished he could put in six months of this, he would be a rich man. He was getting hold of a lot of money. I told him then, 'Don't you think you are taking a chance by me being seen with you so often?' And he told me I don't have to fear. 'When that guy down at headquarters [Police Commissioner Waldo] puts it to me about meeting you, I'll simply tell him I was meeting you for a purpose—to get information from you.'

"He came to my office very often during the months of January and February and he used to tell me a lot of things about

28

how much money he was making and that he was making it awful fast. So I told him in the latter part of February, 'I want to borrow $1500 from you.' He said, 'You're on, on condition you'll give me 20 per cent of your place when you are open.'

"So I told him that was satisfactory to me, so he said, 'Well, you go down to my lawyer in a week or so and he will give you what you want and you sign a chattel mortgage on your household furniture,' and he said for me to bring my wife down with me for her to sign. So I pleaded with him I wouldn't do that.

" 'I don't want her to feel as though you didn't trust me with $1500 without signing over my home,' I said. He said, 'All right.' So I went down to see a lawyer he named in the St. Paul Building, and he says, 'Are you Mr. Rosenthal?'

"I said, 'Yes, I suppose you know what I am here for.' He said, 'Yes, but how do I know you are Mr. Rosenthal?' So I said, 'Why, call Charlie up.' So he called up 3100 Spring and he asked a man to connect him to the C.O. squad and this conversation followed:

"He said, 'Charlie, that party is down here.' And the lawyer said, 'Yes, he has on a brown hat and brown tie.' He said, 'All right,' and with that he rang off. Now the lawyer told me, 'You have to sign this note and these papers.' And I did as he told me, signing the note for $1500 to the order of J. Donohue. I also signed some other papers. And I got the $1500 and the lawyer said, 'It will cost you $50 now.' And I said, 'For what?' He said, 'For drawing up the papers.' So I asked him then, 'Will I tell Charlie about it?' So he said, 'I would rather not, if I were you.' Well, I said, 'All right, I'll come and see you sometime.'

"Well, I went along for a few weeks when finally Lieutenant Becker met me by appointment and told me what a hard job he has got in stalling Waldo. That Waldo wanted him to 'get' me. 'I have told Waldo that I have got my men trying to get evidence, and by doing so I kept stalling him.'

"I met him three nights after that again. He told me I must give him a raid. He said, 'You can fix it up any way you like. Get an old roulette wheel and I'll make a bluff and smash the windows. That will satisfy Waldo, I suppose.' I told him that I would not stand for it. That if he wanted to raid me he would have to get the evidence. That I would not stand for a 'frame-up.' 'Well,' he said, 'I'll do the best I can to stall him.'

"Two nights afterward he called me on the wire at my home and he told me to go and see a certain party at half past ten in the evening at 59th Street and Broadway at a place called Pabst's. When I reached Pabst's there was nobody there to meet me. Then I suspected that something was wrong, so when I came back to my home I found the windows broken, the door smashed and the patrol wagon waiting outside. I wanted to go in when policeman James White told me to get away, not to come. 'It's all right. Everything is all right. It's Charlie making the raid and it's all right.'

"So I stood across the street and waited until everything was over and went into my house, when my wife told me that Charlie said he had to make this raid to save himself. That it's all right, not to worry, 'And tell Herman to go down to the St. Paul Building tomorrow and get the papers from the lawyer. You tell him I am standing the expenses of this raid, $1500. You tell Herman that he and I are even, and I'll see him to-morrow.'

"They arrested James Fleming and Herbert Hull and charged them with being common gamblers. The next day in court Charlie told me to waive examination, that he wanted to make the raid look natural and that he would turn it out in the grand jury room. I said, 'Can I trust you?' He said, 'Why, it's all right. You can.' So I had the case adjourned to the next day to think it over. So I waived examination next day. I met Lieutenant Becker three or four nights later and hired a taxi cab from Fawley's on 45th Street and Sixth Avenue and met him by appointment at 46th Street and Sixth Avenue. He jumped into the taxi with me. We rode downtown very slowly, talking over different things and we finally had an argument. When we left we were on very bad terms.

"The last word I said to him that night, 'You know your

promise.' 'Well,' he said, 'we'll see.' About a week later the grand jury handed in an indictment against James Fleming and Herbert Hull. I called Mr. Becker on the phone that afternoon and I asked him what he meant by not living up to his promise. He told me, 'Aw, you talk too much. I don't want to talk to you at all.' I said, 'You had better consider. You know what you are doing.'

" 'Aw,' he said, 'you can go to hell.'

"I have never spoken to him since, but I tried to right this wrong and sent some people to Commissioner Waldo to explain things to him without any satisfaction. I went to District Attorney Charles Whitman and I laid the matter before him. He told me it wasn't enough evidence to indict Becker. But he said, 'I'll investigate the matter thoroughly.'

"I have repeatedly sent persons to Becker to ask him to take the policeman out of my house and he told them to tell me that as long as he was in the police department he would see that the copper was not taken out. I believe the reason Lieutenant Becker wants to drive me from New York is because I have not hesitated to tell anybody the truth regarding my own experiences with Lieutenant Becker as representing the police."

Appended to this were the names of a dozen gamblers, saloonkeepers and friends whom Rosenthal swore could and would substantiate his story, and the names of more than two dozen members of the police force and the municipal government whom Rosenthal charged were deeply involved in the graft system.

The document was interesting, of course. As evidence, however, it was worthless without corroborative testimony and after what had happened to Rosenthal, how many of these witnesses could be persuaded to talk? In fact, it was even doubtful that they could be found—now. Even Dollar John Langer, for instance, a gambling hall operator whose hatred Becker had long ago incurred, was on Rosenthal's list. But Langer had gone to Canada and he let it be known that he had no intention of returning.

31

3. Country Boy Makes Good

LIEUTENANT BECKER *wants to drive me from New York.* . . .

Herman Rosenthal dictated this odd sentence in the same flat, rambling rush as the rest of his statement. He sat back, mopping his face. The stenographer was still writing but the two witnesses—young lawyers who were members of Whitman's staff—looked at their boss for permission to withdraw. Whitman nodded, dismissing them. He looked thoughtfully at Rosenthal and wondered if the man would have sense enough to ask for protective custody. If not, should he, Whitman, offer it? It would be a generous gesture and it would serve Herman well. On the other hand—well, on the other hand—the plain fact was that with city tensions building toward a foreseeable climax, Herman was almost worth more dead than he was alive for his death would confirm his accusations, morally if not legally. Best to let him go uptown, at least for tonight, and see what happened—a calculated risk that Herman would be alive for the grand jury in the morning.

. . . *drive me from New York* . . .

It had been a curious statement. Heard in an executive office, in the presence of sane individuals, it should have had

the emptiness of a small boy's threat, or a lunatic's babbling—
yet to nobody in that room had it seemed either mad or empty.
For, if he didn't kill him first, to drive Rosenthal, his enemy,
from New York was not only the logical thing for Becker to do,
it was also precisely what he would do, and as Whitman and
everyone else at City Hall knew, it lay easily within the range
of his power.

In the tightly organized, politically unified city of New
York, Charles Becker had made himself into a one-man dis-
senting party, ruthless enough and fearless enough to defy
Tammany's hold on prostitution and gambling and to divert
into his own pockets—in defiance of age-old tradition and all
party rules—the immense flow of boodle from these sources.

Becker could, and he most certainly would, if tested, drive a
man out of New York, or out of this vale of tears, with
no qualms at all. He had become a gang lord, the first of his
kind, and he operated under the threat of a code he had personally created. He was a bad man to fool with. If, as Lord
Acton wrote, power corrupts, and absolute power corrupts absolutely, Lieutenant Charlie Becker was the most corrupt in-
dividual to be found between Albany and Ellis Island, but it
must also be admitted that he had certain qualifications for the
dark eminence he had achieved. He was quick-witted. He was
trained in brutality. He was a crooked cop, a loving husband,
and an insatiably ambitious man, far more interested in the
reality than in the show of power (he rejected promotion, clung
to the nominal rank of lieutenant long after he might have obtained any place in the police force, or the city government, for
that matter, which his whim might have chosen). He was a
grudge bearer and a torturer. He was also charming, handsome
and persuasive, a natural leader, an adroit coordinator, and an
arrogant, impossible bastard. He was, above all, a country boy
who had made good.

Callicoon Center is a scattered, picturesque farming community, wooded and hilly, at the foot of the Catskills in Sullivan
County, New York. Its 500 inhabitants, more or less, are pri-

33

marily engaged in the production of apples, Holstein dairy products and the bucolic amusement of vacationing New Yorkers who just about triple the population every summer.

Callicoon Center has not changed much, essentially, since 1855 when a young German immigrant named Conrad Becker, entranced by letters from relatives who had preceded him, arrived in town at the age of thirty with ecstatic hopes and a bankroll derived from liquidating the family farm in Bavaria. He bought a prosperous acreage from a fellow countryman, built a house on it and inside of two years felt equipped to propose marriage to a distant cousin who ultimately bore him ten children, four of them boys.

Conrad Becker's hopes never quite materialized. Farming was never as profitable as he had inferred from his relatives' propaganda and by the time his sixth child was born, in 1870, Conrad Becker had grown somewhat despairing. It was his first son and he had named him Charles. The boy was a discontented and quarrelsome youth erasing to some extent his father's delight over the fact of his birth. When Charles was eighteen he went to New York to make his fortune among more enlightened people.

Charlie Becker naturally gravitated to the German section of Manhattan, in the old Seventh Ward just north of the Bowery, where he found a room in a boarding house occupied largely by railroad workers, and a job in a bakery whose owner, unfortunately, reminded him of his father. The baker, however, had an unmarried daughter several years older than Charlie and she had two profound effects on him: She saved his job for him repeatedly and she introduced him to sex. The whole arrangement was a consuming one and Charlie did not escape from it for almost a year.

By this time he was nineteen, strikingly handsome and, notwithstanding the baker's daughter, shy. The affair had not enlarged his personality, it had merely fulfilled a hitherto unrecognized hunger for feminine tenderness.

Charlie's next job was that of a porter in the Atlantic Gar-

34

dens, the most famous German beer garden in New York. It was the best place in the Bowery, at any rate, and it could accommodate more than a thousand people. Originally, its patrons had been respectable Germans who brought their families and spent the day. After the Civil War, with its general demoralization and the deluge of immigration, the Atlantic began to attract thugs and hoodlums who came with their own pocket flasks of hard liquor to enjoy the free music, entertainment and games, and to molest the young German girls who traditionally served the huge five-cent mugs of beer. With the thugs came prostitutes who further contributed to Charlie's education. Because of his powerful physique, Charlie was often called upon to quell disturbances and he soon developed a devastating facility with his fists. This, in turn, gained him a higher-paying job as a bouncer at a nearby beer hall and, by the time he was twenty-one, he had earned a singular reputation in this field.

To Charlie, however, there was nothing admirable about his work or the people with whom it forced him to associate. Through a beer hall patron with whom he had become friendly, he got a job as a traveling salesman with a firm that manufactured working clothes. His territory extended from Philadelphia to Albany, and from his fellow salesmen he learned about gambling. He decided it was a fool's pastime.

His shyness prevented him from being a good salesman, but he must have done an adequate job for he stayed with the company for a year and a half. In the main, however, it was a frustrating experience. He met people who were superior, he felt, to the inhabitants of the lower East Side and this, coupled with the enforced improvement in his manner of dress, provoked new feelings of inadequacy in him which he sought to remedy by reading; this further estranged him and deepened his longing for success.

Withal, in his loneliness, Becker could not help but identify himself with the people and the causes of the lower East Side. In his bouncer days, he had met Monk Eastman who headed the most brutal, ruthless gang of criminals in the city, and who was the special pet of Timothy (Big Tim) Sullivan, the Tammany boss of the East Side.

Eastman admired Becker's ability as a fighter. He was amused that Becker had no apparent desire to capitalize on it. He took his new friend to the Sullivan Club where he met people like Arnold Rothstein and Herman Rosenthal (whom he saw at this point only once and immediately forgot) and the hoodlums who helped Tammany perpetuate its control of New York. Becker was inwardly puzzled by the disparity between the renowned charities and lofty principles of Sullivan and Tammany's ruler, Richard Croker, and the gangsters with whom these men surrounded themselves. Then, too, most of them were Catholics, as was Becker, and they all went to Mass regularly. Becker resolved his puzzlement, for all practical purposes, and became a frequent visitor to the Sullivan Club. Before long he had attracted the interest of Big Tim who was aware of the mystified awe in which Becker was regarded. He also recognized that Becker was no ordinary thug and in 1893 he arranged to have him appointed to the police force. This service was regularly performed by Tammany for a fee. In Becker's case, however, there was no charge.

Becker had seen enough of policemen in the Bowery to have no great respect for them, but he also acknowledged that the job held promise. Many policemen, especially officers, were wealthy. Further, because of his deep sense of inadequacy, Becker allowed the authoritarian image of the badge and gun to sway his judgment.

Becker was not altogether a good policeman but Big Tim remained his patron and he progressed steadily. His younger brother, John, had come to New York, meanwhile, and Becker had Sullivan appoint him to the force too.

As a patrolman, Becker was assigned to Fulton Street where he became acquainted with a grocer named Jeremiah Mahoney whose store was on Becker's beat. Mahoney had a pretty, dark-haired daughter, Mary, who was just eighteen. Becker began courting the fragile little Irish girl and her admiration for the handsome, stalwart policeman was unconcealed. They were married on February 6, 1895, in St. Peter's Church. Mary caught cold the night of their wedding and eight months later, after a ravishing illness, she was dead of tuberculosis.

There is no record of the extent of Becker's grief. He never discussed Mary with anybody after the funeral which was held from the same church in which they had been married.

Misfortune dogged him. He was patrolling his beat late one rainy spring night in 1896 when he saw a man emerging from the side window of a store on Washington Street just south of Fulton. Becker was about 200 feet away, across the street. He began to run toward the store, drawing his gun and shouting for the burglar to stop. Instead, the man fled with astonishing speed down the walkway alongside the store, turning north in the alley, the distance between himself and Becker fast increasing. Becker reached the alley as the thief turned east on Fulton. By the time Becker ran from the alley, the fugitive was almost a block away.

Becker stopped, leveled his revolver and emptied it at the running figure. Midway in the fusillade, a man stepped from between two store buildings into the path of fire and fell dead with a bullet in the heart. Momentarily panic-stricken, Becker gave up the chase and ran to the fallen bystander. He searched the young man's pockets but found no identification. Becker called for the police wagon and when it arrived he told the sergeant the dead man was the burglar he had been chasing. The police identified the victim as John O'Brien, a notorious burglar, they said.

The next day's newspapers hailed Becker as a hero but the accounts of the chase also included, unfortunately, a description of the victim. His family soon identified him correctly and he turned out to be John Fay, a plumber's helper. Becker was suspended for a month. Big Tim saved him from dismissal from the force.

About a year after his wife's death, Becker married a girl named Vivian Atteridge. They were divorced in 1905 and two years later she married Becker's brother, John.

Charlie's next excursion into the public print occurred in the summer of 1898 after his promotion to sergeant. He was walking along the Hudson River just above 10th Street when he saw a man stumble on a loose pier plank and plunge head-first into the water. Becker ran out on the pier and saw the man foundering, obviously unable to swim. He threw off his coat, dived in and rescued him.

The man he had saved was James Butler, an unemployed clerk, and he was most eloquent in praise and gratitude of Becker who remained a hero for only a week. Butler complained to the newspapers that Becker had promised him $15 to jump into the Hudson and permit himself to be rescued and that Becker had never paid him. Charlie denied the story as preposterous and no action was taken against him other than to transfer him to the 47th Street station, just off Broadway— the heart of the Tenderloin. Nothing could have been more to Charlie's liking.

The Tenderloin district embraced the area bordered by Fifth and Ninth Avenues, and 48th and 28th Streets. It contained the bulk of New York's estimated 500 gambling houses, in varying states of elegance and squalor, and about 30,000 prostitutes. It also contained the majority of legitimate restaurants, night clubs and theaters.

It was here, in 1901, that Sergeant Charles Becker ran afoul of the fearsome Captain Max Schmittberger and was introduced to success.

But there were interruptions and obstacles that would have discouraged a less resolute (or less patronized) man. He arrested a woman for soliciting on the street late in the evening. The woman was the wife of a textile manufacturer from Paterson, New Jersey. She said Becker had tried to blackmail her. Becker was undismayed. "I don't care who she is," he said afterward. "I know a whore when I see one." The chief of police apologized to the woman and her husband, but only Big Tim Sullivan could persuade them not to sue for false arrest.

In a raid on a gambling house, Becker shot and killed a dealer. There were no witnesses. Becker was suspended for thirty days.

If the customs of police discipline seem indifferent, it must be remembered that such matters were not solely the province of the police. Tammany Hall had ruled the city for forty years with patronage financed by graft taken from virtually every function of city government. It was impossible to erect a building, start a business, dock a ship, or do anything else that required municipal sanction without first paying Tammany's fee. The police department alone, by its licensing of brothels, saloons, gambling houses, pickpockets, pimps and burglars, collected more than three million dollars annually in protection payoffs. Rebellious forces occasionally found a victim such as Boss Tweed, whose inspired direction of Tammany at the close of the nineteenth century had made it the most powerful political entity in the country, but as fast as the perfidious were dragged from power others arose in their places and quickly profited by their predecessors' mistakes.

All this was no secret, especially to the average patrolman whose problem was how to grab his share. Protection was controlled by precinct captains who, in turn, were under the thumb of the district inspectors and, above them, the chief of police. The police commissioner might be honest, which was often the case, but he had no effective means of controlling the echelons below him. The average policeman's discontent over his meager income was assuaged at intervals with ten- and twenty-dollar bills. When some of the more infamous officials like Big Bill Devery or Inspector Alexander (Clubber) Williams were caught and ousted, they were found to be rich men.

The captain in command of the Central Broadway, or Tenderloin, precinct in 1901 was Max Schmittberger, whose confessions of police shakedowns during the notorious New York State Legislative investigations of 1894 had resulted in wholesale police reform under Police Commissioner Theodore Roosevelt, who was then en route to the White House.

Although one of the key perpetrators of the old graft system, Schmittberger had been retained on the force on the theory that he was fundamentally honest. He had simply been conforming, diligently it was noted, to the order of things as they were. Directed to clean up the force, Schmittberger did so. As a reward, he was given back his old district and when graft was subsequently restored he conformed again.

Becker, painfully aware of the money that was pouring into Schmittberger's office for allocation up the chain of command and on to Tammany while he himself received only driblets, asserted himself one afternoon. He walked boldly, in uniform, into Dollar John's, a 38th Street saloon enhanced by a gambling hall of mediocre stature on the second floor, and addressed himself to the proprietor, John Langer, a heavy, moon-faced man, who was behind the bar polishing glassware.

"I'm here," said Becker, "to let you know that the price of the fix has gone up."

"Yeah?" said Dollar John, eyeing him blankly.

"Yeah," said Becker, "besides the $300 to the captain every month it's $20 to me."

"Yeah?" said Dollar John.

"Your business has been good and the heat is on from downtown. There's no reason we should stall all these people without getting paid for it."

Dollar John reached into his pocket and threw a $20 bill onto the bar. Later that afternoon he walked over to the station house on 47th Street and told Captain Schmittberger all about it. Becker, meanwhile, had visited a dozen other gambling halls and extracted altogether $150. It satisfied him for the moment and provided a graphic realization of how neatly the system worked.

He was not prepared, however, for the next morning when he was summoned to Schmittberger's office. The captain was a

40

bigger and more powerful man than Becker but he showed no anger. He seemed astonished by Becker's nerve.

"What you've done isn't allowed," said Schmittberger, without preamble, his long, white mustache quivering.

Becker did not answer. His expression was surly.

"Give me the $150," the captain demanded, extending his hand.

Becker, taken aback by the captain's knowledge of the exact amount, withdrew a fold of bills from his inside coat pocket and dropped them on the desk.

Schmittberger picked it up and counted it. Then he counted off $15 and handed it to Becker.

"That's your share," he said, "ten per cent. From now on you're my collector. You'll get ten per cent. Some of the joints can stand to pay more than they are and if you can get it so much the better for you. But remember, I'll always know exactly how much they paid."

Becker was an outstanding collector and his share was soon increased to the customary twenty per cent. At the end of his first year at it he had $7,000 in the bank. His salary was $1,500 yearly. Five years later, when he was promoted to lieutenant, he was well-to-do and had begun to buy real estate in Queens and in Williamsbridge on the east side of the Bronx.

It was during his ascendancy in graft that Becker met Helen Lynch, a pretty, wispy, doe-eyed, dark-haired school teacher, an introverted girl, one of ten children whose father apparently had given up all hope of Helen ever landing a husband. As an alternate form of security, he sent her through normal school and she went to work in the New York public school system teaching handicapped children who had stirred her compassion. There is no record of how Charlie met Helen but he courted her furiously, appearing outside PS 90 on 148th Street at the end of the school day, whenever he could. Becker was overcome by this shy, gentle, intelligent girl and she by the contrast between his occupation and the tenderness he displayed toward her. They were married in less than a month.

41

"For the first time in my life I am happy," said Helen in a letter to her father. "Charlie seems like the only friend I have ever had."

Charlie and Helen remained always devotedly, sentimentally, and anxiously in love. They lived in Becker's flat on 159th Street and Edgecomb Avenue, and dreamed of a house in the country. He called her My Queen and she called him Charlie-Boy or Charlie-Lover. It is perhaps to Becker's credit that nobody ever joked with him about his adoring wife.

As the budding baron of the bawdyhouse and casino world, Becker introduced his naïve and innocent wife to the more showy aspects of his associations—newspapermen, theatrical people, wealthy politicians, stockbrokers, and a few of the more successful gamblers. She was, of course, awed and excited by it all. They dined almost every night in places she had only heard of—Rector's, Luchow's, Sharkey's, Sherry's—and they traveled about in a chauffeur-driven limousine owned by Col. Henry Sternberger, commander of the New York National Guard, a broker and dabbler in gaming ventures who was shrewd enough to recognize Becker's great potentialities.

As Schmittberger's bagman, Becker found that the captain's position with the gamblers and brothel keepers was being supplanted by the effect of his own personality in constant contact with them. They soon spoke of the Becker payoff, not the Schmittberger. When a gambler balked, Becker acted without a word to Schmittberger and the money flowed. Schmittberger was getting old and Becker anticipated the day when the captain's power would be available to the most qualified heir.

Becker's effectiveness as a bagman revived Tammany's interest in him and Sullivan summoned him frequently for conferences, and discreetly had him promoted to lieutenant. It was said that Sullivan saw in Becker a strong man who could fill the shoes of the fabled Clubber Williams or Big Bill Devery and perpetuate Tammany's omnipotence. Sullivan erroneously assumed that Becker would always remain grateful to Tammany.

In the 1909 elections, Democratic Tammany, as usual, swept its slate of candidates into office—with one exception: Republican District Attorney Charles Seymour Whitman, the fearless foe of Tammany. Whitman's plurality of 30,000 votes was attributed to two factors. He had been the vote-splitting fusion party candidate and his courage, youth, handsomeness and virtue combined to create an image of considerable popular appeal.

The mayor was William Jay Gaynor, an irascible old judge who, although he owed his victory to Tammany, soon repudiated the Wigwam and noisily set about to clean up New York. He discovered such an undertaking was impossible. Tammany minions were so numerous and the system so deeply entrenched that the best Gaynor could hope for, as he often said, was "outward order and decency." His first police commissioner, an iron-willed ex-judge named John Cropsey, might have done more than anybody to reform the force but he fought continually with Gaynor who finally fired him. His successor, even more honest than Cropsey, was Rhinelander Waldo, a retired Army colonel, a hero of the Spanish-American War. He was more a police academician than an administrator, inspired with the idea of transforming the department into a replica of the Metropolitan Police of London which he admired above all else. His most memorable acts as police commissioner were to allow voluntary retirement after twenty-five years' service, and to enlarge the pockets of police overcoats so that New York's Finest could keep their hands warm. He cut a fatuous figure and was frequently the butt of newspaper cartoons. The *Tribune*, his constant tormentor, once caricatured him standing, headless, next to Mayor Gaynor who said, "With one exception, Waldo, you are the Creator's noblest work."

Waldo had no idea of what was happening at the operational levels of the force and no accurate way of finding out. He was at the mercy of his more knowledgeable subordinates.

Nevertheless, with a wary eye on the vengeful Whitman and uncertain of Waldo, gamblers and bawdyhouse keepers curbed their operations until late in 1910 when Charlie Becker, at Tammany's masterful connivance, was given command of the semiautonomous vice squad. It was familiarly known as the "strong-arm squad" because of its violent methods of raiding. This entity, removed from precinct and district control to the direct control of the police commissioner, was Mayor Gaynor's idea. He believed it would take the opportunity for graft away from the police at large and limit it to a single squad which he naïvely assumed Waldo could supervise.

In fact, all this did was to make Charlie Becker an emperor.

Becker wasted no time. He had been ready for the throne for months, even though he did not know just how he would occupy it. He shut down the unprofitable gaming houses and brothels and kept them closed. This established his reputation with Waldo and the reformers whose criticism the commissioner feared. Then he gave carte blanche to the remaining purveyors of vice after substantially raising their payoff costs. To enforce his rule, he engaged the services of Jacob (Big Jack) Zelig who had succeeded Monk Eastman as the principal underworld terrorist.

Zelig's real name was William Alberts. He was the son of respectable Jewish parents. He started his career at fourteen as a pickpocket and by the time he was twenty-one he had become Monk Eastman's aide-de-camp and, next to Eastman, the most feared man in New York. When Eastman was unaccountably abandoned by Tammany and imprisoned for robbery, the least of his sins, Zelig replaced him. The nature of Zelig and his followers was typified by Zelig's bodyguard, Harry (Gyp the Blood) Horowitz, who boasted he could break a man's spine over his knee and frequently performed the feat on inoffensive strangers to win a $2 bet from drinking companions.

Becker, however, had no trouble controlling Zelig or his gang. He simply utilized the famous Sullivan Act, thoughtfully created by Big Tim during his state senatorial days for this very purpose. The law provided an eight-year prison term for carrying concealed weapons. The moment a thug disobeyed, he was arrested and taken to the police station where a pistol was declared to have been found in his pocket. Becker kept a supply of old revolvers for this use. Gunmen had long since given up arming themselves unless they were working.

In no time at all, Charlie Becker was the uncontested overlord of New York vice whose quantity and variety were such that, only a few years earlier, a Congressional investigating committee had declared New York the wickedest city in the world.

Becker still owed practical allegiance to Tammany, but he paid no homage, in cash or courtesy, to anybody but Big Tim Sullivan. Between them, they had organized crime for the first time and were running it as a business.

Becker no longer did his own collecting. He had a staff of bagmen headed by a veteran Broadway gambler and stool pigeon whose real name was Jacob Rosenzweig. He was universally known, however, as Bald Jack Rose because he had neither hair, eyebrows nor eyelashes. His chalk white skull was a roving Broadway landmark. Rose himself brought in a total of $120,000 during the first three months he worked for Becker.

Becker was annoyed, a fact he barely concealed, when an East Side gambler and Tammany loafer named Herman Rosenthal was given, by Big Tim, a Tammany gambling concession known as the Hesper Club. Rosenthal installed the club in a three-story brownstone at 104 West 45th Street, just off Sixth Avenue, furnished it in a grossly lavish way with thick rugs and period furniture, and equipped it with the latest gambling devices. Rosenthal's service to Tammany extended back some twenty years and he was a favored recipient of Big Tim's patronage and affection.

Becker called on Rosenthal the night he opened the house.

"No payoffs here," Rosenthal told him, "this is Big Tim's house."

Becker did not remember Rosenthal personally, but he recalled that Sullivan had often expressed a paternal interest in him, and Arnold Rothstein.

"They're smart Jew boys," he would say, "they're gonna go places."

Rothstein did, but Rosenthal was an abject failure in every gambling venture he attempted and he was continually falling back on Sullivan for help.

Becker remonstrated with Sullivan often over the sacrosanct status of the Hesper.

"Leave him alone for a while," Sullivan decreed, "let's see how he does."

Becker waited about a month, until late in February of 1912. The Hesper was prospering and Becker grew increasingly irritated. Two events precipitated him into action.

Ever since he had taken command of the strong-arm squad, Becker had employed the services of a Broadway bookie and erstwhile gossip columnist as his press agent. His name was Charles Plitt and he earned his living largely as a newspaper tipster. His job also was to plant Becker's name, often and favorably, in the papers. Plitt had been playing in a private crap game. There had been a fight and one of the players was stabbed to death. Plitt was arrested, over his protests of innocence, and charged with the murder. Fearful that the irate Plitt might talk too much, Becker set about raising a legal defense fund for him. He levied assessments against all the gamblers. Rosenthal's assessment was $500. This had nothing to do with protection, Becker reasoned, and Big Tim would not object. As it was, Big Tim never knew about it. He had fallen ill—with paresis, it was said—and his mind was affected.

When Becker heard this, he did not hesitate in any respect. He sent Zelig around to Rosenthal's to collect the $500 plus the first of what would now be regular protection payments. Zelig had known Rosenthal for years and had been friendly with him.

"You better pay," he warned Rosenthal. "Sullivan's out and Becker's the boss now."

Rosenthal refused and headed for Sullivan's office. There he found Sullivan's desk occupied by a triumverate—Florrie Sullivan, who was Big Tim's brother, Jim Sullivan, his nephew, and Frank Farrell. The three of them together did not begin to equal Big Tim and Rosenthal realized that Tammany was, for the moment at least, of no use to him.

Zelig reported Rosenthal's refusal to Becker.

"Now, don't tell me he won't pay," Becker snarled. "Make him pay."

Rosenthal was threatened repeatedly and then savagely beaten one night in front of the Hesper Club. Still he would not pay. He went back to Sullivan's office and begged Florrie to help him.

Big Tim's brother shrugged his shoulders. "You better make a deal with Becker," he advised.

Rosenthal began negotiations with Becker. He could not pay the $500 assessment, he pleaded, nor could he afford $500 a month in protection fees. The club was not as profitable as it should have been.

"All right," said Becker. "I'll take twenty per cent of your gross. It's either that or you can close up."

Rosenthal loudly damned the new alliance as a form of robbery. He told everybody he knew. He was even more outraged when Becker installed in the club, to protect his twenty per cent, none other than Bald Jack Rose, whom Rosenthal hated.

Becker's new grasp for power did not stop with Rosenthal. Sullivan was gone and there was no longer any reason to consider Tammany. Becker grew richer and richer.

Rosenthal's bleating complaints about Becker, meanwhile, were reaching too many ears and attracting too much attention. Word reached the ear of Police Commissioner Rhinelander Waldo in slightly distorted form. In a terse memorandum, Waldo informed Becker that there had been complaints about a gambling house at 104 West 45th Street. He ordered Becker to close it up. "I can't understand how this could have escaped your attention," he wrote.

Becker promptly complied. He raided Rosenthal's house and stationed a policeman inside it day and night to make certain it remained closed.

Rosenthal went to the New York *World* and told them everything he could think of about Becker. Then he went to District Attorney Charles Seymour Whitman and amplified it all in great detail. He was the first informer in years who had been so well versed in his subject or so willing to talk.

Then he was murdered.

4. Most Likely to Succeed

IN HIS confession, Herman Rosenthal had not told the truth. In his tapestry of exposé there was only one thread of fact: Herman Rosenthal, a gambler, had had mutually profitable dealings with Lt. Charles Becker, a police officer sworn to suppress gambling. Beyond that, it was a self-redeeming fiction.

District Attorney Charles Seymour Whitman suspected this and did not care. It was enough that for the first time in half a century a party to the alliance of crime, politics and law enforcement had been eager to stand up in court and expose it.

To Whitman, there was only one important truth: Tammany Hall had created, ruled, and perpetuated this corruption and should be destroyed. Whitman devoutly believed this for Whitman was a moral man. He was, however, keenly aware of a subsidiary truth, that the man who destroyed Tammany could, at the same time, catapult himself to political eminence. It was a heady idea and because of it, perhaps, Whitman did not hesitate to use as the instrument of Tammany's destruction a fat, whining, absurdly self-righteous failure of a gambler whose story, in more ordinary times, would not survive a great deal of scrutiny. But these were not ordinary times and if a jury could be made to believe Rosenthal's story the end would be served and the means would make no difference at all. The principle of presumed innocence could be suspended. There was, in fact, no real question of Tammany's guilt. Justice had been defeated merely on a technicality— Tammany's corruption had never been established in a court of law.

But Herman Rosenthal had been ready to satisfy that technicality. His accusations, with all their self-vindicating invention and embroidery, had become the more believable by his murder. More important, they had been directed at one man who embodied, represented and symbolized the evil: Lt. Charles Becker. With him, Whitman believed, the system might stand or fall. But Becker was cunning. In many ways, it was all too obvious. Was Becker so cunning that he would murder a man who had publicly accused him?

For a moment Whitman entertained his misgivings. Charlie Becker, the ruthless country bumpkin who had outsmarted everybody; was he also so dumb that he would bring ruinous suspicion down upon himself? Or was he so vain that that is exactly what he would do? Men who had achieved vast power were often deluded by it into believing in their own power and grossly inflating their assessments of its effects.

Whitman had to admit, however, that his knowledge of power was academic. It was nothing he had ever sought for himself. His impetus was achievement. He was a striver and a go-getter—and a moral man.

Even his father had to admit, not without pride, that Charles Whitman was a moral man, fiercely obedient to fundamental ethics. The Reverend John Seymour Whitman was pastor of the Congregational Church in Hanover, Connecticut, and as such had conscientiously reared his only child in the God-fearing tradition. He may have puzzled, however, that he had been less successful in conveying to the youth a commensurate amount of tolerance. A studious, self-disciplined boy, Charles was said to be impatient with churchly exhortations to a hypocritical public and argued that morality was a matter for enforcement rather than persuasion.

In Hanover High School, where he was an honor student, Charles Whitman was regarded as too good and aloof and when he was graduated in 1885 he surprised nobody by announcing that he was going to become a lawyer. He spent a year at Williams College and then transferred to Amherst where he completed his prelegal studies. He was still aloof, although more determined than haughty, and was graduated, as expected, with high honors and a Phi Beta Kappa key. He declined to be pledged to a fraternity on grounds he had no time for it, but succumbed to Alpha Delta Phi in his senior year. He had a few close friends who shared his academic perseverance, but was popularly thought to be a trifle odd.

The Whitman family had no more money to continue their son's education, so Charles got a part-time job teaching Latin and Greek at Adelphi College in Brooklyn, to pay his own way through New York University Law School.

Whitman hung out his own shingle and subsisted for months on small cases sent to him by friends of his family. In his spare hours, Whitman visited the Criminal Courts building to watch trials and try to understand the opportunities that should be available to eager, articulate, quick-witted young lawyers. He visited the magistrates courts in lower Manhattan and became acquainted with the abuses that he would later stop.

Most magistrates were the recipients of Tammany patronage and were miserably unqualified. They and the police worked together with bail bond brokers in an extortion pact against the ignorant, poverty-ridden immigrant inhabitants of the lower East Side. Suspects in even the most trivial misdemeanors could be held for weeks without a hearing, and an acquittal was often based not so much on evidence as on the defendant's ability to satisfy the greed of the judge and the police.

Whitman began to defend, without charge, prostitutes, pickpockets and an occasional burglar whose civil rights had been

51

especially trampled. His pleas to the bench consisted of thinly veiled outrage and before long he had succeeded in antagonizing every magistrate south of 42d Street. He seldom won a case, except on an appeal, but he received considerable publicity.

New York's newspapers, for the most part, had begun to attack what they termed "the system" and were shrilly demanding governmental reform. Whitman's effectiveness as an opponent of judicial corruption was far less than the press made it out to be but he was building a reputation as a courtroom Don Quixote.

Whitman was a slight man of medium height, with a thin and drooping mouth, craggy nose, wide and deeply set hazel eyes, a broad, high forehead and wavy, luxurious brown hair which he parted in the middle. His jaws were thick and he had a way of setting his chin slightly forward that emphasized his determination and irritated judges.

In the 1899 elections, Tammany was ejected by the voters in favor of a reform slate headed by Seth Low, former president of Columbia University and mayor of Brooklyn before it became a part of Greater New York. Low set off on one of the most sweeping municipal cleanups ever undertaken. At the outset, it was conspicuously efficient. For perhaps the first time since the Civil War, the government of New York was scrupulously honest. Low purged every appointed official from the municipal payroll and replaced them with personally hand-picked experts in finance, tenement improvement, social welfare, taxation and the law. He dismissed almost all police court magistrates and appointed to the benches a refreshing array of lawyers who, by Low's standards, were also gentlemen. For assistant corporation counsel, a title denoting the city's second-ranking legal advisor, he chose the fighting young nemesis of the Tammany magistrates, Charles Seymour Whitman. Whitman was sent to Albany as the city's legal watchdog over the state legislature. His primary job was to be on the alert for laws promoted by special interests which, in Mayor Low's mind, would be detrimental to the interests of the people of New York. There was a flood of it and it kept Whitman running up and down the Hudson. He discovered, however, the effectiveness of publicity. To stop the passage of unwanted legislation, Whitman simply went to the capitol press room and released a somewhat melodramatic account of the potential menace to the people of New York City. Since he was usually quoted as the source of the story, Whitman benefited by the advertising it gave him as a guardian of New York's welfare. He even let it be known that he was frequently offered bribes to relax his vigilance.

In 1902, just before he left office, Low asked Whitman to accept a post as magistrate.

Whitman hesitated. Among the people he sought to impress —reformers, honest politicians, church groups, the city's minuscule body of civil intellectuals—the job of magistrate still carried unflattering connotations despite Mayor Low's reforms. In the end, Whitman decided he could not only live down the stigma, but that he could raise the level of the job. He became judge of an architecturally famous Victorian Gothic pile known as the Jefferson Market Court, at West 10th Street and Sixth Avenue, dispensing justice to women delinquents for whom the court was reserved.

Mayor Low had severely curtailed the graft in most city departments but he had not had time to root out the deep decay in the police. The shakedown prevailed and Whitman's recognition of it was acute. He issued loud, angry and occasionally vitriolic denunciations of the system in general and Tammany in particular, and his court was popular with newspapermen.

It soon became apparent to Whitman that the majority of miscreants brought into his court were victims of the popular custom of railroading for bail bond graft. The most frequent target of this was the streetwalker. Police would arrest on sight any unaccompanied woman. For five dollars, a bail bond broker would guarantee her appearance in court and she would be released. If she could not pay the broker's fee, she would be convicted on perjured testimony. If she paid the five dollars, the arresting officer would admit in court that she had been picked up on suspicion and that he really had no evidence. The bail bondsman would keep two of the five dollars for himself, and give three to the policeman who, in turn, was allowed to keep one dollar. The remaining two dollars went to the precinct captain for further distribution.

Whitman's discovery of this special graft came when a prostitute named Bertha Vernon appeared in court for the third time in a month.

"I'm going to dismiss you," he said, in a mildly pontifical tone, "but first I want you to tell me why you are so frequently arrested."

She told him candidly.

"Do you always pay the bondsman?" he asked her.

"The bondsman is *always* paid," she said, wearily.

Other independent lawbreakers such as pickpockets, burglars and lone gamblers were also victims of this device. But never saloonkeepers or gambling house operators. They paid their protection fees by the month. Under the state excise laws, saloons were required to close at 1 A.M. Few did. Most, in fact, never closed. Whitman began cruising the streets of his district in the early morning hours. He would pick up a policeman walking his beat and together they would raid the open saloons, much to the cop's chagrin. Soon, the newspapers were calling him "the raiding judge."

In three months, Whitman had documented 400 cases of bail bond railroading and he went to Albany, persuaded the anti-Tammany legislators to enact a bill establishing night courts. Fearful that Governor Charles Evans Hughes, later the eminent U.S. Supreme Court Justice, might somehow be pressured into vetoing the measure, Whitman called on the Governor, armed with his 400 documents and an impassioned argument. Hughes, who was almost as rigid a moralist as Whitman, signed it. The night court did away with the bail bond graft and also with unlawful detention, a practice common to police to give them time to beat or sweat a confession from a suspect.

Whitman's justice was uniform.

The wife of a prominent businessman was arrested for shoplifting. The store owner had been pressured into withdrawing the complaint and Whitman was besieged with potent pleas that he dismiss the case.

When the humiliated woman appeared before him with her attorney, Whitman said:

"Is it conceded that the defendant is guilty?"

"It is," her attorney replied.

"Within a few days," said Whitman, "I have held men and women, without friends, on this same charge. I would not have it said that in this court there is one law for the poor and another for the rich. I hold this defendant for trial."

Whitman was similarly pressured to be lenient with a favorite Tammany Hall thug up on a charge of strong-arm robbery. The thug was a valuable election-day worker, for in whichever precinct he might be stationed not a single opposition vote would be cast.

Whitman gave the gangster twenty years.

This occurred shortly after Governor Hughes had asked Whitman to resign as magistrate and accept a temporary appointment to the Court of General Sessions. When the term expired, Whitman ran for re-election on the Republican ticket. He was defeated by the Tammany candidate but he ran 12,000 votes ahead of his party, which to him was pure prophecy.

Throughout his judicial career, Whitman never let up his bitter assaults on Tammany. His favorite now was: "Someday, I will smash all of this rotten system." Newspapers constantly quoted him.

Whitman had been enthusiastically gratified by Low's election and his subsequent reforms, many of which remained in effect even if Low did not remain in office. He was correspondingly disheartened when Low was defeated by Tammany's George B. McClellan, son of the Civil War general, and he bridled openly when corruption resumed at a wholesale pace.

Tammany's first act, under McClellan's administration, was committed by its major sachem, the publicity-shy Charley Murphy, who owned a trucking company. Murphy leased most of the New York shipping docks from the city and then re-leased them at profits that ran as high as 5,000 per cent. He also had the city force the Pennsylvania Railroad into awarding his contracting firm the job of excavating the site of the new Pennsylvania Station at 8th Avenue and 33d Street.

Although they could not hold office in New York City, the Republicans dominated upstate New York and the Legislature and were often responsible for the shifts of power that occurred in the city. The means by which they accomplished this was a circuslike performance known as a legislative investigation of sin-ridden New York City. It was motivated not by morality, but by cynicism. The Republicans' machine was fully as corrupt as Tammany, but it believed that nothing appealed more to voters than blatant virtue. Tammany believed simply in purchasing voter loyalty. An investigation was, of course, not aimed at annihilating Tammany, but merely to gain a momentary advantage. A genuine investigation would have led to the inner councils of both parties and destroyed them together. Therefore, to protect the interests common to all politicians, investigations operated by unwritten ground rules. They would go so far and no further. A few lesser thieves would be sacrificed, the cause of virtue would be served and corruption could continue.

Mayor Low had been elected in the wake of just such an investigation. But, as the old Tammany boss, Richard Croker, once observed, "Maybe people can't stand corruption, but they can't stand reform either." They tolerated Low and good government for two years and then put Tammany's grafters back into office. Low and good government had hurt business, it was said.

The Republican party meanwhile, which had benefited little from the honest Low, and not at all from Tammany's Mc-

Clellan, began demanding some patronage from Tammany. It wanted some judicial appointments made to Republicans in New York City, for instance. Its demands went unheard, so the legislature ordered a new investigation of New York. Judge Whitman knew this inquiry, like all the others, would be meaningless and it rankled him. "If I were counsel for the investigating committee," he said, his jaw set sternly, "I would go all the way."

In the famous Mazet probe of 1898, the committee's counsel had almost gone too far. He was Frank Moss, like Whitman a fearless fighter, and he had made the mistake of subpoenaing Tammany Boss Richard Croker and tearing him apart in the witness chair. Afterward, Moss was curbed by the committee and the inquiry went its inconclusive way. The Republicans got their judgeships.

Yet in later years, Whitman was to remember the dauntless Moss and to make use of him.

In the meantime, Whitman kept up his articulate campaign and slowly built a public image and a reputation. Among those attracted to this clean-cut, courageous champion of truth and justice was a pretty, blond social worker named Olive Hitchcock. They were married in 1908 and they moved into a six-room apartment at Madison Avenue and 25th Street where they remained for many years. Now relatively famous, Whitman returned to private practice and prospered.

New York's newspapers by this time were all but united in a vendetta against Tammany and the system and were howling for reform. Loudest among them was the *Journal* whose publisher, William Randolph Hearst, had tried unsuccessfully once to outrun Tammany for the mayorship and, still entertaining visions of one day being President, was willing to try it again.

Hearst had lost the first time, in 1906, by fraud. Tammany simply brought in illegal voters from as far as Philadelphia and cast ballots for several thousand dogs and cats. To extend its margin, Tammany gangsters seized the ballot boxes from several Hearst precincts and threw them into the East River.

Hearst was not acceptable to the Republicans who this year, 1909, were running not as Republicans but as a fusion party with purity and goodness as their platform. Their candidate was a tedious banker named Otto Bannard. Hearst took the position that Hearst was the voter's only alternative to the crooks of Tammany and the Big Business minions of the fusion ticket. Tammany's candidate for mayor, however, was not a crook. He was William Jay Gaynor, a Democrat to be sure, but a Supreme Court judge far more independent in fact than Hearst and infinitely less inclined to make deals. He was a rich and colorful talker and had the support of at least one paper, the *World*, which hoped (as Tammany feared) that Gaynor might repudiate the Wigwam if he was elected.

Hearst ran a poor third in the race and Gaynor won, along with the rest of the Tammany slate with one notable exception: the fusion party's appealing candidate for district attorney, Judge Charles Seymour Whitman, who was elected by an amazing plurality of 30,000 votes.

His election was applauded by all the press. *Outlook*, the intellectuals' organ, declared: "Judge Whitman's record is a fine one. . . . He has displayed courageous support of justice, honor and integrity in performing his duties in the face of political and personal influence. . . ."

Installed in office, Whitman immediately announced his plans for ridding the city of white slavery, gambling houses, brothels, police graft. His morality glistened on the subject of streetwalkers.

"Women of the streets," he said, "are the most dangerous factor in the spread of crime . . . She seldom reforms, for she is criminal in all her instincts. She is the greatest of unfortunates, but she is also the recipient of much misplaced sympathy. It will be impossible to drive all of them from the streets, but their operations can be confined to a restricted area. The grafting of the police in this regard will be stopped."

He made the customary vows to protect the innocent as well

as to prosecute the guilty, but he also promised that he would never persecute to satisfy public clamor. The first man he hired for his staff was Frank Moss, the counsel for the Mazet Inquiry of 1898.

In all, the election was a bother to Tammany. Mayor Gaynor did, in fact, turn his back on the party and Whitman interfered to an irritating degree with the machinery of the system. He haunted the courts to discourage the restored abuses he had once abolished, and he often bypassed the police department with a squad of his own investigators. His efforts, however meritorious, were eclipsed in the press by Mayor Gaynor's more dramatic fights with Tammany and with the press itself. Gaynor, the newspapers charged, had failed in his promised reform of the police department.

It was almost axiomatic that a politician who had proven his appeal in the chaotic politics of New York had indefinable but also incalculable advantages if he aspired to the presidency. Theodore Roosevelt had demonstrated this, and there were a host of others who believed it to be true—Gaynor and, before him, McClellan, and of course, Hearst. Whitman had never said that he wanted, or hoped, to be president, but it was obvious that he found politics beguiling and rewarding, and he must have been impressed with his own success at it. A high-brow magazine, *The Review of Reviews,* in acclaiming him said:

"In the turbulent politics of New York, there is always opportunity for new leaders to come forward in American life. . . .

"They must have courage, honesty and a wide knowledge of human nature. . . ."

Whitman's first two years in office were uneventful ones. He despaired that his causes could not find recognition in the daily papers.

He may have regarded it as a reward for good works, therefore, when Herman Rosenthal came to him with his story about Lt. Charlie Becker.

Whitman knew of Becker, but had never gotten close enough to the higher criminal echelons to understand Becker's place in it. His excitement over Rosenthal had been aroused by a third person, Herbert Bayard Swope, the New York *World's* star reporter of crime and politics. Although Swope was personally friendly with the gamblers, gunmen, crooked politicians and policemen, as well as the honest ones, he did not hesitate to sacrifice his friendships in the interests of a story or the *World's* campaign to clean up New York. It was Swope who virtually delivered Rosenthal to the district attorney. He knew Rosenthal and was fully aware of his fight with Becker. He also knew that with Sullivan sick and Tammany adrift, Becker was the key to police corruption. He told Whitman:

"Becker may not know it himself, but he controls the police force; at least, he controls the graft. Tammany is temporarily out of the picture; they're mad as hell but there's nothing they can do about it. I'm telling you, Judge, if you get Becker, you've got them all."

Whitman had never sought help before, nor had he ever been tempted to strike bargains. But this time, for all his confidence, he didn't want to drown his reputation by getting in waters that were over his head.

"What can I expect from you?" Whitman asked.

"All the help in the *World,*" said the debonair Swope, unashamedly pleased at his pun.

5. The DA Plays It Close

DISTRICT ATTORNEY CHARLES WHITMAN strode from the 47th Street Precinct house, in his mind attempting to assay the significance of the scene. Coroner I. L. Feinberg had arrived and in a perfunctory manner was removing Rosenthal's body to the morgue for those last documentary formalities that separate the dead from the living. Becker had long since gone, his unnerving presence supplanted by an uneasy quietude. But as Whitman reached the sidewalk, a large red touring car pulled up at the curb. In it were Second Deputy Police Commissioner George S. Dougherty and Chief Inspector Edward Hughes. Whitman knew that Captain Day, the precinct commander, would soon be relieved of all concern for the matter at hand. Whitman would have to work fast, for the police must not commandeer the initiative in the investigation.

It was almost dawn. The first dreary gray streaks now appeared in the sky and Whitman, noticing them, lamented to himself that it would be another hot day. Hurrying on toward Broadway, he could already feel the sweat congealing under the band of his straw hat. At Broadway he turned south. The Great White Way was deserted, its glistening façade bleak and pale in the half light.

The late Herman Rosenthal's home and now-defunct gambling casino occupied the second position in a row of three-story brownstones running west on 45th Street from Sixth Avenue. These buildings were an architectural hallmark of the affluent 1880's and at one time the symbol of economic respectability. Under the pressure of New York's exploding population, the neighborhood in less than a decade had been engulfed by beauty parlors, chop suey restaurants, theatrical costumers and delicatessens, and many of the homes had become rooming houses. In this environment, Rosenthal's house was a pathetic example of hopelessly struggling opulence. Its paneled front door, almost four inches thick with the customary peephole, still bore the scars of the axes of Lieutenant Becker's raiding squad. The door was ajar when Whitman reached the top of the steps. He hesitated a moment, peering into the dark and cool interior. There was no sound. He stepped inside, pausing again while his eyes adjusted to the darkness. His feet sank stickily in the thick carpeting. The hallway smelled of dead heat and stale cigar smoke. Whitman walked on. A door on his left was open and he stepped into the room. By the front window, where the policeman had been on duty for three months, an armchair had been pulled out from against the wall and placed alongside a heavy table. It was a teakwood table, and very expensive, but Whitman did not know that. He had the impression that the house was cheaply furnished in imitation of luxury. On the table were two huge saucer ashtrays, both filled and overflowing with cigar butts.

From the hallway the sound of voices drifted to him. He moved back into the hall, following the sound to the rear of the house, past half a dozen closed doors. There was a lamp on a table by the door, its glow spilling out into the hall. The sound of the voices, muddled when he first heard it, was still incoherent. As he reached the room, the light flared up in his eyes and blinded him. The voices he reduced to one, its incoherence now understandable. It was a woman sobbing; weary and convulsive, so long at it that the sobs broke in rhythm with her breathing. At last he could see her, a large, wilted, round figure face down on a davenport against the far wall. At her feet sat another woman, silent, staring blankly up at Whitman. Relieved for the moment of explaining himself, he surveyed the room. In contrast to the rest of the house he had seen, it was shabby and disheveled. A worn Oriental rug covered the floor. At each end of the sofa were semicircular tables, each with a cut glass lamp resting on a lace doily. At one end of the room was a heavy carved desk and at the other end a stuffed chair, the innards of which were squirming through a slit in the front of the seat cushion. The walls, papered in a buff floral relief, were bare. It was obviously the Rosenthals' sitting room.

The sobbing woman roused herself jerkily. Her head, which had been buried in the crook of her arm, swung about. She squinted at Whitman, her eyes swollen, her face puffy with red welts. Strands of wet black hair were strung across her forehead. The other woman had not moved. Her chin was cupped in her hands, her elbows propped on her knees.

"You're not a newspaper reporter," the fat woman whined accusingly. "You're the district attorney."

Whitman removed his hat, holding it at his side.

"I told them reporters and I'll tell you. I blame the police and nobody else. They killed him."

Her voice, which had been flat and formless, began to rise in pitch. The curved folds of fat beneath her chin quivered pendulously as she moaned.

"I knew it. I knew it. I told him not to go. I told him to stay home. I pleaded with him. It was that man he went to see. I knew it when he left."

Whitman's stomach tightened. What man? Rosenthal had not said anything about meeting a man and Rosenthal, he thought, had told him everything.

"What man was that, Mrs. Rosenthal?" Whitman said it calmly, quietly, trying to pierce the woman's stream of babbling. "What man did he go to meet?" He asked it again. She was just as melodramatic as her husband, he thought. He asked again, louder, more firmly, insistent. "What man did he go to meet?" Mrs. Rosenthal had begun to sob again and Whitman crossed the room, kneeling down. He grasped her forearm. "What man?" She jerked her arm away and took refuge in her anguish.

The other woman spoke. "I'm Herman's sister. She doesn't know who called. Somebody phoned and told Herman to come to the Metropole."

"When did he phone?" said Whitman, rising.

The woman shrugged. "I don't know. Sometime early in the evening." Before he went to Whitman's office then.

Whitman left, frustrated and more anxious than before. He took a taxi home, shaved and bathed, ate a hurried breakfast and reached his office shortly after 7 A.M. By this time, the police department had already fulfilled Whitman's fears. They had arrested two men, a fact of which Whitman was not informed for several hours.

By some extraordinary reasoning, Commissioner Dougherty had taken the license number of the murder car, as noted by cabaret singer Charles Gallagher, and traced it. At exactly 4 A.M., two hours and ten minutes after the killing, Dougherty learned that the gray Packard, bearing New York license 41313, was registered to one Louis Libby, 15 Stuyvesant Place, on the outskirts of Greenwich Village. Dougherty knew that Libby operated the car for hire and he also knew that one of his best customers was Big Jack Zelig, the gang chieftain. In fact, the car itself was somewhat famous. Its original owner had been John L. Sullivan, the pugilist, who toured Broadway nightly in it for a few weeks before becoming bored. He had sold it to Libby who profited substantially by buying it. People liked to ride in Sullivan's old car. Actually, Libby had even made the car more romantic by coincidentally renting it to Zelig the day he was unsuccessfully ambushed in front of the Tombs by Jack Sirocco's gang. The tonneau bore two bullet holes which Libby frequently pointed to with pride.

Dougherty and four members of the detective bureau,

which he commanded, left headquarters in the commissioner's big red car and headed for Libby's apartment. They broke in the front door, dragged the sleeping Libby out of bed and carted him off to headquarters. Another contingent of detectives descended on the Washington Square garage where Libby housed the car. The frightened attendant, an immigrant named Gino Montani, admitted after a moment's bullying that the car had been returned to the garage after 2 A.M. but that the driver had paid him $10 to say, if anybody inquired, that it had been in the garage since midnight. It was not Libby who had brought the car in and paid him the $10, Montani said, but a young man he knew only as Shapiro.

At headquarters, meanwhile, considerably more pressure was being applied to Libby, a slender young man whose chief attribute was not courage. Confronted with the garage attendant's statement, Libby admitted that his partner, William Shapiro, had driven the car since ten o'clock the previous night. Shapiro woke him about 2 A.M., he said, and told him the car had been involved in a shooting. Beyond that he knew nothing. Dougherty dispatched the entire detective force on a man hunt for Shapiro. At 7 A.M., detectives found Shapiro sleeping in the Lafayette Baths. He was taken to Dougherty's office and, despite some manhandling, refused to say anything. He and Libby were held as "suspicious persons" and confined in headquarters all that day. Dougherty refused to allow them to notify anyone or to call a lawyer. The following morning they were formally accused of the murder of Herman Rosenthal and were jailed at the Tombs. Their bail was set at $25,000 by Coroner Feinberg.

On the afternoon of July 16, infuriated by Dougherty's refusal to permit him to question Shapiro and Libby, Whitman called in the press. To the assembled reporters, he issued the following statement:

> I accuse the police department of New York, through certain members of it, with having murdered Herman Rosenthal.
> Either directly or indirectly it was because of them that he

65

was slain in cold blood with never a chance for his life. And the time and place selected were such as to inspire terror in the hearts of those the system had most to fear. It was intended to be a lesson to anyone who might have thought of exposing the alliance between the police and crime.

Just as he was about to give important additional evidence and to give the names of eight or ten men who could and would support his charges; just as the situation shapes up most dangerously for the police involved, he is killed and with him dies his evidence.

But the case against Lieutenant Becker will be pushed through with all possible vigor, even though it is apparent that no conviction can result.

Whitman did not believe this, but he injected a note of futility in the hope of provoking further public outrage. The grand jury's hands might be tied, he said, but at least the public could return a moral indictment.

"The big thing in this case is not the death of Herman Rosenthal, but the death of public confidence in our system of justice. Why, twice today, witnesses going before the grand jury hung back and told me they were afraid . . . that Rosenthal's death had frightened them."

Whitman was asked by a New York *World* reporter if he thought he could have convicted Becker had Rosenthal lived.

"I cannot answer that," Whitman replied, "because it relates to matters that are to be put before the grand jury. But I will say that Rosenthal had placed in my hands valuable evidence and had supplied important leads which brought forth new material. He was a source of grave peril to the system. He knew conditions in the city as few men did because he was a part of the things he intended to expose."

Asked for the specifics of police complicity in Rosenthal's murder, Whitman said:

"It is a curious thing that four or five policemen were within 300 feet of the place of the shooting yet they cannot give a corroborative account of it. Not one of them is certain that an automobile took the murderers away, nor are they certain of the license number of the car. It remains for an outsider—Charles Gallagher—a man who is not supposed to have his faculties sharpened for such tests of observation, to save the situation."

William J. File, the handsome young police detective who had been in the Metropole when Rosenthal was shot, gave a fairly accurate account of the murder, insofar as he was able and with due regard for his own skin. He did not at first give it to Whitman, but to Commissioner Dougherty and Chief Inspector Edward Hughes. File was permitted to be interviewed by Whitman the following day.

Among other things, File said that he had seen Bridgie Webber in the hotel not only before the murder, but afterward. Dougherty was impressed. He already knew that Webber and Rosenthal were not friends, but business and political rivals. Two of Dougherty's stool pigeons amplified this. They said they had been present, with Webber, and scores of other gamblers, on the Sunday outing of the Sam Paul Association, a Tammany social club whose membership consisted largely of gamblers. Rosenthal had been the principal subject of discussion, the informers reported, and at one point during the Long Island excursion Webber had said, "If Herman doesn't keep his mouth shut, somebody is gonna get him and get him for keeps."

Dougherty sent detectives out to bring Webber in and told a crowd of clamoring reporters outside his office that Rosenthal's death had been the result of a gambling war, that the police had already arrested two persons (whom he declined, for the moment, to identify), and that the killing would be solved in a matter of hours.

It was now midafternoon of July 16, thirteen hours after the murder. Whitman watched the police competently surround the crime and isolate it from him. He knew he could not wrest it back, and his accusatory outbursts had provoked nothing. He could only hope that they served to put the police further on the defensive in the public mind. Whitman put great faith in public opinion. It had served him well. It had made him district attorney. It was his strongest ally and, for that matter, his most influential friend. It would bring its pressure to bear through members of the grand jury who were as easily swayed by emotional climate as anybody else.

As for investigating the case himself, Whitman had neither the time, knowledge nor the facilities. His investigative staff, consisting of a dozen men whose primary function was to serve subpoenas, could not cope with it either. Nor was he certain that they could be trusted. He was reasonably confident, however, that he could rely on one, a burly ex-cop named Emil Klinge who had served under two previous DA's. Klinge had proven his loyalty to the office during the tenure of the famous Travers Jerome, Whitman's immediate predecessor. Klinge had once served a gambling warrant on Herman Rosenthal who had offered him $100 to withdraw it. Klinge accepted the money and reported the matter to Jerome who arrested and convicted Rosenthal for bribing a public official.

Whitman called Klinge in and guardedly asked his counsel.

"There's no use trying to fight this case yourself. You could hire private detectives but I don't think you'll have to. Just keep the pressure on the cops and don't accept the case for prosecution until you know it's right. Just sit tight."

Klinge's advice proved remarkably prophetic. By waiting until the morning of July 17, Whitman found the case in his office. It appeared in the portfolio of one Aaron J. Levy, a Tammany attorney who was later to become a state assemblyman and who, with Alfred E. Smith, eventually ruled the New York State Senate.

A short, sinewy man with dark and nimble eyes, Levy told Whitman that he was representing the two men arrested by the police, Louis Libby and William Shapiro. If his clients were brought to Whitman's office, Levy said, they would make a full statement. Levy was accompanied by a handful of reporters to whom he related his offer, explaining, "It is better that these prisoners turn their information over to the district attorney rather than to the police."

68

As a Tammany politician, Levy reportedly had also extracted a promise from Whitman: That he, Levy, would cooperate fully in the case provided that Whitman agreed to keep Tammany and certain of its officialdom out of it. Whitman denied this, with some success, but the police exploited Levy's gesture for the time being. "I don't care *who* gets caught," declared Commissioner Dougherty. "We will push this case to the limit."

At Whitman's demand, Dougherty had Libby and Shapiro brought from the Tombs to Whitman's office. The two slight young men, thoroughly frightened, dirty, unshaven, their dark eyes darting apprehensively around Whitman's office, only listened in silence as Levy read to Whitman their prepared statement. Whitman questioned them further for more than an hour and then, satisfied, dictated a revision of the statement to a stenographer. In an hour it was typed. Whitman opened the door to his office to a contingent of impatient reporters which had followed the two prisoners from the Tombs. Levy read them the statement.

Louis Libby turned the car over to William Shapiro at 10 P.M. at the Café Boulevard, on Second Avenue at 21st Street. A few minutes afterward, Whitey, who is the starter at the Café Boulevard, received a telephone call to send the car to Tom Sharkey's saloon on 14th Street near Fourth Avenue. Mr. Sharkey is the former heavyweight prize fighter. Shapiro drove to Sharkey's where three men got in the car and ordered it to an address on 95th Street where a fourth man got in. Then the car was ordered to Bridgie Webber's pool room at 42d Street and Sixth Avenue. All the passengers got out there, and Shapiro was told to wait. Half an hour later, seven men came downstairs and six of them got into the car. One man remained on the curb and said to the others, "Now make good." Shapiro was then told to drive to the Metropole and pull up opposite the entrance. Two men got out of the car, telling Shapiro to wait, and disappeared into the hotel. Two more men got out of the car and stood on the sidewalk, blocking Shapiro's view of the entrance. After a few minutes, Shapiro heard loud voices and several shots were fired. Two of the men jumped back into the car and ordered Shapiro to "get out of here." Shapiro hesitated and one of the men in the rear seat leaned over and struck him on the side of the head with a pistol, shouting, "Go on, you bastard! The cops are all fixed. It's a clean getaway."

Shapiro drove as fast as he could to Sixth Avenue, south to 34th Street and east to Madison where he turned north, shooting up Madison at 35 miles an hour, hoping he would be stopped by a policeman. Somewhere in the 80's, he was ordered to stop and all the men got out of the car and told him to "beat it." He was never paid for his services.

Levy paused here, apparently for dramatic effect. A reporter anticipated him and called out, "Does Shapiro know who hired the car?"

"Yes, he does," Levy answered, slowly. "The car was hired by Bald Jack Rose."

"You mean Becker's stool pigeon?" the reporter shot back.

"I don't know his relationship to Lieutenant Becker," said Levy, dryly. "All I know is that he hired the car."

Levy said Rose was not in the car, however, when it went to the Metropole. Shapiro had never seen any of the other men before.

Whitman proposed a reduction in bail on both Libby and Shapiro but Shapiro said it didn't matter. "I wouldn't live for more than half an hour if I walked out of here now," he said. Libby nodded silently.

Shapiro's fears found their way on to the front pages of all New York's twelve daily newspapers and, in time, to the journals of Europe. Berlin newspapers were especially censorious, concluding that the police were indeed guilty. Raged one editorial, "New York is a shriekingly scandalous city."

6. The Forgotten Man

WILLIAM SHAPIRO, chauffeur of assassins, was not the only man seized by fear. It had been steadily infesting, to one degree or another, hundreds of unrelated and unacquainted people ever since news of Herman Rosenthal's bloody end reached print.

Fear flickered through the public mind in the form of a growing suspicion that the police would kill to protect their interests. Fear of greater proportions gripped the entire police force, 10,000 strong; exposure was in the air and even the innocent smelled danger for their jobs.

In response to their own special fears, gambling house proprietors and brothel keepers closed up shop, and railroad trains to the Catskills were suddenly crowded. Gunmen and thugs who were known to the police either left town or pulled down their window blinds and stayed in bed: somebody had to be hung for this killing and it could be anybody. Although there were as many as a dozen eyewitnesses to the crime, not one of them volunteered the fact.

Fear, triggered by vast and vague uncertainties, echoed through the halls of Tammany. In Albany, Governor John A.

Dix, a Tammany man, heard them and gave clarion calls into the darkness.

"Anyone would think that New York was on the verge of anarchy," he said. "I have no intention of interfering in the internal affairs of New York City." He expressed full confidence in Mayor William Jay Gaynor and made some oblique reference to martial law which he said he had no intention of invoking. Nobody had suggested it, but New Yorkers recalled that it had happened once during the Civil War and they seemed intrigued by this precedent.

Gaynor himself, while giving no evidence of fear, moved to shore up the bulwarks of public confidence. With the paranoid attitude that he so frequently displayed, Gaynor regarded the Rosenthal affair, and the conduct of District Attorney Whitman, as a personal affront. He vowed anew his faith in Police Commissioner Rhinelander Waldo and minimized everything. The victim and the entire element of society identified with him Gaynor dismissed as a gang of "lawless and degenerate foreigners." Since a large percentage of the gamblers and better-known hoodlums were Jews, his remark not only failed to ease the public mind, it also embroiled him in an acrimonious fight with the noted Rabbi Stephen Wise, who called Gaynor an "arch quibbler" and termed his outbursts "shrill and vulgar."

Waldo, meanwhile, was bridling in self-defense at Whitman's accusations against the police department. Since they reflected on him personally, he fired off a rebuttal in a letter to the district attorney, with copies to the press. He demanded that Whitman "proceed without further delay to resolve the matter." He also pointed out that the district attorney had condemned the reputations of 10,400 honest policemen on the alleged behavior of a mere handful who had the opportunity to profit by gambling law enforcement.

Whitman retreated, but not from fear. He at last had found a chink in the police department's monopoly of the case and he thought he could enlarge it. Or, he may have simply reconsidered strategically. He withdrew his charge that the police killed Rosenthal by insinuating that he had been misquoted.

"I have never accused the police of murder," he declared, "and my own opinions in the matter are unimportant." However, he reiterated the belief that the policemen at the scene had been singularly negligent.

He answered Waldo's letter, forbearing its "insulting tone," and he again neatly laid the crime at the commissioner's doorstep.

"The awfulness of the situation," he wrote, "cannot be lessened by *your* urging *me* to 'proceed without further delay . . .'

"It is up to you to defend the reputation of your 10,400 honest policemen. Their defense rests in unraveling this murder mystery and you have a small army of detectives and a fund of money . . .

"Since you published your letter to me, I give this answer to the press."

Whitman might not be able to find Jack Rose before the police did, but he would have access to him through Shapiro and, in the meantime, he had discovered other points of leverage. Among them was the mortgage that Rosenthal, in his now-impotent exposé, had said he had given Lt. Becker in return for the $1,500 loan. Whitman sent Emil Klinge out to find it. The mortgage had been canceled but Klinge went directly to the County Clerk's office where the mortgage had been dutifully filed by the law firm of A. E. Lesinsky and Robert Hibbard of 220 Broadway. Klinge handed Hibbard a summons for an immediate appearance before the grand jury.

Hibbard, a former policeman who had laboriously put himself through law school, was attorney for Becker's brother, John, also a lieutenant on the police force, and for Becker's wife. Hibbard said he had known Becker while on the force but that he had never done any legal work for him. He declined to discuss the nature of his services for either John Becker or Mrs. Becker.

Hibbard told the grand jury that the money for the mortgage had been supplied by Jack Rose. A law clerk named John J. Donohue had given his name as the mortgager in return for a $10 fee. Donohue, Hibbard said, did not know any of the parties involved. Hibbard added that when he told Rosenthal the money came from Rose, Rosenthal replied, "Oh, no. It's from my friend, Charlie Becker." Hibbard said he was surprised to hear it.

Whitman fed all this to the newspapers and when it appeared in print the following morning, July 18, Mayor Gaynor and Commissioner Waldo summoned Becker to City Hall.

Becker arrived shortly before noon. He stepped from his chauffeured car and sullenly pushed his way through a crowd of reporters on the front steps. He refused to answer any questions. He shook his fist menacingly at a photographer who blocked his path and the photographer did not take his picture until after he had passed. He was in Gaynor's office for an hour, emerging in the same snarling mood in which he had entered and the newspapermen gave him a wide berth.

The portly, bewhiskered mayor and the gaunt, soft-spoken police commissioner appeared in his wake. The reporters turned from Becker to Gaynor who raised his hand in a regal gesture, motioning for quiet. Waldo stood respectfully by his side.

"I am weary of this clamor for sensationalism," shouted Gaynor angrily, his beard quivering. "This tempest of evil insinuation. Nothing has occurred to shake my faith in Commissioner Waldo personally or in the police department generally. I will not allow political capital to be made of a foul crime perpetrated by degenerates on a member of their own calling."

Gaynor spun his big bulk about and strode back into his office, Waldo at his heels, and slammed the door.

Three hours later, Commissioner Waldo announced that Lt. Becker had been relieved of command of the strong-arm squad "until his name has been cleared of all suspicion." Becker, he said, would be transferred to other duties. He was immediately assigned to desk duty at the 47th Street station and two days later was transferred again, also to another desk, at the Bathgate Avenue station, near 117th Street, in the Bronx.

Waldo's announcement had no sooner cleared his lips than Bald Jack Rose walked into Commissioner Dougherty's office in police headquarters. He was as nattily dressed as ever, but he appeared paler than usual. His hairless skull glistened. To the desk sergeant, Rose said, in his hissing voice, "Is Commissioner Dougherty in?"

"No," said the sergeant, "he's out. Who are you?"

"Never mind," whispered Rose, airily, "I'll be back."

He returned an hour later and was warmly received by Dougherty.

Reporters soon heard that Rose, the number one suspect in the case, had wandered into police headquarters and then had been allowed to wander out again. The incident was the subject of a cartoon next day in the *Tribune*. It showed the interior of a police station with a large sign above the desk sergeant's head reading, "Criminals will not be received unless properly introduced."

The desk sergeant involved was indignant. "I don't know who Jack Rose is," he complained. "I never saw him before."

Dougherty greeted Rose in a disarming fashion, inquiring after his health and wealth and, in a protracted way, casually brought the conversation around to the matter at hand. He did not, however, ask Rose why he had come. He appeared to understand. Rose seemed relieved.

Asked to review his movements on July 15 and 16, Rose said he had left his home on West 110th Street late on the afternoon of the 15th. He ate a leisurely dinner at Luchow's, he said, and then went to the Turkish Baths where he encountered Harry Vallon and Sam Schepps. The three of them sauntered over to the home of Dora Gilbert, Rosenthal's ex-wife, on east 27th Street. On the way they picked up Charles Plitt, whom he identified as "Becker's press agent," since acquitted of his murder charge. The purpose in calling on Miss Gilbert, Rose explained, was to obtain from her an affidavit detailing Rosenthal's alleged moral lapses while he was married to her. Rose said that since he, too, had been named in Rosenthal's exposé, he felt he must take some steps to protect himself by discrediting Rosenthal.

Midway through this inquiry, Dougherty's phone rang. Whitman, tipped off by a reporter of Rose's surrender, demanded that Dougherty deliver him instantly to the Criminal Courts Building. Dougherty complied.

While Dougherty's questioning had been gentle, Whitman plunged to the point.

"Did you go to Miss Gilbert's at Becker's direction?" he asked Rose.

"No," the gambler whined, "'I wanted the affidavit for myself because Rosenthal was hitting at me, too. If Becker wanted to use it, it would have been all right by me."

From Miss Gilbert's, Rose related, the four men went their separate ways. Rose returned to the Lafayette Baths, and from there telephoned Shapiro to have a car meet him at Sharkey's Saloon. Then to the home of his brother-in-law, Max Blauner, on 140th Street, then back to Jack's restaurant at 43d and 6th Avenue. No, he had not gone to Bridgie Webber's poker parlor, although he had intended to, just to Jack's and then home.

"That's all I did that night. I heard about Rosenthal in Jack's. I was sorry because we had been friends in the old days. I wasn't too surprised though. I think it was in the air, with Rosenthal acting the way he was."

It is a failing of all of us that we want to be believed, no matter how high principled our truth or how debased our lie. Rose saw that he was not believed. A smile flitted ever so subtly across Whitman's stern features. Dougherty and Hughes had retreated to separate corners of the room, withdrawn from the scene. Rose looked at them and received only impassive stares. What was worse, Rose wanted a cigarette. He fished out one from his shirt pocket and fumbled in vain through his clothing for a match. Whitman had a match. He was holding it in his hand, across the broad desk from Rose. Whitman made no move to light it. Rose stared at it. Whitman looked bored. Rose fidgeted. He knew he was being manipulated but he couldn't seem to stop it. If he could only convince them that he told the truth.

"What time did you learn about Rosenthal?" Whitman asked, quietly.

"I don't know, maybe two o'clock, maybe later. I don't know exactly."

"How long were you in Jack's?"

"I don't know, exactly. I had one or two drinks."

"Which was it, one or two?"

"Two, I think."

"Don't you know?"

"Yes, two drinks. I had two drinks."

He knows something that I don't know, thought Rose. What did that bastard Shapiro tell them that wasn't in the papers? Whitman's droning voice cut into his thoughts.

"Where have you been for the last two days?"

Oh, thought Rose. He just isn't satisfied. He wants me to admit something, some little thing. Then he'll be satisfied.

"Well, I wasn't afraid, exactly." His tone is conciliatory and a little resigned. "I felt that because I was in the car I might be suspected. When I read in the papers that Shapiro had pretty much told the truth, as far as I was concerned, I thought I might as well come forward. I don't know why or by whom Rosenthal was killed."

"You know, of course, that Shapiro says you went up to Bridgie Webber's?"

Now I give him what he wants, thought Rose. It will be even more plausible than denying it. This DA will be satisfied and then I can go. He smiled, a gesture of sheepishness.

"I was in Bridgie's before I went to Jack's. I played a couple of hands of poker and then I left. Bridgie wasn't there and I didn't see him. I went right home after I left Jack's."

But Whitman did not let Rose go. He took him before Coroner Feinberg on a technical holding charge. Feinberg committed Rose to the Tombs for seventy-two hours without bail. Rose appeared dumbfounded.

The following morning, still wearing his nonplused air, Rose was brought from the Tombs to the office of Commissioner Dougherty. He had not been able to shave and he felt untidy. He sat down facing the hulking Dougherty, ready to deliver himself of injured protest. The commissioner was absorbed in an array of papers spread across his desk and Rose waited for his attention. The door to Dougherty's office shot open suddenly and a policeman beckoned from the hallway. Dougherty stepped outside, closing the door. Rose waited, fidgeting. At that moment, an inner door to the commissioner's office, leading to a row of adjoining offices, opened slowly. Rose looked up at the sound. Framed in the half-open doorway was Lieutenant Becker. He stared blankly at Rose for a few seconds and then withdrew, shutting the door behind him.

Rose's indignant and bewildered manner was instantly replaced by an expression that could only be described as one of terror.

When Dougherty returned to his office that afternoon from lunch, he found Bridgie Webber, flanked by two detectives, waiting for him. Wearily, laboriously he led Webber through the tangle of facts and half facts. Webber was willing, helpful and anticipatory. He had nothing to conceal. He and Rosenthal were old friends. Their friendship had been strained in recent years by inexorable changes in their lives, but he bore him no ill will.

Webber had indeed been in the Metropole a few minutes before the murder; he had, indeed, seen Herman, even spoken to him. He had gone to the hotel, however, looking for William Pinkerton, the famous private detective, to discuss various matters. Pinkerton was not there, so Webber went back to his club. "I was sitting in front of the door. About two thirty someone came running in and told me Herman had been shot. That's all I know about it."

78

Whitman asked the dapper little gambler only one question.

"What time did Jack Rose come into your club?"

Webber's reply was instantaneous. "I didn't see Rose at all that night."

Rose's story remained an unknown quantity.

Dougherty told Webber he was free to go, but not to leave town.

By ten o'clock on the morning of July 19, 45th Street between Broadway and 6th Avenue was choked with people squirming, pushing, and shifting. The temperature was 83. In front of the brownstone at No. 104 stood a black horse-drawn hearse, shimmering in the bright sun, its black and gold tassels quivering as the two chestnut horses to which it was attached fidgeted in the stifling heat. Behind the hearse, reaching to the corner of Broadway, stood three carriages provided by the undertaker for members of the immediate family. Even the long front stairway to the house was filled with onlookers, pressed two deep against the iron railings. Through a narrow passageway down the center, moved an endless flow of flower-laden visitors. On the stairs the heat was intensified by the heavy cool fragrance that heaved in waves out the open door. Inside, a hundred persons gasped quietly for breath in the clammy, perfumed air. Rosenthal's casket, a velvet black, stood in the corner of the front room, partly concealing a roulette table that had been draped with a dark green cover. Next to the coffin stood the Reverend Samuel Greenfield, of the Washington Heights (Reformed) Congregation, a large, severe man, garbed in black, his face fixed in studied sorrow.

The widow's entrance was prolonged. She appeared in the doorway, her great girth engulfed by folds of black taffeta, leaning heavily on the arm of Rosenthal's plump, young sister, Minnie. Mrs. Rosenthal was sobbing heavily, a wadded handkerchief pressed against her mouth. In slow, trembling, agonizing steps, she crossed the room to the coffin. It was the first time she had seen it. The undertaker had done a creditable job of restoring Herman's face and he was plainly recognizable. Mrs. Rosenthal, her shoulders heaving, looked at her husband. She screamed. She turned and faced the staring mourners. "That's not Herman!" It was an accusation. "There's been a mistake." Then she turned to Minnie, grasping her by the shoulders. Her crumpled handkerchief fell to the floor. "Isn't it a mistake?" Now she was pleading. "Tell me it's a mistake. Tell me it isn't my Herman." Then she fainted.

Solicitous hands closed in upon her, carried her to a nearby row of chairs where, stretched across them, she revived. Her conduct set off an epidemic of uneasiness in the room, and a knot of friends surrounded the Reverend Mr. Greenfield, needlessly urging him to begin the service and get it over with. Mrs. Rosenthal sat wrapped in Minnie's arms. Alongside her, in a solemn row, their heads all turned disapprovingly toward the widow, were Herman's brother, Edward, a General Sessions Court clerk, and Herman's four other sisters, all brooding replicas of himself. How many of them heard what Reverend Greenfield was saying in his thick, sonorous voice?

"It is not given to us all to round out the term of our creation, and Herman Rosenthal was cut down at a time when he was most needed." This was the only reference, however veiled, to the dead man's new prominence in New York. For the rest, the Reverend Mr. Greenfield found solace in the trials of King David who, like Herman, "also had no place to hide his weary head from the darts of his enemies." Herman Rosenthal was a good man, devoted to his family and friends, and compassionate to a fault with the poor and needy.

The undertaker had been unable to find sufficient of Herman's friends to serve as pallbearers, for fear either the police or Herman's killers would read significance into the gesture, and the undertaker and his assistants carried the casket out to the hearse. It took a squad of police almost twenty minutes to clear a path through the sweating crowd for the funeral procession. After that, Herman and his family traveled alone, plodding the three miles down Broadway to the Brooklyn Bridge and then across it to Washington Cemetery in Herman's home-land.

Seldom has the finality of death rested so heavily on a public figure. With his burial, Herman Rosenthal ceased even to be a memory. There was no one who could recall to mind, with any reality, the image of Herman Rosenthal, the precipitator of great and monstrous events. For a time his murder was only an impersonal symbol of the fate that henceforth awaited squeal-ers. Soon even the symbol grew hazy and Herman Rosenthal remained in death what he had been in life—a failure. His cause paled before a new and living cause: The cause of District Attorney Charles Seymour Whitman, dramatically fighting the powers of evil.

But there was nothing theatrical about it, as far as Whitman was concerned. He told his wife:

"I'm going to get Becker if it's the only thing I ever do. New York is supposed to be the greatest city in the world. People came here expecting it to be and many of them can help make it so. But as long as Becker and all those like him are allowed to defy and corrupt every law by which decent people live, New York will never be anything but a human sewer!"

7. Dawn of a Private Eye

DISTRICT ATTORNEY CHARLES WHITMAN had potent allies in his crusade: the newspapers of New York, all twelve of them. Whitman, of course, appreciated the value of a friendly press and he perpetually fanned the embers of this mutual affection. Each paper had as many as ten reporters working on the story and Whitman took the entire horde into a kind of selective confidence. Nothing, naturally, was withheld from the *World* and its urbane expert on crime, Herbert Bayard Swope. In general, however, Whitman's doors were always open to reporters and no question was beyond an answer. He arranged for portions of grand jury testimony to be disseminated among them and illegal as this act was in itself, the only criticism came from the mayor's office and from the police. Everyone else, it seemed, was on his side.

Whitman soon acquired the allegiance of another virile force: Money. Within a week after Rosenthal's murder, there appeared in Whitman's office one day the tall, dignified person of William Jay Schieffelin, chairman of a wealthy civic pressure group known as the Citizens Union. Principal backer of the

Citizens Union was J. P. Morgan, the banker who, a few weeks later, admitted to a Senate investigating committee that he donated $150,000 to Theodore Roosevelt's presidential campaign fund without a thought of reward.

Schieffelin, in effect, offered Whitman a blank check in support of his crusade.

Matching Schieffelin's dignity, Whitman thanked him and conditionally declined.

"It is my feeling," he said, "that the city of New York should pay the costs of this investigation."

H. C. Curran, chairman of the finance committee of the New York Board of Aldermen, heard about Schieffelin's offer and Whitman's gesture of refusal and agreed. He began circulating a petition among his fellow aldermen to create a special appropriation for Whitman and to launch an aldermanic inquiry into the morals of the police department.

Mayor Gaynor waived aside the whole proposition at first as mere political horseplay. He became downright vehement, however, when he learned that the money would be used principally to hire the famous private detective William J. Burns and a platoon of his operatives. It was, he said, another rank plot to embarrass him personally. He shot off one of his famous letters to Police Commissioner Waldo, denouncing "the corrupt scamps who are trying to defame you . . ." and, to make certain his invective would be publicly applied to Whitman, he attributed the entire furor to "weak public officials, scheming for some higher office for which they are unable to recognize their mental and moral unfitness."

Whitman wore a bemused expression when he faced reporters anxious for a reply to the mayor. Holding a copy of Gaynor's outburst in his hand, Whitman said:

"I have only one concern in this matter. Herman Rosenthal, as he had publicly announced, was to come to my office last Tuesday morning with his wife to supply evidence of the corrupt alliance between the police and the lawbreakers of this city.

"He was butchered last Monday night in the most brilliantly lighted street in New York because, I believe, he was coming to me. He was shot down by four or five murderers in a block literally swarming with policemen.

"Notwithstanding their presence, there was not a semblance of an effort to apprehend the murderers and the pretext of a pursuit is so silly and transparent that it ought not to deceive a ten-year-old child.

"A week has elapsed and the actual murderers are still at large. Any further comment by me on the police of New York seems quite superfluous."

Mayor Gaynor made no reply. Police Commissioner Waldo, however, responded. Without any explanation, he sent Deputy Commissioner Dougherty and Chief Inspector Hughes to Whitman's office. His motive was apparent: if you can't beat them, join them.

"Commissioner Waldo," said Dougherty, wading through the reporters, "has instructed me to work under the direction of the district attorney."

Dougherty thus brought to Whitman the army of stool pigeons on which all police, honest or dishonest, relied, as well as his own private and highly developed pipeline into the underworld.

Within an hour, Dougherty, Hughes and the district attorney were in conference with William J. Burns. The newspapers heaved a collective sigh of relief. Burns, fresh from notorious exposures of civic corruption in San Francisco and Detroit, was on the job. He and Whitman would save New York from the police department's inability, or refusal, to solve Rosenthal's murder.

Dougherty's sudden subordination to Whitman had other effects. It eliminated the nucleus of the district attorney's competition and it gave Dougherty fresh incentive by delivering him from the wild pressures of City Hall. Whitman could now feel that his crusade was well launched.

Although the killers themselves might still be free, Whitman had custody of three wellsprings of vital information, if he could break them down. Shapiro had driven the murder car, as it was now being called. Libby owned the murder car. Rose had hired the car and his denial that his purpose was assassination was not altogether acceptable. Shapiro, obviously, had not told everything. It was inconceivable that he could have spent more than an hour with the killers in the confines of an automobile and not know more about them than he confessed. His attorney, Aaron J. Levy, the Tammany strategist, was obviously trying to strike a bargain. He wanted Shapiro to turn state's evidence and . . . What else did he want? Was the price of Shapiro's and Levy's cooperation going to be an assurance from Whitman that Tammany itself would not be involved? It seemed farfetched.

Still, there was Levy in the district attorney's outer office, regaling reporters with sensational innuendo. Tomorrow's headlines would be that Shapiro the chauffeur might lead the investigation into the bowels of the police department—if Whitman would let him.

"I will give Shapiro immunity from prosecution," replied Whitman to this subtle pressure, "provided he was not one of the murderers and provided he tells me all he knows."

At the same time, Whitman ordered Dougherty to arrest three more persons: Bridgie Webber, the natty pool-hall keeper in whose club the killers had assembled; Sam Paul, wealthy owner of the infamous Sans Souci Music Hall on Third Avenue and host at the Sunday gamblers' outing where Rosenthal's death had been predicted; and Jacob Reich, alias Jack Sullivan, the newsboy monarch who spent the murder night with Lt. Becker and then showed up at the Metropole minutes after the shooting. In fact, Reich had remained at the scene until the police arrived. He even volunteered the information that he had been sitting in the soda fountain next to the Broadway entrance of the Cohan Theater when he heard the shots. He ran around to the hotel, he said, found the streets full of wildly excited people and Rosenthal lying in a widening puddle of blood.

85

"I kneeled next to him," Reich related, "and I asked him, 'Who done it, Hermie?' But he was dead arreddy."

Dougherty and a handful of detectives were already looking for Harry Vallon and Sam Schepps, two other Broadway gamblers that Shapiro claimed had been in his car that night at one time or another.

Dougherty's outward support of Whitman was just that, and it took William J. Burns and his platoon of detectives to obtain the names of people who had been loitering in the 100 block on West 43d Street before, during and after the murder. However, even if Dougherty had tried, he might have failed. Names of witnesses were information a police stoolie might hesitate to pass along. It was too dangerous. Burns immediately got two names. One was that of Thomas Coupe, the Elks Club clerk who had seen the shooting from the doorway of the club, directly across the street from the Metropole. Coupe had left the country. The other name was that of John Reisler, barber and occasional prize fight promoter, who had had dinner in the Metropole just before the murder. Reisler, whose shop at Broadway and 44th was a hangout for the sporting set, was known familiarly as "John the Barber." He was picked up by Burns and brought to Whitman's office. He was vague, evasive, and thoroughly frightened. Finally, he admitted that he had just left the Metropole and was walking down 43d to Broadway. As he reached the corner, he said, he heard the shots. He stopped and looked toward the hotel. People were swarming in the street and Reisler could not tell exactly what had happened. As he was standing there, he said, Bridgie Webber ran past, fleeing from the direction of the hotel. This put Webber also at the scene of the crime and Whitman could scarcely conceal his elation.

It was the first of two major breaks. The second came later the same day when Shapiro, his immunity from a murder charge now guaranteed by Whitman, named the killers and put Jack Rose plus the still missing Harry Vallon at the scene of the crime. Sam Schepps's role was not clear.

Levy announced Shapiro's willingness to tell all to Whitman and then waited, surrounded by reporters, while Shapiro was brought over from the Tombs. Levy was smug and boastful.

"My client," he declared to newsmen, "can lay this case in Commissioner Waldo's office."

"What about Jack Rose?" a reporter asked.

"Rose is not the big factor in this case," said Levy, arrogantly. "There is Lieutenant Charlie Becker and a few others." He smiled mysteriously.

Shapiro arrived, handcuffed, and was pushed by two guards through the swarm of reporters and on into Whitman's office. Levy followed him and slammed the door. Dougherty and Burns were already inside.

"Tell them what you told me this morning," Levy directed.

Shapiro licked his lips nervously. His eyes flickered around the room.

"Go ahead," Levy urged. "Tell them everything you told me. Everything."

Shapiro began, haltingly. He had picked up Vallon, Rose and Schepps at Tom Sharkey's and had taken them to Webber's pool room. It was shortly after 10 P.M. They remained at Webber's a few minutes and then Shapiro drove them to 134th Street and Seventh Avenue where a man named Dago Frank got into the car. Dago Frank's real name was Cirofici and he was well known to Dougherty as a young killer who worked for Big Jack Zelig. Shapiro drove them all back to Webber's where he was told to wait. About twenty-five minutes later, he said, Rose came down from the pool room with six other men.

"I started across the street—I was parked on the other side of the street from Webber's—but Jack waved his hand at me meaning to wait.

"I had heard a lot of funny things said earlier in the evening when Rose, Vallon, and Schepps were riding around in the car and I was wondering what they were up to.

"They all got in except Rose, Vallon and Schepps. Rose walked on down Sixth Avenue toward 43d Street. After a minute or two I was told to drive to the Metropole. As I turned the corner of Sixth Avenue into 43d Street I saw Jack Rose standing in the shadows on the north side of the street. His hat was pulled down low over his eyes and he was talking to someone.

"Someone said, 'There's Jack now,' and one of the others said, 'Close your mouth, you damn fool.' I was told to go to Broadway and turn around and park across from the hotel. Four of the men got out of the car and one of them told me not to move away. Another man leaned over from the back seat and jabbed me in the ribs with a gun. 'He won't go anywhere,' he called out. Just then I saw Webber go into the hotel. He came right back out and then I must have dozed off for the next thing I knew there were shots fired."

After that, Shapiro said, the getaway was ordered, as he had previously related.

However, his memory for names had improved considerably. He recalled that among those in the car were men addressed by their companions as "Lefty," and "Whitey" and "Gyp."

Dougherty identified them in greater detail. Lefty Louis was Louis Rosenberg, Whitey Lewis was Jacob Seidensheiner, Gyp was none other than the terrible Harry "Gyp the Blood" Horowitz, the bully terrorist who was still breaking backs as a bar-room pastime. All of them were Zelig's men. They were proclaimed as fugitive murderers in the papers the next morning.

Although Whitman's case grew stronger, it was by no means solved. Under New York law, an accusation is worthless if it cannot be corroborated by witnesses who themselves are neither principals nor accessories. All those arrested, or sought, were presumed to have taken part in the murder. However, Whitman knew, as did the entire New York underworld, that all of them had not participated. Any one of them, therefore, could become the corroborating witness. This gave Whitman a certain flexibility, but it set the underworld's nerves on edge. If somebody in custody broke down, there was no telling how

88

far he would go. Webber, it was known, was a "weak sister" who, like Rosenthal, knew too much. Criminal careers by the hundreds hung in the balance. It was no problem, therefore, for the gambling and bawdyhouse fraternity to raise, among themselves, a $50,000 defense fund. And they began spending it on lawyers the morning of July 22 when Rose, Webber, Paul, Shapiro, Libby and Reich were arraigned before Coroner Feinberg on charges of murder. The hearing was, as well, the Broadway spectacle of the summer season. The coroner's court adjoining the Tombs was filled to capacity with gamblers and assorted criminals two hours before the hearing. Those who were unable to get in the court, a crowd estimated in excess of 5,000, jammed the streets for a block in all directions. When the suspects' lawyers arrived, there was no room for them and not much for the defendants themselves. Coroner Feinberg adjourned the proceedings to the more spacious General Sessions courtroom across the street. For all its contradictions, there was an air of the Roman arena about the hearing. The five lawyers, carrying briefcases and indignant manners, strode down the aisle like gladiators. Through the side door came the six prisoners who, however, acted more as lions than in a martyred role. The district attorney and his staff, despite their duties of oppression, appeared to be presiding. The spectators seethed not with anticipation, but with apprehension.

Coroner Feinberg, a shaggy, quiet man, sat on the bench with what could be described as a bored air.

Whitman opened the hearing with a perfunctory request for a continuance of three days for Libby and Shapiro. Levy smiled an assent and Feinberg nodded to the clerk. The six prisoners, seated in a row of chairs along the railing separating the court from the spectators, turned their heads at intervals to scan the audience and wave at friends who did not wave back. Photographers clustered about them and the stench of burned magnesium soon filled the room.

Without warning, a woman draped in black, a shawl

wrapped about her head, rose from near the front of the court-room and walked falteringly, arms outstretched, toward the row of defendants.

"My son, my son," she cried.

Shapiro jumped to his feet and whirled about.

"Mother! Mother, please go home."

"My son, my son," she cried again, drawing nearer.

"Mother, please, please go home," said Shapiro, his voice cracking.

A bailiff stopped the woman and led her toward the door. Shapiro dropped back into his chair and buried his face in his hands, sobbing. Webber, seated next to him, drew away, look-ing in near-horror at the weeping chauffeur. Then he glanced over his shoulder into the crowd and saw his pretty wife, a shapely brunette with a hard veneer of cosmetics. She smiled and winked. Webber turned away and hiding his eyes with one hand, began to cry.

Whitman asked that Rose's arraignment be continued three days and that Rose be held until then without bail. His attorney, James L. Sullivan, who, like Rose, was a short and dapper man, shot out of his chair and across the floor to the bench. He ges-tured with clenched fist toward Whitman.

"I object to my client being shut up in the Tombs while the district attorney goes fishing for evidence," he shouted.

Rose himself watched through slitted eyes. Resplendent once again in his gaudy finery, his hairless head scented and powdered, Rose was, observed an erudite reporter for the *Trib-une,* "a study in light, reddish brown—an artist who painted him would certainly have to be post-impressionist."

All other eyes were on Whitman.

"I have plenty of evidence," he said, quietly.

"Well, submit it then," snarled Sullivan. "I demand my client be admitted to bail."

Whitman called Deputy Commissioner Dougherty to the witness stand. There was an explosion of whispers among the spectators as he lowered his bulk into the chair, smiling. Coro-

90

ner Feinberg banged his gavel. Whitman led the police official through a brief recitation of the case. Rose was arrested, Dougherty explained, on the strength of Shapiro's statement that it was Rose who had hired the murder car.

"You'll concede Herman Rosenthal was murdered?" asked Whitman sarcastically, facing Sullivan.

"I concede nothing," the lawyer replied.

There was an instant of silence and in that instant a man immersed in the crush at the rear of the room called out, "Herman wasn't murdered; he committed suicide." A chorus of laughter erupted.

Feinberg slammed his gavel angrily.

"If there's another disturbance, I'll clear the court."

The buzzing of the crowd subsided to a murmur that rolled eerily back and forth across the sweltering room in waves. Sullivan's voice shot above the sound.

"The district attorney has given us hearsay. There's no evidence to hold my client for first degree murder."

"Very well," said Whitman, grinning. "I'll consent to second degree." A flutter of laughter at this.

Exasperated, Sullivan turned to the bench, his hands outstretched in supplication.

"Your Honor, I beg of you, your Honor has a mind and brains. Your Honor is not a-a-a-a-a-"

"An automaton," said the smirking Levy.

"Ah yes," said Sullivan, "that's the word. Now your Honor . . ."

Feinberg raised his hand. He was a man of few words under any circumstances.

"I'm satisfied," he said, wearily, "that there is enough evidence to hold Mr. Rose for three more days."

He motioned Sullivan to sit down. His refusal to be thus swayed by anger or oratory intimidated the other lawyers and within a few minutes Webber and Paul had been formally arraigned on murder charges. Jacob Reich, alias Jack Sullivan, the newsboy king, was the last to be arraigned. Whitman said that

Reich's alibi had been confirmed. He asked that Reich's status be changed from that of a suspect to a material witness and that his bail be set at $100.

As Feinberg nodded approval, Reich's attorney stepped forward and laid two fifty-dollar bills on the court clerk's desk. He was Benjamin Reass, a former deputy state attorney general and one of Tammany's more saintly politicians. Sullivan clapped his straw hat on his round head and strolled airily down the corridor and out the door. Unfortunately for Reich, his exit was purely a theatrical one and he could not stay away from the case. Before it was over, he became a hinge on which it turned.

Dougherty, meanwhile, was pulling potential witnesses—waiters, cab drivers, gamblers—in off the streets and from the ranks of the police force and Whitman was taking them before the grand jury. Oscar Cauchois, a prosperous real estate man who was foreman of the jury, followed the district attorney from the jury chambers one afternoon and announced to the inevitable crush of reporters that the jury wanted to talk to Lt. Charles Becker provided he would waive immunity from any prosecution that might result.

"What if Becker won't testify?" a reporter asked.

Whitman answered him.

"It would be a sad state of affairs if a policeman refused to testify before a grand jury on grounds he might incriminate himself."

None of the policemen questioned before the jury thus far had refused to talk, although many had been evasive and forgetful. One, however, had been so voluble he had to be told to stop. He was Lt. Daniel Costigan, a handsome, black-haired, pink-faced young Irishman who had been in charge of one subdivision of the strong-arm squad during Becker's reign and, before that, in sole command of a raiding squad. What he had to say became the day's sensation.

Costigan testified that, by his own count, there were at least

150 gambling casinos operating, unhampered, in New York at that very moment and that this would be impossible without the connivance of the police. He said his own efforts to suppress gambling had been stopped not by Becker but by Police Commissioner Waldo. Even the jury gasped at this and at his claim that all his reports, accompanied by evidence sufficient to obtain raiding warrants, ended in pigeon holes in Waldo's office.

"All gambling raids were ordered by the Commissioner," he told the jury, "and we were forbidden to make raids without his order."

Becker did not escape incrimination. In more instances than he could remember, said Costigan, he and his men would be in the process of gathering evidence for a raid, visiting a gaming hall incognito, when Becker and a squad would come crashing in without a warrant and thus destroy the evidence.

"We were deliberately double-crossed," said Costigan.

Waldo sniffed at reporters' questions about Costigan's testimony, saying, "It doesn't merit discussion."

Costigan himself seemed a little shocked on reading his words in the newspapers and his colleagues on the force shunned him as a Judas. He bawled that he had been misquoted. Whitman did nothing to help him.

"Newspaper reports of Lt. Costigan's testimony are essentially correct. Perhaps the lieutenant objects to some of the phraseology used."

Costigan was enraged.

"The hell with that," he shouted, "I never told the grand jury any of that stuff."

As usual, the denial never did catch up with the accusation and the score against the police, as far as the public was concerned, continued to rise. And, as usual, Police Commissioner Rhinelander Waldo was moved to prove his own unimpeachable character. He suspended Dectective William J. File, whose pursuit of the killers had been the only overt gesture the police had made, on charges of gross neglect of duty. Later, he demoted File to patrolman. File was astonished. He appeared before the grand jury with an air of injured innocence, proclaiming that he had made every effort to nab the killers.

"Why shouldn't I? It would have meant a medal and a promotion."

Members of the jury murmured their sympathy.

Whitman also took Rosenthal's widow before the jury. She was an excellent witness. She fainted twice. She reiterated her dead husband's accusations against Becker, declared that Becker controlled vice in New York virtually singlehanded and said that Rose was Becker's head payoff collector and informer. In addition, said Whitman, she named several policemen as associates of Becker. That night, she and her late husband's brother Edward, the court clerk, had dinner with the Whitmans in their Madison Avenue home.

Of all the grand jury testimony, one key fragment failed to reach the newspapers in detail. It was that of the chauffeur, Shapiro, who at last told all. Of the testimony, Whitman would only say:

"Shapiro's story is amazing. It proves that this was one of the most carefully planned murders in criminal annals. It was not plotted by mere criminals."

The intimation was clear. The arm of suspicion, which for days had been waving all over town, began drifting back in the direction of Lt. Charles Becker, now impotently presiding over a desk in a Bronx stationhouse and, on the advice of his lawyers, keeping his mouth shut. It was a difficult role for him. He was, however, far from idle. He hired an old friend, ex-cop and private detective named Valentine O'Farrell, and assigned him to the herculean chore of finding witnesses to keep Becker's own name out of the thickening mire. Whatever his success, he was no source of assurance to Becker.

"You can get any kind of witness except the kind you want," O'Farrell told him. "Whitman's after you and he isn't gonna let any witnesses get in his way."

8. Any Well-Dressed Person

CONDITIONED by half a century of lawlessness in New York City, criminals in 1912 took pains not to conceal their occupation but to declare it. They had been successfully defying the police for so long that they could not help but be proud of their calling. Their dress was garish and the fastidiousness with which they attended to their persons was almost effeminate. If you could not see a prosperous gambler, gunman, or thief, you could certainly smell him for his consumption of cologne, toilet water, and hair dressing was stupendous. Although many of them spent a substantial part of every day in a Turkish bath ("They are members of the Order of the Turkish Bath," sneered Richard Harding Davis), a daily manicure was a status symbol reserved for such important figures as Big Jack Zelig. All, however, wore tan shoes, silk socks, silk ties and bedecked themselves with as much jewelry as they could buy or steal. A really accomplished criminal, of course, bought his ornaments.

Bald Jack Rose was the epitome of underworld exquisiteness. Harry Vallon, the fugitive suspect in the murder, aspired to this but, unhappily, could not afford it. When he walked into Commissioner Dougherty's office on the morning of July 24, however, he was at his most splendid, carrying a black cane with a silver head. He had been resting, he said, at a resort near Big Indian in the Catskills. He came back to town because he read in the papers that he was wanted. He was puzzled. He had seen Rose, Webber, and Paul on the night of the murder, but parted company from them about midnight and retreated to the familiar Lafayette Turkish Baths. He was quite drunk, he explained. He rubbed his long bulbous nose thoughtfully.

"Shapiro says you were in the murder car in the getaway," lied Dougherty, hopefully.

Vallon's answer was calm and a trifle haughty.

"He is mistaken. My word is as good as his."

Vallon denied knowing Dago Frank, Lefty Louie, Whitey Lewis or Gyp the Blood. Dougherty took Vallon to Whitman's office and after four hours of questioning, Vallon admitted only that he had often been a partner of Bridgie Webber in various gambling enterprises and that they frequently employed the protective services of Big Jack Zelig. As far as his fellow fugitive Sam Schepps was concerned, Vallon hadn't seen him, didn't know where he was.

"He'll be here," he said, confidently. "He ain't got nothing to hide for."

Vallon was lodged in the Tombs on a charge of murder. Shapiro had placed him at Webber's just prior to the crime, and Whitman hoped he could somehow place him at the Metropole too. Rose was in similar straits and so was Bridgie Webber. Whitman closed the noose more tightly about Webber later that day when he received a phone call from a restaurant owner at Coney Island. One of his waiters, a Hungarian who spoke very poor English, had been standing across the street from the Metropole throughout the murder and had seen the whole thing. He hadn't come forward before because he couldn't read newspapers. The waiter, a scrawny, balding little man named Louis Krese, was the star witness next day when Vallon and Rose were taken before Coroner Feinberg to be arraigned on murder charges.

Crowds began gathering outside the General Sessions Court on Center Street at midnight and a detachment of police was sent over to maintain order. The Coroner's office decreed the next morning that admission to the courtroom would be by ticket only and it began issuing them, in the form of blank white cards, an hour before the hearing to "any well-dressed person." The audience, as before, consisted largely of members of the underworld.

Webber was the first to be arraigned and Whitman put John Reisler, the Broadway barber, on the stand. He was a large, red-faced man with a scraggly mustache and glistening black hair. He was sweating profusely despite the electric fans Feinberg had installed to moderate the heat. He gasped for breath as he climbed into the chair and his hand shook violently as he placed it on the Bible to be sworn in. He was terrified. He admitted to knowing Webber and, to satisfy legal formalities, pointed him out. Webber sat impassively, studying the barber's sweat-soaked face.

Whitman's voice was quiet, matter-of-fact.

"Did you see the defendant, Mr. Webber, running from the Metropole Hotel on or about 1:50 A.M. on the morning of July 16?"

Reisler, his hands gripping the arms of the chair, stared at Whitman through rapidly blinking eyes for almost a minute without answering.

"Please answer the question," said Coroner Feinberg.

"No," said Reisler, in a low voice, his eyes now on the floor.

Whitman spun about in astonishment.

"Didn't you just tell me, before this hearing, that you saw Mr. Webber 'running like hell,' to use your own words?"

Reisler stammered.

"I-I-I was excited and I didn't know what happened."

Whitman's face reddened in anger.

"Didn't you just tell me, before this hearing, in the presence of my assistant, Mr. Moss, that you were afraid to testify here?"

Reisler gasped and choked.

97

"I don't know. I'm not sure."

Whitman ordered Reisler to step down and he put Frank Moss on the stand. Moss repeated Reisler's statement that as he approached the Metropole immediately following the shooting, Webber passed him, running away. Reisler was recalled to the stand and questioned by Webber's attorney, Hartford T. Marshall, a popular Tenderloin counsel. Reisler was more composed.

"How long have you known Webber?"

"For many years."

"Did you see him running away?"

"I did not."

"Are you willing to swear you saw Webber at all that night?"

"I'm not sure about it."

Whitman stepped forward and Reisler began to squirm.

"Do you understand you are under oath?"

Reisler hesitated, avoiding Whitman's eyes.

"I do."

"Do you know what perjury is?"

"I do."

"Did you or did you not see Bridgie Webber running away?"

"I think I did."

Whitman ordered Webber to stand up. His voice rose steadily. Reisler's answers were low, muffled.

"Is that the man you saw?"

"I think I saw him."

"Did you see him?"

"I-I-I-I-I'm under oath and I'm not sure."

"Did you tell me that the man who testified against Webber would not live?"

"I did not say any such thing."

"That's all," snapped Whitman. "I ask that this witness be held without bail. I charge him with perjury. I also ask that this examination be continued for twenty-four hours."

Feinberg nodded assent. A bailiff stepped up and led the barber from the room.

Webber looked down at the floor. He was smiling. Rose, seated next to him, stared at the wall behind the coroner, his face blank.

The scene, in all its aspects, was repeated the following morning. Reisler, however, was not in court. Another Tenderloin barrister, Henry Goldsmith, wizened and taciturn, silently handed Coroner Feinberg an affidavit, signed by Reisler, repudiating his denials of yesterday. He had, indeed, seen Webber in full flight from the Metropole.

"My client," explained Goldsmith, without emphasis or elaboration, "was afraid for his wife and six children."

Rose and Webber appeared puzzled. Webber's expression dissolved into one of shock moments later.

Whitman called Louis Krese, the Coney Island waiter. On July 15, he had been locked out of his job at the Waldorf Astoria by a waiters' strike. He was walking the streets, looking for work, and he happened by the Metropole shortly before 2 A.M. on July 16. He was walking on the opposite side of the street and as he neared the Metropole, a gray car roared up in front of him and swerved to a halt. He stopped to watch. Krese became excited at this point and his heavy accent thickened. He had to be asked to repeat his answers and Whitman's questions often had to be rephrased. Finally, the district attorney asked him simply to tell what he saw occur in front of the Hotel Metropole.

Men got out of the car, he said, and went inside the hotel. As he stood there, a man approached him.

"Whatta ya lookin' at?"

Krese ignored him.

"Beat it," said the man. "Mind your own business."

"It's a free country," Krese replied, testily. "Perhaps you own the street."

The man started to say something else, Krese related, when suddenly a fat man carrying an armload of newspapers came out of the hotel and was immediately shot down by men standing in the street. The car roared away toward Sixth Avenue, the waiter said, and men began running in front of the hotel.

"Do you see anyone in this room who was there at the time?" Whitman asked.

"Yes, sir," said Krese, pointing at Webber. "That man over there. He ran right past me."

Panic charged across Webber's face and he licked his lips nervously. Sweat broke out on his forehead. Rose stared at him, wide-eyed. Feinberg beat on the bench with his gavel, vainly trying to stop the outburst of noisy consternation among the spectators.

Whitman pressed on, his voice loud and firm.

"Are you sure?"

"Yes, sir. He ran as fast as he could to Broadway and turned north."

"Was he waiting near the hotel before the shooting?"

"Yes, sir."

Krese, suddenly at ease, began to study the faces of spectators nearest him. His eyes paused on Jacob Reich, free on bail and enjoying his safe notoriety as a material witness.

"Do you see anyone else in this room who was there that night?" Whitman asked suddenly, as though an afterthought.

"Yes, sir," said Krese, pointing at Reich. "That little man over there. It was he who told me to mind my own business."

Dougherty vaulted the railing and seized Reich by the arm. Reich struggled for a moment, his face distorted in panic.

"It's a frame-up," he screamed.

Spectators were jumping from their chairs and scrambling for the exit. Bailiffs trying to stop them were roughly pushed aside. Feinberg slammed his gavel again and again but it could barely be heard above the pandemonium.

The story exploded the next morning across the front pages of all the newspapers. America's progress in the summer Olympics and Germany's growing war menace were relegated to inside pages. But for the next two days, the papers had to struggle to keep the story going. Whitman and Dougherty withdrew into enigmatic silence. The press, to fill the void, ran photographs of everybody involved, attacked and insulted the mayor and his loyal police commissioner, interviewed "authoritative underworld sources" in endless number, and speculated interminably on the significance of the stream of noted and notorious criminal attorneys visiting the Tombs.

There were frequent allusions to a marathon grilling of Rose, Webber and Vallon by the district attorney and his staff. William J. Burns lurked in the background like some avenging specter. Reporters tailed him everywhere while police detectives tailed his operatives. It was impossible to link Burns or his men directly to any developments in the case yet they were obviously deeply embroiled, conferring constantly and furtively with Whitman. In the end, all America was titillated to learn that Burns had installed hidden Dictographs, a recently invented electric listening device, in the cells occupied by Rose, Webber, and Vallon.

All the underworld, meanwhile, was in a collective sweat and a new exodus to Catskill hideaways began. It was apparent to every gambler and gunman on Broadway that Rose, Webber, and Vallon were going to be charged with Rosenthal's murder —unless they could hang it on somebody else. Rose and Vallon were inextricably linked to the killing by Shapiro, the chauffeur. Webber was implicated beyond hope not only by Shapiro but by two other witnesses. It was only a matter of time before Whitman and his now vast forces put Rose and Vallon in the same spot. Bravery was not their strongest virtue. Confronted with the prospect of the electric chair, how long would any of them stand alone? Juries were composed these days of men and women who were expressing their repugnance with the flagrant state of crime and corruption by sending people to the electric chair. In one week alone, in New York City, a total of nine men had been handed the death penalty. All juries, it seemed, were hanging juries.

For Whitman, however, the momentum he had generated in the case was beginning to lag. The prospect of convicting three gamblers for murdering a fourth was not one likely to mean much in his political future. Destroying the tools of a criminal conspiracy would avail him nothing unless he also got the conspirators. He must get Becker. While Rose, Webber, and Vallon stewed in the Tombs and squirmed under the pressure of endless questioning and threats, Whitman threw out an irresistible bait and, at the same time, sent new terrors surging through the veins of the Tenderloin.

"I don't want the small fry in this murder. I want the big fish. I'd give anybody immunity if he will lead me to the real culprit. That goes for Rose, or Webber, or anybody who can help me show how far they were aided by influences and activities outside their own circles—by the police, for example."

He had given them a perfect out, albeit an expensive one. It had no sooner appeared in print than Deputy Commissioner Dougherty received an anonymous phone call. A rasping voice advised him that Dago Frank was occupying an apartment at 523 West 134th Street in Harlem. Dougherty and a squad of detectives, armed to the teeth, raced to the address. Their precautions were needless. Dago Frank was sound asleep in an unmade bed, a cold opium pipe on the floor beside him. Two revolvers lay on a bedside table. Dago Frank had not been awakened by the crashing entrance of the police and, in fact, he remained in an opium stupor for two days, unable even to state his name coherently. New Yorkers waited impatiently for him to confess. They were diverted momentarily when Police Commissioner Waldo, no longer defensively maneuvering around the jabs of the press, sued the *Tribune,* the *Press* and the *Herald* for libel. He asked damages totaling three quarters of a million dollars.

It was somewhat less newsworthy when a Negro domestic named Mary Carter sued Lt. Becker the same day for $15,000 damages for the death of her twenty-five-year-old son, Waverly, shot in a gambling raid conducted by Becker four months previously.

The following day the newspapers fell back on the announcement that Alderman H. C. Curran was going to court for a writ of mandamus to force the mayor to order an aldermanic investigation of the police department.

And the next day, July 29, was, as the *Tribune* proclaimed it in a banner, "A Red Letter Day in the History of Crime."

Lt. Charles Becker was indicted at 9:30 P.M. by the grand jury for the murder of Herman Rosenthal. Two detectives from Whitman's office found him half an hour later on duty in the Bathgate Avenue station. They gave him ten minutes to change from his uniform into a natty brown suit and then took him directly before General Sessions Judge J. P. Mulqueen for arraignment. His Panama hat in hand, he entered a plea of "not guilty" in a toneless voice and was led away to the Tombs.

A handful of reporters present had difficulty hearing the brief proceedings because of a thunder and lightning storm which broke just as Becker stepped before the bench. It was inevitable that one of them would make note of this heavenly manifestation and attribute it to the wrath of God.

Wrath of another source fell two days later on a Harlem saloonkeeper whose name, according to the police, was either George Hendricks or George Fredericks. They didn't really care. All they knew was that two men had come into the saloon, which adjoined the rooming house where Dago Frank had been arrested, and George had greeted them as patrons. They had greeted George by putting eight bullets into his chest. He was dead before he hit his sawdust-covered floor. His killers knew what the police didn't: That George had been the anonymous cause of Dago Frank's arrest.

9. The Big Squeal

IT WAS several days before New Yorkers understood fully how Becker had been indicted. Even after the newspapers uncovered it, the story was difficult to explain. Essentially, of course, Becker was indicted on the confession of Bald Jack Rose— and not the timid Webber. However, Webber also confessed soon afterward and so did Vallon. They said they had hired the four murderers—Dago Frank, Whitey Lewis, Lefty Louie and Gyp the Blood—but only because Becker had forced them to do it.

Rose's monumental squeal came out in daily fragments of sensation released with theatrical timing by the district attorney. It was not until August 7 that his thirty-eight page handwritten confession appeared in full in all the papers. It gave a detailed, if somewhat ungrammatical, picture of police shakedowns in New York generally and Becker's ruthless role specifically.

As Becker's chief bagman, Rose said, he had no choice but to obey when the lieutenant directed him to arrange for the murder of Herman Rosenthal, the squealer. Of course, Rose explained, he didn't have any experience with this kind of a thing and he had to get help from Webber and Vallon. They sought out Zelig, who knew how such matters were accomplished, and thus got in touch with the four young men whose guns they had hired for $500 each. Webber had put up the execution fund, Rose explained, because Becker didn't have that much change on him although he promised to pay it back.

"It was a generous fee," commented Commissioner Dougherty, sardonically. "They don't usually charge that much."

The public delight over Becker's downfall was a tribute to Whitman's wisdom in cloaking the police lieutenant, metaphorically, in the hide of a dragon. At the same time, Becker's wife, stunned into grief over her husband's arrest, succeeded briefly in spreading misgivings among New Yorkers. Her eyes brimming with tears, she met reporters in front of the Tombs where she went faithfully every day to visit her husband.

"I am certain this will all be cleared up," she said. "Anyone who knows Charlie will realize that he is not capable of such a foul crime."

It wasn't long, however, before these same sympathetic New Yorkers began to wonder if they didn't know Charlie better than she did. Whitman had restored Becker's image of evil by releasing to the press the text of Bald Jack Rose's confession, grammatical horrors and all. It was a persuasive document with the ring of sordid truth. Rose had taken Rosenthal's own story of the alleged partnership between Becker and the slain gambler and simply extended it logically.

"Becker told me almost every day," Rose wrote, "that Waldo was after him to raid Rosenthal. I begged and pleaded with him not to do it because I knew what would happen. . . .

"His reply was that he had to do it and that he was going to make Rosenthal a present of the $1,500 Rosenthal owed him to cover expenses in the matter. . . . Well, he raided the place . . . .

"After that Rosenthal and Becker had several meetings but

could not fix the matter up and the policeman continued to be stationed at Rosenthal's house. . . .

"Rosenthal was growing desperate. . . . He began threatening to tell what he knew. . . .

"Becker told me to find Zelig's friends and tell them that if they wanted to save themselves that Rosenthal is the man who is stirring up all the trouble in New York and that Becker wants him murdered. . . .

"I went to see Lefty Louie and Whitey Lewis and told them Becker would frame them if they didn't kill Rosenthal. . . . They said, 'We are willing. We'll go tonight. . . .'

"I saw Becker that night and told him everything was all right, that Zelig's friends were on the job. . . .

"Becker said, 'Tell those fellows to drop everything else. There is nothing to worry about and nothing to fear. I will take care of anybody and everybody who has a hand in the thing.'

"I thought it would all blow over but Becker kept demanding. . . . He kept asking me why the job wasn't done. . . .

"'All that's necessary,' Becker said, 'is to walk right up to where he is and blaze away at him and leave the rest to me. Nothing will happen to anybody that does it. I will take care of that. . . . Walk up and shoot him before a policeman if you want to. There ain't nothing to fear. . . .'

"Becker was furious at the delay. . . . Rosenthal had gone to the district attorney and had issued affidavits exposing Becker and naming me as Becker's collector. . . ."

On the night of July 15, 1912, said Rose, Becker informed him that Rosenthal was going to appear before the grand jury the next day and that he would have to be killed immediately. Rose said he and two other gamblers, Harry Vallon and Sam Schepps, rented a car and driver and picked up the four killers, taking them to Bridgie Webber's pool hall at 42d Street and Sixth Avenue, a block and a half from the Metropole Hotel.

"We all went upstairs and sat at a table for refreshments. Webber went out and when he returned he said, 'Rosenthal is at the Metropole.' Everybody got up from the table and started for the door. I stayed and Schepps stayed with me. Soon the word came that Rosenthal had been killed. . . .

"I went to the Times Building and telephoned Becker's house. I asked him if he had heard the news. He answered, 'Yes, and I congratulate you.' He said a newspaperman had called him. I told him I was at Webber's and he said he would be down soon. . . .

"Becker came along about daybreak. He said he had been to the 47th Street station and that District Attorney Whitman was there. . . .

"He said he went to the back room and took a look at Rosenthal. His exact words were:

" 'It was a pleasing sight to me to see that squealing Jew lying there and if it had not been for the presence of Whitman I would have cut out his tongue and hung it on the Times Building as a warning to future squealers. . . .'

"Then he said, 'The only thing to do now is to see that those fellows get away and lay low for a few days until this thing blows over.' "

Rose said that Webber, at Becker's instruction, handed him $1,000 to pay the killers. Rose said he delivered the money to Sam Schepps and then went home, "sick in body and mind." Two days later, still ailing, he went to the home of a friend where Becker contacted him by telephone.

"I asked him, 'What's the news?'

" 'News?' he said. 'There are 200 cops looking for you. But don't worry and don't get excited. This will all blow over. . . .'

New Yorkers may have wanted to believe that Rose turned state's evidence in response to Whitman's virtuous strength, but Rose had another explanation. It began, he said, that day in Dougherty's office when he looked up suddenly and saw Becker staring at him.

"I had seen Becker look like that when he told me to get Rosenthal. I did some quick thinking and saw I was to be jobbed by the whole police department. I knew I would get a square deal from Whitman so I waited until things shaped up right and then I talked to him.

"While I was in the Tombs, Becker sent word to me that my life wouldn't be worth a dime if I squealed. Five or six other cops sent me the same message. I waited until I was absolutely sure that Becker had turned me down—that he had put me in the bag and was tying it up. Then I hit in self-defense and I'm going through with the thing although I am certain they will get me for doing it."

Zelig's involvement in the case brought an outraged denial from his attorney, Charles F. G. Wahle, a former Tammany magistrate. This whetted the grand jury's curiosity and they issued a subpoena for Zelig. The lean, hawk-nosed gang chief cheerfully complied and later, emerging from the jury's chambers, he snarled at waiting reporters.

"I don't know who killed Herman Rosenthal and if I did," he said, "I would find him and break his leg for him. Herman Rosenthal was my friend."

Never had he been so indignant. He barely knew the four gunmen, he said, "but they are decent chaps compared to this fellow Rose. He would hang his brother to clear his own skirts.

"If Rose ever tried to frame me," Zelig said, "my friends would kill him."

"He means his friends would avenge him," corrected lawyer Wahle.

"Yeah," agreed Zelig, climbing into a taxi, "avenge me."

Rose's motives to confess were now clear. He could no longer endure the pressure Whitman applied because of Rose's alleged link with Becker.

Shortly after his arrest, Rose was waiting alone for his lawyer in the Tombs' counsel room when a man he had never seen before stepped through the door and approached him.

"I've got a message for you," he whispered to the startled Rose. "Whitman won't stop. The best thing for you to do is to kill yourself."

He left before Rose could recover his wits and reply.

Next, the celebrated criminal lawyer, Max D. Steuer, after repeatedly announcing that he wouldn't touch the case with a pole, became Webber's attorney and publicly accepted a $10,000 retainer from the dainty hands of Mrs. Webber.

The *World*, attempting to explain Steuer's change of mind, said that he "yielded to the persuasion of friends who felt the interests of someone whose name has not been mentioned in the case would not be safe unless a lawyer of Steuer's ability was on hand to represent them."

It was all very mysterious, and the mystery heightened when Steuer spent most of his time conferring with the district attorney instead of Webber.

The day after Rose's confession and the admissions of Vallon and Webber bulwarking it, Whitman said that it was Steuer who had so nobly brought about this triumph of justice.

Added James Sullivan, Rose's counsel:

"Rose is not a squealer in the ordinary sense. No matter how low he may be, no matter what his crime is, let it be understood that he held out and refused to entertain any proposition for a confession until the men who should have stuck with him deserted him and he found himself without friends or money and his family without aid or financial assistance."

Rose's fair-weather friends were not identified.

"He has implicated Charles Becker directly in this hideous murder," said Sullivan, "and a great step has been taken in the furtherance of the ends of justice. The thanks of the community are also due Mr. Whitman for his unrelenting search for the true criminals."

And the avalanche of accusation and insinuation against Becker rolled onward. Nor could his lawyer, John D. Hart, a noted Broadway barrister, protect him. Hart himself was summoned before the grand jury to be questioned about a rumor that he had been in contact with Bald Jack Rose while Rose was still a fugitive. Hart refused to answer questions on the grounds that to do so would be to violate the bonds of secrecy between a lawyer and his client. Whitman, charging that Hart "isn't a lawyer, he's a witness," dragged him immediately before Judge Mulqueen who ordered Hart to answer all questions. He did so but when he came out of the jury's chambers he told reporters:

"I was subpoenaed to testify before the grand jury in the case of the People against Becker, et al. It is most unusual to ask an attorney to testify against his own client!"

It was two days before Hart could hit back. He submitted motions before Judge Mulqueen asking that the indictment be dismissed as illegal, on grounds the entire jury had not been present, and he asked for the right to inspect the minutes of the grand jury meeting to determine the question of the indictment's legality on other grounds.

Both motions were denied.

Hart then issued, with considerable conviction, a charge that Becker was the victim of a diabolical frame-up.

"These three," stormed Hart, with a contemptuous wave in the direction of the Tombs, "have had it dinned into their ears since they were arrested that the only chance for them to save their own bacon is by confessing. They have been told again and again that if they will swear that Becker conspired with them they will be granted immunity.

"They showed yellow and they threw Becker to the wolves. They have nothing on him and they made the story up. We won't have any trouble proving it. We have five witnesses to the fact that just four days ago, in the Tombs, Rose turned to Webber and Vallon and he said, 'My God. I can't stand this any longer. Why, they're trying to send me to the chair. Just how bad do they want Becker? What'll they do for us if we give him to them?' "

There was silence among the reporters. They were obviously impressed.

"You don't think that Becker is the kind of damn fool who would trumpet his intentions from the housetops, do you? Even if he had made up his mind to murder Rosenthal how many people do you think he would tell? He would try to keep it this

110

side of the Brooklyn Bridge at least, but to listen to those three fine fellows in the Tombs you would think he had told everybody in the eastern states."

The reporters themselves may have been moved by Hart's words, but the city editors were not and they continued to play the story against Becker. The presumption of guilt clung to him like a bad odor.

And to counter whatever effect the frame-up charge may have had, Whitman embarked on a galloping exposure of Becker's financial resources. For three days he fed the newspapers itemized reports on Becker's private finances. He uncovered deposits in eleven New York city banks which altogether totaled slightly more than $100,000. Everybody laughed when Hart said Becker had made his money on the stock market. And Whitman had found only a handful of all Becker's bank deposits.

Becker's own efforts to strike back were no more successful. He offered his exclusive story to a succession of newspapers and magazines, all of which scoffingly declined, and the dozens of interviews he gave to the nation's press did nothing to help him. Editorial revulsion toward civic corruption was at a peak. Everything he said emerged in print as the incredible utterances of a dangerous social specimen. He could agree for the first time with Mayor Gaynor, also smarting under the journalistic lash, when he ranted, "The black plague was nothing compared to the yellow press."

Helen Becker was the only redeeming element to his story. A frail and pretty woman, demure and courageous, she continued to give reporters heavy doses of uneasiness, for her selfless dedication as a teacher was widely known. Reporters tried to bridge the gulf between Mrs. Becker and her ruthless husband but she remained an enigma. Her loyalty was more than admirable, it was incomprehensible.

On the day of his arrest, Becker had just finished moving himself and his wife into a rustic little home at 3239 Olinville Avenue in Williamsbridge near the Bronx Botanical Gardens. It was the beginning of the fulfillment of their domestic dreams. There was a garden where Charlie planned to spend his weekends and there was even a nursery, she confided one day to a lady reporter from the *Daily News*. Mrs. Becker's pregnancy was not reported to the public until it became obvious several weeks later. By that time, it had lost some of its sentimental value.

Mrs. Becker lived alone in the little brown frame house, stoically ignoring the curious crowds who clustered about the front gate. Letters by the hundreds poured into her mailbox, asking for money, offering money, proposing marriage, naming non-existent witnesses who could clear her husband, letters aimed at blackmail, letters born of psychopathic cruelty. She obtained a large white mongrel watchdog named Bum, who, inordinantly zealous, bit the milkman and was promptly shot by a policeman. Then the Beckers' maid, a Negress known only as Lena, inexplicably committed suicide with rat poison one afternoon in the Becker dining room. Finally, Helen's brother, John, came to stay with her which set the neighborhood afire with rumors that she was living with a strange man.

"I think the house is bad luck," she said, "despite all our dreams about it. Nothing good has happened to us since we got it."

Helen made the three-hour round trip by subway to the Tombs every day and spent from 10 o'clock to noon with her husband. On Sunday she was not permitted to visit him, but she came anyway carrying a basket of food, usually a roast chicken, some fruit and homemade bread and preserves.

Becker began to lose a little weight but the effect was to make him more muscularly trim. Aside from his prison pallor, he actually looked much more fit than before. At first, he assumed the air of a man about whom a terrible mistake has been made, but a man who is confident that vindication is at hand. As the weeks wore on and the mass of testimony mounted against him, he became increasingly hostile. At the same time, the press began to lose interest in him and even his ineffectual opportunities for rebuttal were soon gone.

112

Only one paper quoted him when, peering through the gates of the Tombs' yard, he spotted a handful of reporters and cried out:

"Whitman thinks he can become Governor by killing me. That's what he wants. He wants to be Governor."

It was the first and last time that Becker's nerve failed him.

10. How Are Things in Hot Springs?

HOT SPRINGS, ARKANSAS, was a nationally famous resort even in 1912. Among the relatively few Americans who could afford to go there, spend several weeks and take the baths, were criminals. They might be wanted in earnest anywhere else but the people of Hot Springs not only ignored this, they seemed to like it. Sam Schepps, whose status as the fugitive key witness in the Rosenthal killing was being trumpeted on the front pages of a majority of U. S. newspapers, strode confidently into the Hot Springs post office on the morning of August 10 to mail a letter. He had spent the previous evening at a gala formal dinner at the home of the district attorney and was in a pleasurable mood. He dropped his letter into the outbound mail slot and had started to leave when he was tapped on the shoulder. Fate, in all her perversity, had chosen him as the exception to the rule.

Schepps stopped and turned his pleased countenance amiably about. He was smiling. Still resting on his shoulder was the hand of Fred Johnson, postmaster of Hot Springs, who was also a deputy U. S. marshal.

"Sam Schepps?" asked Johnson, his hand pressing down.

"Who wants to know?" retorted Schepps, his smile fading.

Johnson steered Schepps into his office and summoned Police Chief George Howell who searched Schepps. In the gambler's hip pocket was a letter, undated but postmarked in New York four days earlier, from Bald Jack Rose. It read as follows:

Dear Sam:

I don't know what you have heard or read, but it has got down to the stage where the electric chair stares us in the face. The first man to try and get from under was Becker. There were many people who saw everything that night and the next day the district attorney knew what part everybody played in the thing and nobody could have gotten away. I was deserted like a dog by Becker. When I saw what the situation was I opened up negotiations with the district attorney, who offered me a sort of cover that I cannot go into details by writing. I insisted that the same protection given me be extended to Harry, Bridgie and you, to which he finally agreed. We are all pleased with the agreement and all our worry has been to get you to come in and go before him before it is too late.

My advice is to let me send a representative of the district attorney to bring you here. This would prevent the police getting you and putting you through the third degree. Don't say a word to anyone. You know, Sam, that you have been too loyal and too dear a friend of mine for me to ask you to do this if I wasn't positive that you haven't got a chance otherwise. On receipt of this wire me to my brother, Louis Rose, what you want to do.

Jack

Postmaster Johnson, meanwhile, retrieved the letter Schepps had mailed a few moments earlier. He opened it and read it aloud. It was Schepps' reply to Rose. It said:

Dear Friend Jack:

Your letter followed to me and contents noted. All I can say is that I am mighty sorry it has turned out this way for you, dear old pal. However at this stage of the game I can dispense with sympathy as it can't help any now. I have read little about the case so far and I can't bear to think about it any more. What you asked of me I considered very carefully and looked at it from all sides and find I am in very bad regardless of the leniency you say Mr. Whitman holds out for me.

That you had a guilty knowledge of the facts before its perpetration is a fact from your confession. So why do you want me to corroborate a few lies, for instance, such as that I paid $1,000 to L.L. (Lefty Louie, one of the killers) on 42d Street and a few others I dare not mention? However, Jack, my name is Sam and I don't go back on a pal such as you. If you had trusted me with more of your confidences this terrible state of affairs would never have come to pass. But what is done can't be undone. I have no right to preach to you and I can't. I am at present in poor health having taken treatment and am all broken up with worry and sickness. However, if you decide to state truthfully the entire state of affairs and what part you had in same, I will come gladly for you, Jack, because you know what I think of you.

Yes, I have been, and am very sorry for it, as now to prove my loyalty to you, I must be a squealer. Still I am willing even at that cost, on these conditions: that you will only expect me to tell the truth, and nothing but the truth, or else to write word for word what you expect of me. Also, I will not be ready to see Mr. W. representatives until after the 19th of August. If the foregoing is satisfactory, I will come, but you must send me a wire to this effect before the 19th; then I will be ready to meet the man and go back to N.Y. with him. He won't find me if I don't get this wire. I shall change my address today, but if O.K. I will meet on the 19th in the Arlington Hotel the man he will send. Let me know his name in advance. I am sick of being hounded and seeing my mug in the papers every day. Best wishes to you and may God help us.

Sam Franklin

Postmaster Johnson never explained why he had singled out Schepps from among all the other fugitives he knew were in Hot Springs. Whitman later claimed he had asked Johnson to make the arrest on the strength of an informant's tip. After notifying Whitman and the New York police, Chief Howell took the gambler not to jail but to a suite in the Marquette Hotel and kept him under guard there until the arrival four days later of a trio of Whitman's aides. Whitman, meanwhile, was fending off a police demand that Schepps be surrendered to them. Schepps's importance in the case was obvious. He was the corroboration to the confessions of Rose, Webber and Vallon which might otherwise never survive in court. The three had made it clear—or had been instructed to make it clear— that Schepps knew nothing about the killing beforehand.

Reporters converged on Hot Springs from Chicago and St. Louis and laid siege to the Schepps suite. Carried away by his now leading role in the case, Schepps graciously granted a number of contradictory and indiscreet interviews that astonished everybody. He paced the room in a red silk dressing gown, smoking cigarettes incessantly. He seemed to have plenty of money for he kept his police guard busy running gastronomic errands for him.

On one day he told reporters, "I don't want you fellows to think we killed a man who was of any account. Rosenthal was a dirty cur."

The next day he said, "As regards the killing of Rosenthal, I have nothing to confess. Mr. Whitman knows I had nothing to do with it."

Then he declared that until he had met with Whitman, he would say nothing. In the meantime, he talked his head off. He voiced the fear that if he returned to New York he was doomed. He became increasingly and morbidly preoccupied with the drama of this possibility. He made the ominous announcement that "Rosenthal had a more powerful bunch of gunmen at his command than any other man in New York. And I don't doubt they are as loyal to his memory as to his command."

He was counting on Whitman, he said, to protect him, adding, to reinforce this picture of peril: "There are 10,000 police officers in New York and 9,000 of them wouldn't hesitate to put me out of the way if they got the chance."

He literally fell into the arms of the Whitman delegation when it arrived to take him back to New York. Whitman himself boarded the train at Albany and prevented a squad of police detectives from seizing Schepps in Grand Central Station.

A month later, both Whitman and Becker's lawyers realized that Hot Springs was a font of information and they all went there for an orgy of depositions. In their absence, Commissioner Dougherty took two squads of his detectives and thundered into a flat on Ridgewood Avenue in Brooklyn and arrested the two remaining fugitive killers, Lefty Louie Rosenberg and Gyp the Blood Horowitz who were dining in their undershirts with their wives. They had never left town, they said, and didn't know anything about any murder except some astonishing fiction they had read in the newspapers. Whitey Lewis, the second of the suspected gunmen, had been bagged by detectives a few days earlier while waiting on a Kingston, New York, railroad platform for a Chicago-bound train. He would answer no questions and, in fact, asked one.

"Who," he cried, "was the lousy stoolie who told ya where I was?"

The arrest of Gyp and Lefty, which Dougherty explained with a complex tale of superb police work, was a headline sensation for two days thanks to Whitman who, on the second day, let go a blast from St. Louis.

"The fact that they were arrested in New York," he said, "establishes convincingly the truth of my contention, which I have held from the first, that they were always within easy reach; nor am I at all satisfied that the police have not known all along just where they were."

Detectives certainly knew where Whitey was. They had been following him through the Catskills for two weeks pending orders to arrest him. There was no explanation for the delay.

On August 21, the four gunmen were formally indicted by the grand jury for Rosenthal's murder. And the next day Governor Dix appointed Supreme Court Judge John W. Goff to preside over the trials of all those indicted for the Rosenthal murder as well as any other trials arising out of the general investigation of graft and police corruption.

118

Goff's appointment intensified underworld fears anew, for this white-bearded, steely-eyed jurist had been terrorizing criminals since 1894 when he served as counsel for the Lexow Committee of the State Legislature in the first full-blown investigation of New York. The witness chair in this almost legendary inquisition had come to be known as "Goff's Gridiron."

Goff's appointment also gave a large and influential segment of the police department fresh incentive in raising a $50,000 defense fund for Becker. It was the only way they could think of to buy his silence now. With this fund, Becker was able to retain as his chief counsel the eminent John F. McIntyre, the leading criminal lawyer of his time. He had served during the 1890's as an assistant district attorney and emerged from the office with a record of more first degree murder convictions than any other prosecutor in history. The statistics on this were, as well, a measure of the morality of the times. In less than ten years, McIntyre had prosecuted a total of 614 murder trials and obtained convictions in 580 of them. That he should now oppose Goff—and an opposition it was, with Goff dedicated like Whitman to the destruction of the system—must have struck both of them as ironic and their antipathy for each other grew as McIntyre became increasingly convinced of Becker's innocence and of Goff's determination to destroy him, if for no other reason, as a symbol of civic corruption.

Goff was sixty-three, McIntyre fifty-two. They were both eloquent and distinguished with unimpeachable pasts. They were, in addition, fellow Irish Nationalists, their allegiance long since given to Ireland's struggle for freedom from England. They were both members of Clan-Na-Gael, the Irish secret society which believed this freedom could come only by violence.

Goff had once organized a guerrilla band known as Goff's Irish Rescue Party which chartered a New Bedford whaling ship in an unsuccessful scheme to liberate half a dozen Irish revolutionaries from an Australian penal colony.

McIntyre's personal strike for the cause had been to obtain an acquittal for Edward Ivory who had been accused of the

119

famous plot to blow up Parliament and Queen Victoria. He was a big man, hefty rather than portly, with a short, thick neck. A brush mustache and heavy-rimmed glasses gave him a gruff appearance.

The color of Goff's conduct of Becker's trial became apparent the moment McIntyre entered the case. The grand jury had returned a second, superseding indictment against Becker in an effort by Whitman to eliminate the possibility of legal error in the original indictment which Becker's other attorney, John Hart, had already challenged.

McIntyre's objections to the second indictment were summarily overruled along with his request for a two weeks' continuance to prepare motions. He was given, instead, six days.

It was during those six days that McIntyre concluded that the case against Becker was "a diabolical plot."

Becker was finally arraigned on September 3 before Judge Goff, sitting as a special trial judge in the criminal branch of the Supreme Court. Whitman and his staff came up from their offices on the floor below and Becker was brought from the Tombs across the street, over the "Bridge of Sighs," accompanied by two amiable guards. He conferred briefly with McIntyre in the counsel room adjoining the court and then entered the court. McIntyre and Becker had no sooner seated themselves than the case was called.

"To which indictment are we pleading?" asked McIntyre, a facetious tone in his voice.

"To the superseding indictment of August 20th," responded Goff stiffly, not looking at McIntyre.

"I request one week's adjournment," said McIntyre. "There are certain motions to be made and heard before we plead."

"I object to a continuance," interjected Whitman, rising to his feet. "Counsel for the defendant has had ample time—"

Goff interrupted him.

"The application is denied."

McIntyre grew red in the face.

"The defendant refuses to plead," he said, angrily.

Goff beckoned to the court clerk, who hurried up to the bench. Goff whispered in his ear. The clerk returned to his desk and announced:

"The court directs that a plea of not guilty be entered."

Becker sat impassive, his eyes on McIntyre who moved up to the bench. There was no pleading in his voice, only indignation.

"The defendant will not be ready for trial. The defendant needs ample time. His life is in danger as your Honor has ordered him to plead before his case is ready. There are many persons in the Tombs charged with murder in the first degree who have not been brought to trial. Why should this case, important as it is, be rushed to trial? If it goes to trial in this period of hysteria and clamor the defendant cannot have a fair and impartial trial. We have had no time to prepare. . . . I ask that the defendant be given the same rights as any other defendant. . . ."

Goff's eyes were fixed on McIntyre. He appeared to be listening intently. When McIntyre stopped, Goff responded instantly.

"Trial of the defendant is set for Tuesday next, September 10."

Becker showed no reaction. McIntyre appeared stunned and the next day he filed a motion for a continuance to October 3 before Justice George Bischoff, sitting in another department of the court, who granted it, noting that the motion was not out of order "in the instance of a defendant on indictment charging a crime, the penalty for which is death."

McIntyre had requested the continuance on grounds that the delay was necessary to enable the taking of depositions of people in Hot Springs with whom Schepps had talked following his arrest. It was no secret now that Whitman's case hung on Schepps.

In his petition, McIntyre had accused the district attorney

121

of having defied both law and tradition by releasing to the newspapers secret grand jury testimony to "poison and contaminate" the public mind.

The public mind was being influenced as well by the behavior of Rose, Vallon, and Webber, who had been transferred from the Tombs to the West Side Prison on 54th Street for fear Becker would kill them if they remained with him in the Tombs. Now, it seemed, things were at the other extreme. The three men spurned the prison food and had their meals sent in from Sherry's, Rector's, Delmonico's, along with a variety of other personal comforts. They entertained their lawyers, their wives, their friends and each other day and night. When Schepps joined them, he had a rug and furniture sent in and broke the spell. Whitman ordered a return to austerity. New Yorkers were beginning to laugh.

Schepps's spirits remained high, however, and he dispatched jolly telegrams to the police chief, the mayor and the district attorney of Hot Springs, thanking them for their courtesies and hospitality and expressing the hope that he would be seeing them all again soon.

McIntyre and Hart, meanwhile, as Becker's chief counsel, pointed to the West Side Prison activities and renewed their charges of careful, calculated collusion among the four informers.

Whitman responded by putting an end to all special privileges for Rose, Webber, Vallon, and Schepps. They were not permitted to visit with each other, or even with their lawyers except through the bars of their cells with a guard in attendance.

Jacob Reich, alias Jack Sullivan, King of the Newsboys, was also transferred to the West Side Prison, apparently to keep him away from Becker on whose behalf he was obviously going to testify. Sullivan had no sooner arrived in his new confinement than he made a determined assault on Webber during the morning exercise period. He slugged him twice on the side of the head screaming "the vilest of epithets," as the newspapers said, before guards separated them and took Reich back to his cell.

The newsboy urchins of New York, meanwhile, were collecting a defense fund for Reich whom they were describing as their great and selfless benefactor, a sentiment that derived largely from his building the Newsboys' Home with funds personally begged from a dozen New York millionaires, including the Whitneys, the Guggenheims, and the Belmonts. Reich often posted the property as security on bail bonds for friends.

By mid-September, Whitman and Becker's attorneys had ceased maneuvering for newspaper headlines. The trial was nearing and the desperate realities of obtaining evidence and unearthing witnesses overshadowed the satisfaction of trying the case daily in the newspapers. The press, however, deprived of its chief source of sensation, turned to police station gossip, gambling hall rumors and the vastly imaginative speculations of its reporters.

The remnants of underworld leadership (tattered by Whitman, one inferred from the papers) were pulling themselves together in a struggle for survival. All potential witnesses in the case, the *Tribune* solemnly reported, were being ordered out of town under penalty of the sudden rubout.

Becker, it was widely rumored, was trying to talk terms with Whitman and was ready to squeal on the system.

Alderman Curran, his investigation of the police department finally forced to passage by the Board of Aldermen, suddenly gave the climate of exposure new breadth. Patrolmen by the score, municipal clerks, an occasional precinct captain, went before the committee and talked about minuscule peccadillos in the ranks. Mayor Gaynor, invited to testify, refused explosively and described the inquiry as "Curran's newsstand play." Curran responded with a double-barreled threat: to sue Gaynor for libel and to subpoena him. Gaynor testily consented to appear and he harangued the committee for a full day, affixing the entire blame for New York's scandals on "the degenerate press and the abominable reformers." He was neither evading nor concealing. He was utterly sincere.

Curran adjourned the inquiry at this point, "to prevent any possibility of prejudicing the Becker trial."

On September 28, the New York Republican Party, convening in Albany, unanimously nominated District Attorney Whitman as its candidate for Governor. Whitman telegraphed his regrets and declined. The nature of the nomination indicated to him that he could have it any time he wanted it. But first, he told the voters, Becker and the system must be punished.

"Our very civilization is at stake," he cried in a stentorian challenge to a morality-in-government rally held at Cooper Union on his behalf by the Reverend Dr. Lyman Abbott, the leading clergyman-intellectual and editor of *Outlook*, an esoteric monthly. Smiling benignly in the front row while the applause of the overflow audience thundered around them was a key contingent of New York's wealthiest, a group that was to become Whitman's patron.

When it came the Democrats' turn to select their gubernatorial favorite, they did what Tammany Boss Charlie Murphy told them to do; they nominated a vain, oratorial politician named William O. Sulzer who, although he won the election, was subsequently impeached at Boss Murphy's direction for failure to cooperate with the Wigwam. Murphy must have begun to suffer some qualms now for Sulzer, like Gaynor, was a Tammany man gone wrong.

In Washington, the Becker case, the Curran inquiry, and the latest Tammany outrages were debated at length in the halls of Congress. A Republican-born bill, conceived with the notion of crippling Tammany, would have made literacy a requirement for the admission of immigrants to the U. S. To nobody's surprise, it remained in committee.

The newspapers had a hard time of it relating this kaleidoscopic picture of social chaos to Becker specifically and New Yorkers were left wondering exactly what it all meant. Over-

124

simplification became the conversational rule and galloping generalities the watchword of the press. A few people were asking, however, whether Becker was in fact the lord of vice, or whether he was merely a symbol, a graven image of his times. Then, too, there were those who wondered if Becker were the victim of Whitman's ambitions. For Helen Becker remained a disquieting force, her dark and frail figure, gently rounded now with her coming child, a familiar and ubiquitous sight; trekking daily to the Tombs, cheerful and tireless, oblivious of the detectives who followed her constantly wearing masks of chagrin. She ran errands for her husband and for his lawyers; she helped in the search for witnesses, pleading with policemen and newspaper reporters, people who did not want to be involved. Yet it was hard to resist her consuming faith in her husband's innocence. She had no maid now and she arose each morning at dawn, did her own housework and then left for her morning classes at PS 41 in Greenwich Village. In the afternoon she taught at PS 90 at 148th Street. In between she helped Charlie and at night she taught in the women's evening school. Newspapers studied her behavior for some sign of guilty knowledge and in reporting simply her movements they magnified her personal faith into a kind of propaganda. Courageous as she was, being recognized on the subway never failed to embarrass her although she received more smiles of commiseration than stares of condemnation. In late September, she took a year's leave of absence to bring herself and Charlie what they had wanted most—a child.

11. The Good Years

PROBABLY the only opinion shared by nearly all New Yorkers in the autumn of 1912, as they read endlessly about Herman Rosenthal and Lt. Becker over the breakfast table, was that the police had killed Rosenthal or had directed the murder. However, New Yorkers were too inured to lawlessness among those sworn to uphold the law to be shocked by their belief. It was only later, as they felt themselves drawn vicariously into the drama of the case, that they began to transmute their beliefs into opinion and their opinions into action.

The rest of the world seemed shocked more by New Yorkers' beliefs than by the apparent audacity of the police to commit murder in the presence of what amounted to an audience. This was understandable to Lyman Abbott, the scholarly clergyman. In his magazine *Outlook* he bristled as never before and echoed the alarm, "This crime is a challenge to our very civilization." What he meant was that New York had been defiled by virtual anarchy for half a century and that it could not take much more.

As the gateway for nearly all immigration to the U. S. and where perhaps a majority of the early immigrants remained,

New York had always been an island of contained social chaos. The extremes of wealth and poverty were worse than feudal in their relationship. Crime, which had been festering steadily in the immigrant slums, was awesomely inflamed by the general demoralization that followed the Civil War. The word "gangster" had not then been coined but "gangs" had, and there were literally hundreds of them whose depredations if committed today would be cause for martial law. Immigrants continued to surge across the Atlantic in hordes and instead of finding wealth they found each other trapped in the warrens of the lower East Side. Their disillusionment was insulated from public concern by the boom town aura, the frontier air that permeated the city and sustained for some the gleaming image of gold. Wealth was possible, at any rate for saloonkeepers, panderers, gamblers, practitioners of assorted forms of felony and, of course, for Tammany Hall politicians who appeared to be the only people on earth distressed by the plight of the immigrant mass which, by 1910, accounted for more than three-fourths of the city's entire population of four million.

New York's influence upon the rest of the country was at least debatable. The low ebb of its morality, both public and private, appeared consistent with the growing scandals in Washington, those of the Grant Administration particularly, and in the pillaging of the country and the abuse of labor by the barons of industry.

In New York, Tammany's attention to the immigrants was universally recognized as exploitation. Yet this recognition availed nothing. Patronage, financed by millions of dollars taken by graft and outright thievery from almost every municipal office, continually assured Tammany's tenure. Gambling, the principal source of graft, engulfed Manhattan, from 33d Street to 59th, extending for a block on either side of Broadway.

Most of the city's grafting leaders went to church and few reform efforts ever were generated in the pulpit. A singular exception to this was the pulpit of the Reverend Dr. Charles

Parkhurst, whose famous crusades against crime, vice, graft and Tammany were sensationally successful, all things considered, even though they failed to reach their ideal goal because they interfered seriously with the economy.

Legislative investigations, ostensibly aimed at uprooting evil but in actuality aimed by upstate Republicans at Democratic Tammany, exposed but did not destroy their objective.

Congress had conducted a lurid probe in 1868 that produced little more than the observation that a dance hall owner and saloonkeeper named Theodore Allen, whose lewd floor shows were among the most famous, was "the wickedest man in the wickedest city in the world."

However, even as water erodes stone, the cumulative effect of these inquiries was beneficial and resulted, over the years, in piecemeal correction of the most flagrant abuses of the law. At the same time, the lawbreakers learned to be increasingly less flagrant.

Aside from this, there were election years when guilt, or conscience, unexpectedly found its way into polling places and, as though to exorcise themselves, the voters put a reformer into office. Since virtue is a poor substitute for patronage in a jungle economy whose most remembered characteristic is poverty, Tammany would soon return.

Reform was further handicapped by Tammany's employing large numbers of thugs whose reign of purposeless terror had for more than a generation rendered the streets of the lower East Side unsafe in daylight for honest citizens and even policemen in numbers of less than four. Tammany's recognition of these gangs as a political force gave them prestige which encouraged them to prey on other sections of the city. They were the lackeys of politics, the get-out-the-vote committee. They supervised the polls on election day to make certain only Tammany ballots were cast. They stuffed the ballot boxes and, if necessary, raided enemy precincts, stole the ballot boxes and threw them into the East River.

These hoodlums were also used extensively as repeaters at

the polls, for what election clerk could refuse a ballot to an armed thug who wanted one and had no compunction about maiming you to get it? Hoodlums protected vice operations from the maraudings of other hoodlums, and served as bodyguards to the Tammany chieftains. In return for their energies, they were allowed to shake down some of the smaller brothels and gambling dens, giving them a sense of power which they coveted more than money. They were actually paid very little, considering their contribution. The fee for murder was as little as $10, an amount which indicated the large numbers of killers in business, the value they placed on human life, and their utter lack of fear of apprehension.

Murders occurred at the rate of one a day in 1912, an increase of 450 per cent in two decades, yet in only a third of these killings was anybody ever arrested, and of those arrested, less than 10 per cent were ever convicted.

This organized lawlessness and corruption was obviously no secret, for the press of New York had been attacking it since its inception, without effect. The public appeared to be more entertained than aroused. The voters who endorsed it did so under an unarticulated rationale that it was economically necessary. The rest of the voters seemed to have been diverted by the other, more beguiling face of New York. For the era constituted, with all its horrors, the Good Years.

It was an era of elegance and opulence and the gay life among the affluent had a mesmeric glitter. Jack London was astride his socialistic charger but the dynamism of his assaults spent itself in book reviews. Mrs. Cornelius Vanderbilt III had just seized the throne of what was known as Society from the dying Mrs. William Astor, whose tyranny was a thing to remember. Indeed, will anyone ever forget that the ballroom of Mrs. Astor's Fifth Avenue palace held just 400 persons, which represented her considered selection of New York aristocracy and became the numerical synonym for the Social Registry.

It was still the Golden Age of opera and the theater. The Met, under the guidance of the terrible-tempered Gatti-Casazza (who married his diva, Frances Alda) was astounding the musical world with its assemblage of virtuosi. Arturo Toscanini was conducting and no one suspected that the majestic voices of Caruso or Scotti, Louise Homer or Lucrezia Bori, would one day fade from behind the gold curtain. It seemed like an immortal time. Madame Schumann-Heink had left the Met but only for the concert stage. Mary Garden was packing them in at the Manhattan Opera Company. The memories of Edwin Booth and Richard Mansfield were still bright on Broadway, Maude Adams had become Peter Pan in the minds of the multitudes who were also enraptured by Douglas Fairbanks, George Arliss, George M. Cohan, Al Jolson and Billie Burke, a handful among scores. Lionel and Ethel Barrymore were famous and John was about to be. The movies, instead of falling, as predicted, of their own dead weight, were blossoming wildly. Mary Pickford was known as the Maude Adams of the cinema, a parallel that indicated the popular devotion to both actresses and both media.

In another creative area, it was the dawn of ragtime which, before long, would give way to jazz in the irrational progress of these things.

To New Yorkers by the tens of thousands, all of this was infinitely and intrinsically more vital and compelling than the seamy machinations occurring in that blighted area east of Fifth Avenue and somewhere south of 39th Street.

It was further ironic, perhaps, that the very people who talked about the abominations of Tammany were those who, in the natural course of their profitable commerce, happily did furtive business with the minions of the Hall and patronized the gambling dens at night. Then too, it was commonly known that the entertainment world, at all aesthetic levels, was heavily financed by the racketeers and their politician friends. Big Tim Sullivan was deeply involved in the ownership of theaters, hotels, and nightclubs.

The tempo of these contrasts was heightened at the turn of the century by the violent material, intellectual, and spiritual changes that were suddenly being imposed on the western world. No one was more aware of this than the frustrated compilers of dictionaries which, vastly outpaced by discovery and change, remained for a quarter of a century at least ten years behind the language in daily use. Mass production techniques were giving birth to mass distribution techniques whose effects on our culture and philosophy are still accumulating. New York, as the largest U. S. city, the greatest market in the world for products and services and ideas, had become America's tribunal of culture yet it had no culture of its own. Nearly ninety per cent of its population consisted either of immigrants or second generation alien stock who, in trying gamely to become Americans, had abandoned their own codes and mores to emulate, for the most part, the only example of Americana they found: the nebulous, shifting values adopted with the same motives by a previous wave of immigrants. The people of New York were a febrile hothouse in which any new idea, art form, product, way of life, philosophy or taste could and did take root and, in time, find acceptance by the United States at large. From this cultural orphanage emerged the emotional, social, political and moral values that, overlaid with history book precepts and loosely embraced by the general scientific and intellectual awakening, became America's twentieth century traditions.

This all had some effect on corruption, too. It refined it. The scandals involving Tammany occurred with greater frequency from 1890 onward, forcing basic changes in the system of crime and politics.

Lincoln Steffans, immersed in the problem as a reporter for the New York *Evening Post,* described with irritating simplicity the alliance of crime and government as "a system."

By 1910, with the press all but united in incessant cries for reform, it was being called "The System" with capital letters.

Today, half a century later, it is no longer so vividly labeled for everyday usage. Perhaps because it is less understood. Yet it not only still exists, it has assumed a power and a virility undreamed of in Tammany's heyday. Its evolution from awkward and brazen crudity into a highly energized and exquisitely refined organization has come about through the same pressures that created social welfare, enacted women's suffrage and made labor unions respectable. The most influential of these pressures has been simple enlightenment.

At the outset, Tammany made little effort to conceal its use of thugs, largely because it had no reason to. By 1900, however, with scandals becoming increasingly numerous, this practice began to decline. What had been accomplished with force would now be accomplished with money, which was an even greater power. It was a monumental discovery, however obvious, and one from which the country seems unlikely to recover. Graft was divorced from force and made to stand on its own. It was expanded and organized. As for the gunmen, they were absorbed by the embattled labor unions to enforce strikes, or they were hired by employers to break strikes. When enlightenment began to purify labor relations, prohibition saved the thugs from unemployment.

Because of the omnipotent position occupied by policemen, they were the primary enforcers of the graft system. When Herman Rosenthal was murdered, however, politicians realized that policemen were altogether too omnipotent and that some other arrangement would have to be effected. Lt. Charlie Becker was a sterling example of uncontrollable omnipotence.

At the same time, men whose grasp of affairs was considerably broader than Becker's knew that Becker could not remain forever immune to the ambitions of others. Still, Becker had given them an idea. More than that, Becker had put it into operation, perhaps without even knowing it. Becker had organized crime.

There was no telling then where it would all go from here. While Becker paced his cell in the Tombs, raging silently against this obdurate turn in his destiny, other men waited for the ever-rising tide of opportunity they felt was linked to it. Yes, it was truly an age rich with anticipation. It was the Good Years.

12. Big Jack's Big Day

BIG JACK ZELIG was whistling. he was anticipating the trial of Police Lt. Charles Becker, his old friend and faithful employer, which was to open at one o'clock the next afternoon. Zelig had spent a convivial evening with his cronies and associates at Seigel's Coffee House, 77 Second Avenue, and he had strolled out, alone, reeking of gin and goodwill, to savor the dusky Sunday evening and smoke a cigar. The detectives who habitually followed him were nowhere in sight and he was relieved. At first he had welcomed their surveillance because he knew that Jack Sirocco, whose rivalry in gangsterism had blossomed into a grim vendetta, had not abandoned plans to annihilate him. Tonight, however, Sirocco was farthest from his thoughts which were occupied with the manner in which he would testify for Becker. Zelig shared a gunman's instinctive loathing for informers and he could well have focused his testimony on this fact alone, but coupled with it was his affection for Becker and his general contempt for Rose who, if he went unchecked, could well send Becker to the electric chair. Intent in this gratifying contemplation, Zelig decided to prolong it and instead of returning to Seigel's, he walked briskly to the corner and hopped aboard an uptown-bound streetcar. The car was crowded but Zelig spied a space on the rear platform bench between an elderly man and a young woman and he wedged his slender frame into the opening, squirming back to relax, enjoy his cigar and ruminate further. The car started up with a jolt and Zelig was aware that it had left a passenger behind. He turned his head and saw a tall, rangy man running alongside, and slightly to the rear, and he silently urged him along. When at last the man caught the long handle on the rear platform and pulled himself aboard, Zelig turned away. He was completely oblivious of the fact that the tall, rangy man had moved along the platform behind him and that in his right hand he carried a .38 revolver which he expertly placed behind Zelig's left ear and pulled the trigger. Zelig leaped forward in one last spasm, lunging across the knees of the young woman, who was screaming, and then fell dead to the streetcar floor. His assassin jumped off the car and collided with a policeman who took the gun away from him and clubbed him unconscious with his billy.

Zelig's killer was identified in the morning papers as Philip Davidson, alias "Red Phil," age thirty, whose occupation, according to which paper you read, was that of a fruit peddler, a gambler, a white slaver, a narcotics peddler. He was, in fact, a fruit peddler who only aspired to these other callings. He readily admitted killing Zelig, explaining the terrible terrorist had cheated him out of $400. It was an improbable story but it didn't really matter. The only story that anyone would have believed was that Zelig, like Rosenthal, had been killed to close his mouth. But for whose benefit?

"No man's life is safe who offends the system," said the Brooklyn *Standard Union*.

This was the view Whitman's office sought to encourage. "Zelig was a vital witness for the prosecution," the district attorney announced in memorium and Becker's attorneys promptly denied it. Zelig was their witness, they said.

Zelig's death received only the most cursory investigation

and several weeks later his killer, pleading guilty, was sentenced to twenty years in Sing Sing for second degree murder. No one, even the general public, seemed greatly interested in the Zelig mystery. It was all part of the whole, a piece of the complex fabric that could only be fully unraveled at Becker's trial. New York waited for Becker's trial—and the truth.

13. Witnesses from All Over

ON THE NIGHT of October 6, 1912, the eve of his trial, Charles Becker was permitted three visitors; his wife, and his two brothers, John, now a lieutenant of detectives, and Jackson, a Wall Street broker. As they left the Tombs, Mrs. Becker and John deferred to Jackson when two reporters approached. Jackson proclaimed simply, "We believe in his innocence."

Becker slept soundly that night, awakening early on the morning of the 7th. At eight o'clock, Becker's special guard, Deputy Sheriff Henry Spellman, brought him his breakfast and the two men chatted about the trial for almost half an hour. Spellman liked Becker, as did most of the other guards and virtually all the prisoners, to whom Becker was the gallant victim of a dirty squeal. At nine o'clock Spellman escorted Becker to the Tombs' counsel room for a last conference with his attorneys. The trial would not begin until one o'clock that afternoon.

And when the great event finally began, only a privileged few were able to attend. The courtroom held less than 200 spectator seats and Judge Goff refused to seek a bigger court or otherwise contribute to what could be called a spectacle.

While Centre Street was jammed with thousands of New Yorkers, and hundreds filled the corridors of the Criminal Courts building, Judge Goff announced that only witnesses, city officials, and accredited newspaper representatives would be admitted to the trial.

Becker and the six other men accused together under a blanket murder indictment, trooped down from the prisoners' pen at the rear of the courtroom to stand before the bench while Whitman went through the formality, its outcome long since decided, of requesting a separate trial for Becker.

McIntyre had already opposed this in a motion submitted earlier to Judge Goff, and now he reinforced it.

"I submit that the defendant Charles Becker cannot in justice be tried for arranging the murder of Herman Rosenthal unless the persons who, it is alleged, acted at his direction are themselves found guilty of having so acted."

McIntyre spoke dispassionately for, it seemed, he had logic on his side.

Judge Goff's response was instantaneous and, like McIntyre's plea, without emotion.

"Your motion is denied and your objection to the prosecution's motion for a separate trial for the defendant, Charles Becker, is overruled."

Goff's blue-gray eyes bore into McIntyre who moved forward to speak again. He was stopped by Goff's upraised hand and an ominous warning.

"This court will proceed in an orderly manner."

Goff would tolerate no defiance, however well founded legally.

Becker, as always, reveals nothing by either his manner or his expression. He stands motionless, his hands clasped behind him, towering over the other defendants who are crowded in front of him at the bench. Jacob Reich, runted and apprehensive; William Shapiro, tensely licking his lips; the four gunmen, discreetly surly. Becker's head is erect, his body tilted slightly forward as though to hear better. Suddenly, he is alone.

His six companions in custody have been withdrawn by guards and Becker looks across the green-carpeted void to McIntyre, his mooring in this current of inexorable rules and relentless demands. McIntyre gestures with a nod and Becker turns toward the counsel table just inside the heavy mahogany balustrade that encloses the arena. The sun slants in through the tall windows, projecting itself in pleasantly distorted rectangles across the green carpet, here and there relieving the morbid luster of the dark woodwork and furniture with moving streaks of reddish sheen. The room is warm on this brisk October day and Becker seems to have succumbed to a kind of hypnotic lassitude. He sits fixed and motionless, paying no attention as his wife enters the court from Judge Goff's chambers, a bailiff at her side, and accepts a chair placed for her in the far corner—out of sight, as the judge had ordered, from the jury box on the other side of the room. Nor does Becker seem aware as the first twelve prospective jurors are motioned from their seats behind the balustrade and led across the green carpet to the box where some of them will be sitting for several days. Does he hear Judge Goff, beckoning to a bailiff, order that the window shades be drawn lower? "There's not enough gloom in here," says Goff, as though to himself.

Then Becker hears his name and raises his head. McIntyre is on his feet, striding up to the bench. Goff sits a little more erect. He is ready. But McIntyre will not give him satisfaction. There will be no clash of tempers, now.

"I have two motions, your Honor."

"The time for motions has passed."

"I request a week's adjournment because of the illness of Mr. John Hart, the defendant's attorney of record, who is not here today."

"Motion denied."

The occupants of the long, dark rectangle containing these possible jurors are no longer staring at the impassive Becker, but at the exchange between Goff and McIntyre. It is almost a grip of wills, but how is that possible when a judge's will is an exercise of fiat rather than reason?

McIntyre, his eyes now scanning a sheaf of papers in his left hand, does not seem to have heard the denial of his request. He raises his head.

"I request an adjournment . . ."

Goff's hand is raised and his head is turning slowly from side to side.

McIntyre steps aside, as though to talk around the upraised hand. His voice rises at judicial obstinacy.

"Do I understand that we are being forced to trial . . ."

McIntyre's shrieks have caused the members of the press to turn from their pencils and pads to exchange looks with one another.

". . . in the face of unwarranted statements by the district attorney that the murder of Big Jack Zelig was a serious loss to the prosecution when he knows he would have testified nothing for the prosecution but to the contrary would have been a witness for the defense. I protest—"

"Stop, stop. I warn you, Mr. McIntyre. This is a court of justice and we will proceed in an orderly manner with the regular course of justice. There will be no more delays. The unnecessary delays brought about by the tactics of attorneys has become a public scandal."

It is a shout. But McIntyre will not be intimidated. He can shout too.

"But the regular course of justice has been interrupted and the defendant objects to being forced to trial."

(Even more loudly) "I will hear no more of this. I have denied your motions. We will proceed here in an orderly manner. Your long experience should teach you that a courtroom is no place for such harangues. If you do not cease I shall direct an officer of the court to eject you."

McIntyre is silent but not subdued. It appears now that he, too, is on trial.

Becker's attention has returned to the moment. He remains erect in his chair for the first two hours of questioning jurors, then he relaxes, begins to exchange smiles with his wife across the room.

The audience, except for the colony of witnesses encamped on one side of the aisle, is quiet and attentive. The witnesses are apprehensive. It is a trial without responses from the uninvolved. One half of the spectators are frightened; the other half continually expects to hear the worst.

Becker's interest in the selection of the jury becomes more acute, intuitive. It becomes apparent by evening that Becker is insisting on a jury of married men and only one juror has been selected. He is Harold W. Skinner, forty-eight, manager of a branch office of the New York Edison Company. Court adjourns with a warning from Goff that if the jury is not empaneled by 5 P.M. tomorrow he will hold court at night.

A few reporters found time to attend Big Jack Zelig's funeral. It may not have been the most opulent, but even for New York it was impressive. The mourners began gathering in Seigel's on Second Avenue, the same place from which Zelig had departed on his last journey in life, to prepare themselves. The gang chief's intimates walked together, flowers in one hand, revolvers scarcely concealed in the other, to Zelig's house on Broome Street nearby. Such a congregation would surely tempt Jack Sirocco and, despite their grief, the mourners were apprehensive. The police sent a thirty-man detail of detectives who reported later that they had never seen so many gangsters assembled in one place before in all their careers. The city's better pickpockets were also represented and, despite the watchful contingent of cops, they made a grand haul in watches and wallets. It took forty carriages to transport the mourners on a long, wandering procession through the lower East Side and across the Brooklyn Bridge to Washington Cemetery where Rosenthal lay buried and forgotten. The streets were lined with people, many of them aware of the nature of the procession, all of them awed by the large carriage which followed the hearse. It contained four cantors and a ten-voice male chorus chanting the Hebrew service for the dead.

On Tuesday, Becker's interest in the selection of the jury became increasingly acute and because of it McIntyre used up fifteen of the thirty peremptory challenges allowed him—the right to dismiss a juror without cause. Whitman had used only six such challenges. Becker vetoed several without even indicating to McIntyre his reason. He would simply shake his head slowly as he did for a man who smiled at the district attorney. "An apparent flirtation," he said to McIntyre, loud enough for the man himself to hear. Goff scowled down from the bench.

At 6 P.M., the jury was still four members shy. A total of 100 talesmen had been examined. Only fifty remained. Judge Goff ordered an additional 100 on hand for the next day and adjourned court until eight o'clock that night, true to his vow. McIntyre's plea that he was physically exhausted and unable to continue was brusquely denied. His gray hair disheveled and his face deeply lined with fatigue, McIntyre repeated his plea again at nine o'clock and was denied, again at ten o'clock and was denied, and again at eleven o'clock when Goff finally relented. The jury was one member shy.

It was still one member shy at the end of the third day, Wednesday, October 9, again at eleven o'clock at night. A day that dragged for the members of the press, a day that left McIntyre dangerously spent, a day during which Goff did not relax in any measure his ruthless observance for the letter of courtroom conduct. This extended as well to the nature of questioning the prospective jurors.

Please state your name, your address, your occupation and your age.

Are you acquainted with the defendant? Or his counsel?

Are you acquainted with the prosecution or the members of his staff?

Are you acquainted with any member of the New York Police Department?

Are you acquainted with any person in this courtroom?

"Please, Mr. McIntyre, confine your questioning to legal propriety."

Have you read about this case in the newspapers?

You are familiar then with the position the defendant occupies in regard to . . .

"I warn you again, Mr. McIntyre."

Are you married?

"I will not continue to warn you, Mr. McIntyre."

Have you formed an opinion about this case?

[A murmur ripples through the press gallery. "That's the most rhetorical question I have ever heard.")

It is eleven o'clock in the morning of October 10, the fourth day of trial. An accountant named Samuel H. Haas has passed Mr. Whitman's inquiries. Why is it, Mr. McIntyre asks, that you have not formed any opinion? Mr. Haas, it seems, has been traveling with his family and the entire affair has thus escaped his interest. Becker studies Mr. Haas's face and approves.

The jury is complete. Twelve men, all married, who will decide Becker's guilt or innocence solely on the basis of the evidence to be introduced in this courtroom.

They are, in theory, hearing the case for the very first time. Like the audience at a novel first-night performance of a play to which they will provide the ending and the climax and the point of it all. In the meantime, they will not discuss the case with each other or with anyone else and they will refrain from reading newspapers. Their conclusion will be the truth. Or at least it will suffice until a greater truth comes along.

A massive stir, a hush of relief settles on the courtroom and Whitman mounts to the center of the arena to tell the jury the story of Lt. Charles Becker. It was an hour in the telling. An intense, gratifying hour. Becker watched with moderate interest, as though he too were hearing the story for the first time. On Becker's right, McIntyre, who appeared not to be listening at all, and on Becker's left, two of McIntyre's three assistants,

Lloyd B. Stryker and George W. Whiteside, both former deputy district attorneys, both taking notes.

At the counsel table opposite, sit the members of Whitman's staff; a four-man panel of confident avengers, prominent among them the courageous Frank Moss on whose legal skewers hang the bones of many a civic malefactor. The long table is laden with books and piles of papers, but neatly as though to bulwark the determined, orderly, sure manner of their attack.

Whitman is almost through now. His speaking pace has slowed. What is his theme?

"We will prove that in spite of the fact that he may not have been personally at the scene of the crime, that understanding the fact that it was not his hand which held the fatal weapon, that the real murderer, the most desperate criminal of them all, was the cool, calm, calculating, grafting police officer who used the very office, the very power which the people had entrusted to him for the enforcement of law and order, used this power to tempt and force others into the commission of crime and finally for the . . ."

Now. McIntyre is on his feet, gesturing frantically toward the jury box. His words overlap those of the district attorney and they cannot be heard. Something about a mistrial. A juror whispering to another juror.

Goff sighs heavily.

"I have been most tolerant of your objections, Mr. McIntyre. Please proceed, Mr. District Attorney."

Whitman hesitates, reconstructing the sentence. Its impact is dissipated.

". . . and that he used that office for the protection of his traffic and in the purchase and sale of law enforcement and that he wantonly sacrificed human life in order that that might continue."

When court adjourned for lunch, Becker was allowed several minutes with his wife. Then he was taken back to the Tombs where he ate a hearty meal of roast beef, mashed potatoes, green beans, coffee, and apple pie. The gavel had scarcely rung in the opening of the afternoon session when the first witness was moving across to the witness chair; a round, polished wooden armchair, elevated slightly, to the right of and beneath the bench. From where he sits, Judge Goff can see the head of each witness. It is a policeman named John J. Grady, young, red faced, with a rich brogue, in uniform. No one remembered who he was. A policeman on a beat at 43d and Broadway. He heard the shots, came running to the Metropole, saw and recognized Herman Rosenthal dead on the pavement.

No questions by McIntyre.

Police Detective William J. File, handsome in a pretty way, but his expression dour. He is not a detective now, only a patrolman. He was in the Metropole, ran out into the street, saw the fleeing murder car and gave chase in a taxi.

No questions, your Honor.

Dr. Dennis Taylor, bored and low-voiced, middle-aged. He is on the stand no more than three or four minutes. An ambulance physician attached to Flower Hospital. He describes a man lying dead of bullet wounds on the sidewalk in front of the Hotel Metropole, covered with a white tablecloth.

No questions.

Dr. Otto H. Schultze, husky, fiftyish, dark gray hair, a coroner's physician, a performer of autopsies, a technical chronicler of the causes of dying. Two bullet wounds caused Herman Rosenthal's death; one entered Herman's head to the left of Herman's nose, another slightly farther to the left which, in passing, shattered the upper jawbone. Both penetrated Herman's brain.

No questions.

Nothing has been said but we feel we are getting closer, however slowly, to the heart of the matter.

Jacob Hecht, thin, balding, bony. Dark, deep-set eyes, a middle-European accent, a waiter at the Metropole. Looking out the window, heard the shots and saw Herman Rosenthal fall. Wrings his hands, blinks rapidly.

"Did you see the person or persons who fired the shots?"

"No."

"Did you or did you not tell me before this trial that you saw the men who fired the shots?"

"Yah, but I wouldn't know who they were. Just men. I wouldn't know them."

No questions.

There is a surge of sound in the press gallery as the next witness mounts to the stand. He is Louis Krese, the Hungarian waiter whose testimony in coroner's court had put both Bridgie Webber and Jacob Reich behind bars; Webber as having been seen fleeing from the scene of the killing, Reich as having ordered Krese away from the scene. Whitman brings out these points, then relinquishes the witness. This time there are questions.

McIntyre approaches slowly, but confidently.

"When you say you saw Jacob Reich, also known as Jack Sullivan, don't you know you are committing perjury?"

"I am not."

There are signals from the judge, over McIntyre's head, and abruptly from the side door come the four accused killers followed by Jacob Reich and three bailiffs. The judge motions them into a line in front of Krese, who suddenly looks like an owl caught in the daylight. Judge Goff asks him to identify each of the five by name which he does, rapidly and without hesitation. The judge's purpose is not clear. The five men leave the courtroom and McIntyre resumes.

"Isn't it true that you were in Dowling's saloon when you heard the shots and you then ran out and to the hotel?"

"No, sir, I never drink."

"And isn't it true that you consulted a lawyer before you agreed to come to the police?"

"Yes, sir."

"What was the name of the lawyer?"

It is very quiet. All minds are following McIntyre.

"Sullivan."

"James M. Sullivan? Mr. Jack Rose's attorney?"

"I didn't know it then."

"Where did you consult him?"

"Right in a saloon. I was up in his office first. I wanted a lawyer's advice before I should come as a witness."

"How did you know there was such a lawyer as James M. Sullivan?"

"I heard about him several times. I was working in the Waldorf and I heard lawyers mentioned often."

"Don't you know that Mr. Sullivan just came down from Connecticut?"

"Well, I don't *know* him. Only that day I spoke to him."

"Who sent you to Mr. Sullivan?"

"Nobody."

"Didn't you ask Mr. Sullivan for money to leave town; didn't you say you'd be a bad witness against Mr. Rose?"

"That's a lie." [*matter of fact*]

"Do you remember being asked in coroner's court whether you saw the men do anything after the shooting and you replied 'No, I did not.'?"

"It must be a mistake." [*vaguely*]

"Do you remember being asked in coroner's court if you had seen a lawyer and you replied, 'I couldn't tell you his name'?"

Krese is saved by the judge.

"Mr. McIntyre, I notice you are examining what appears to be a transcript and that you wait to frame your questions from that. That should be a matter of preparation before you come into court. There being no further questions to put to this witness, he is discharged from the witness stand."

There seems little fight left in McIntyre today. He closes the transcript and wearily confronts Goff.

"Your Honor, I request that the cross-examination of this witness be continued tomorrow. I am too fatigued to continue."

"No," retorted Goff and adjourned court for the day.

There is something less than orderly about the unfolding of the case, but then perhaps tomorrow some other testimony will make everything clearer. A curly-haired taxi driver,

146

Thomas Ryan, his eyes round with fear and his hands trembling visibly, is on stage as the curtain goes up Friday, the fifth day.

Ryan's identity and the fact that he was standing by his cab across the street at the moment the killing occurred is brought out by Moss. Then the four gunmen are brought in from the side room and arrayed in front of the witness, whose eyes remain glued to Mr. Moss.

"Are any of these men in front of you the same men you saw outside the Metropole on the morning of July 16, 1912?"

Ryan's eyes are riveted to the first assistant district attorney.

"I couldn't be sure."

Moss is not surprised.

"Didn't you tell me that you could positively identify the men you saw shoot Mr. Rosenthal down?"

"Yes, but I'm not sure now."

"Why are you looking at me? Please look at these four men and tell me if you have ever seen them before."

Ryan's eyes flick up the line and pounce back on Moss.

"Well?"

"I'm not sure."

Ryan is replaced by John Stanich, tall, gray-haired, distinguished. He said he had been standing on the sidewalk a few feet west of the Metropole and that he saw the shooting. Confronted with the gunmen, however, he was able to identify only Whitey Lewis but he did so calmly and without concern. He had long, tapering hands which he ran frequently through his bushy hair. McIntyre is before him now.

"What is your occupation?"

"I am an inventor."

"Do you make your living from your inventions?"

"The way in which I make my living is my business."

"Have you ever been convicted of a crime?"

"Never."

"Where were you on the morning of July 16, 1912?"

"I said that before."

"Well, say it again."

147

"I am not a hand organ and I do not have to play the same tune over and over again."

It is a maxim among practitioners of the art of cross-examination that a witness should never be asked a question unless the examiner knows what the answer will be or unless he does not care. This exchange is chalked up to what appears to be McIntyre's weariness.

The next eyewitness is a tall, angular, sallow, dark-eyed man named Morris Luban. He is unknown to the press and his appearance is fraught with expectation. Moss elicits from him a double-barreled blow at Becker.

"Where were you on or about the night of June 23, 1912?"

"In the Lafayette Baths."

"Is that at 405 Lafayette Street?"

"I think that's the address."

"And whom did you see there?"

"I saw him [pointing at Becker] and Jack Rose who I known for a long time."

"Do you also know the defendant, Charles Becker?"

"I know him on sight."

"Were the defendant and Jack Rose together?"

"Yes. They were talking."

"Could you hear what they said?"

"Yes."

"What did they say?"

"Lieutenant Becker said to Jack, 'If that goddam squealer Rosenthal isn't croaked, I'll do it myself.'"

There is no sound of response in the courtroom, but suddenly all eyes are on Becker who gives them no satisfaction. He is simply watching Luban with casual attention.

It is further developed by Moss that Luban was standing in the lobby of the Metropole and that he saw everything. He saw Rosenthal pass through the lobby, nodded to him and then started to follow him outside. He said he could identify "three or four" of the persons who were there. Judge Goff gives his now familiar signal to the bailiff at the side door and there

148

is the tiny, disrhythmic parade across the courtroom again. The four accused gunmen and Shapiro, the chauffeur.

Then McIntyre is before the bench.

"I protest, your Honor, against this kind of identification. It is only fair that other persons not involved in this case be included in this lineup. It has happened repeatedly."

There is a murmur of agreement among the four gunmen. Shapiro is noticeably silent. The judge snaps.

"I do not wish to hear anything further. I have overruled your objections twice before and I hope counsel will interpose no further objections."

The witness is asked by Goff to proceed. Luban steps down, pointing quickly at Dago Frank, then Lefty Louie, then Gyp the Blood, then Shapiro.

"Are these the people you saw take part in the shooting?"

"Yes." His voice is husky, can barely be heard.

"The ones you have just pointed to?"

"Yes."

All heads swivel toward Dago Frank. He is saying something. Loud, clear, but his voice is high pitched like a boy's.

"We are willing to be identified but this isn't fair."

Goff has not heard. He gestures again and the parade leaves the courtroom. Now it is McIntyre's turn. Luban's testimony is very pat.

"Would you please tell us exactly what you did between the hours of 8 P.M. on July 15, 1912, and 2 A.M. on July 16, 1912?"

Luban scratches his chin, shrugs. He was with a young lady and they went to Hammerstein's Victoria Theater, in the dollar seats.

"Don't you know the Victoria was closed on that night, that only the roof garden was open?"

"It must have been the roof garden then." Another shrug.

"What is the name of the young lady you were with?"

"I don't want to break up her home."

McIntyre is holding several letter-size pieces of paper in his hand. He gives one of them to the witness.

"Have you ever seen this before?"

"I don't know."

"Do you have a brother named Jacob?"

"Yes."

"Did he write this letter?"

"I don't know."

Not one letter, but four; all of them addressed to Charles Becker, "In care of the Tombs," and all of them signed "Jake Luban" or "Jacob Luban." In sequence, they develop the fact that the Luban brothers are being held in the Newark, New Jersey, jail on a "trumped-up" charge of forgery; that they both know Becker has been framed and they will testify for him if he or his lawyers can get them out of jail. Judge Goff takes the letters under advisement. McIntyre's manner now can only be described as that of a cat with a tired mouse.

"Did Mr. Whitman or anyone connected with his office offer to intercede on your behalf with the State of New Jersey?"

"When I came over here I expected favors from the State of New York positively."

"Have you ever been convicted of a crime?"

"No."

Luban's sallow face fills with shadows as McIntyre reads a record of Luban's conviction in New York several years previously on a charge of forgery. Luban says nothing and he is excused. How does one go about deducting from the mass of testimony heaped upon the jury's minds the remarks of a lying witness? And to what unknown extent has he lied?

Judge Goff has risen, his black robe billowing about him. Court is adjourned.

A few reporters drift down and through the swinging gate in the balustrade. The bearded Moss greets them with a smile.

"Who's on stage tomorrow?"

"How about Jack Rose?"

"Have you got any witnesses from the right side of the tracks?"

The jesting air vanishes. Moss's face stiffens.

"We cannot pick our witnesses from high places. We have to get them from Becker's own cesspool."

Then he smiles again.

"Well, there's Thomas Coupe, the eyewitness from the Elks Club. He's agreed to come back from England to testify."

There is a flourish of pencils.

"How much did you have to pay him to make the trip?"

Moss is gathering up papers now. He looks around him. Whitman and the others have gone. Becker and his wife are together in a far corner, surrounded by bailiffs. He smiles again.

"You'd better give questions like that to Mr. Whitman."

Anonymous telephone and mail threats of violence against Judge Goff, Whitman and McIntyre, a daily occurrence since the trial began, were now increasing in volume and in savagery. Judge Goff ordered the courtroom guard doubled from six to twelve and the screening of all those entering the room was intensified. In addition, the three were provided with two-man bodyguards to accompany them outside the court.

Most of the prosecution's witnesses had been threatened, too, and Whitman hired operatives from the staff of William J. Burns to guard Stanich and Krese, the two eyewitnesses to the shooting.

This very day, in fact, McIntyre had been assembling his papers after adjournment. He was alone at the table. A short, husky man, his face partly concealed by a derby hat pulled low on his forehead, stepped through the gate and moved next to McIntyre.

"Keep Jack Rose's wife outta this," he muttered, "or I'll blow your head off."

14. The Song of Bald Jack Rose, Part I

ON OCTOBER 13, 1912, a Sunday, *The New York Times* devoted eighteen columns of space to the testimony of Bald Jack Rose against Lieutenant Charles Becker. It was almost more space than the same paper gave to the attempted assassination of President Theodore Roosevelt in Milwaukee three days later, or to the sinking of the *Titanic* the previous April. Near the lead of the story, which broke three columns wide across page one, was this paragraph:

> Lieut. Becker presented a strange spectacle yesterday. Before the eyes of the throng that crowded the courtroom his face went through a multitude of changes. Rose might have been the sculptor. Becker the clay figure on which he worked. . . . It was as though the very composition of his face, the contour, the quality of skin, were passing in a few short minutes through changes that should require years. He entered the room, smiling and unconcerned, as he has always been. His face, once ruddy, had long ago lost its color in the close confinement of the Tombs, but its glow has always been healthy and strong. It was so when he entered the courtroom. But when he arose to leave, wrinkles across his skin had become furrows; the skin

was mottled and the eyes looked out from twin rings of blue, and his lips showed pale and drawn . . . a state bordering on collapse. . . .

Bald Jack Rose made his entrance attired as exquisitely as ever in a dark blue suit with braided edges, a gray tie and dark shoes. He was scented and powdered and, as *The New York Times* reported, "shaven to the blood." His hairless skull, almost the color of chalk, looked like a mask. He walked slowly, purposefully across the green floor, looking neither left nor right until he was seated in the witness chair and had sworn to tell the truth so help him God. He settled back, crossed his hands in his lap and calmly surveyed the courtroom; first the judge, then the jury, then an embracing study of the spectators and, lastly, he looked at Becker. And Becker looked at him, a look, *The New York Times* assayed, "that would have unnerved a different man from Rose. But Rose is said to be the smoothest poker player in New York and he has proven it." Rose occupied the witness chair for ten hours and never once lost his pose.

Frank Moss led him gently into the story of Becker, the Monster, and then gave him his head. Rose's voice was low-pitched, with a hissing quality, but no one had any trouble hearing it. While Rose's expression remained immobile, his tone of voice and its intonations were fluid and eloquent; frankly earnest, heavy with sorrow, angry, disappointed and vengeful. A ballad of lament and disgrace and shame and the dirty truth.

> Do you know Charles Becker, the defendant in this case?
> I do.
> How long have you known him?
> Since the fall of 1911.

Piecemeal, Moss and Rose developed their story. Of how the late Herman Rosenthal and Lieutenant Becker had met, and how Becker had pledged Rosenthal his everlasting friendship during a New Year's Eve party at the Elks Club on the dawn of

1912 and how, subsequently, Rosenthal wanted Becker to go into the gambling business with him.

> Herman Rosenthal had asked Becker to invest $5,000 and told him that with Becker's influence in command of the strong-arm squad and Herman's capabilities in the conducting of such a place, the possibilities of growing rich fast were very bright. Becker consulted me on the matter and I advised against it.
>
> I told him that Rosenthal was unreliable in his transactions in the division of the profits of a place; that I knew that; and I told him not to accept the proposition of this investment of $5,000 in his place, and Becker said: "Well, I guess I will turn it down."

But Rosenthal kept lowering his demands, Rose said, and kept hounding Becker. Finally, Rosenthal begged the police lieutenant to lend him $1,500, that he could open the club with that. Becker asked Rose's advice again.

> Well, my answer was the same: "It is not a question of the amount, Charlie, it is a question of your avoiding tying up in business with him, because it won't take very long before Herman will be telling everybody, 'Becker is my partner.'

Becker said he thought he could avoid that by getting a dummy to take a chattel mortgage on Rosenthal's household goods. In addition, he would require that Rosenthal accept Rose as his partner, giving Rose a twenty-five per cent share of the take which Rose would then split with Becker without Rosenthal's knowledge. The deal was made, Rose testified, and after the first night's play Becker telephoned Rose for a report.

> I told him that the first night's business had been very quiet, and the play had been very quiet. We had not had many customers or patrons, but that I hoped before the place had been open a week that business would be very good.
>
> The next conversation I had with Becker was when I reported to him that the house had had a very good night's business, and that we had won several thousand dollars. Becker then told me to go to Rosenthal, and tell him to give me $500 for

Becker, that Becker needed that much money to pay counsel's expenses in the case of Plitt. [The reference was to Charles Plitt, Becker's press agent, accused of killing a man in a crap game.]

Rosenthal then said: "What does Becker need with $500?" "Why," I said, "Herman, this is part of the money you owe him, and he wants this $500, and he is hard pressed for cash just now. He is looking after Plitt and furnishing money for his defense on the charge of murder, and he would like to have $500. I think you ought to give it to him."

Herman said: "You tell Becker I won't give him any $500. That note on that mortgage is not due for sixty or ninety days yet, and when it is due I will pay it, and you can also tell him for me that the longer I think over the matter the worse I feel about his treatment of me. I don't think he did me any great favor loaning me $1,500 and taking my household goods as collateral."

Q. What did you say to Becker?
A. That Rosenthal refused to let me have the $500 he sent me to get. Becker said, "Well, that is just what I thought about that fellow. Now I will tell you something, Jack," said Becker.
Q. You use the very language, when you give the statements— use the very language, as nearly as you can?
A. As nearly as I can. "Now, I will tell you, Jack," Becker said, "this place has given me a lot of worry and trouble. I am being harped on every day at Police Headquarters about this place. Up to today I have been able to deny its existence, but the time will come very soon when I won't be able to do that. While I was assured I would be dealt fairly with by that fellow, I was willing to go on and do everything I could to protect that place, but this man's treatment of me now when I need money and sent you to get $500, and his refusal of it, relieves me of that worry about that place. The next time my attention is called to that place I am going to raid it."
Q. Was there anything further said at that interview?
A. Yes, sir; I said to Becker: "Now, do not get excited about

the thing, Charlie, and do not jump at conclusions. Rosenthal will fix things up all right with you, because if ever you start looking to raid that place, there is going to be a lot of trouble." He said: "There will be no trouble. Once I start, I will go through with it, and the only trouble there will be will be trouble that Rosenthal will have." I left Becker and told Rosenthal of my interview with Becker and warned Rosenthal to not go too far with Becker.

Q. How long after the interview that you had with Rosenthal did the next interview take place with Becker?

A. The following day. My interviews with Becker were daily on that subject. I told Becker that I had told Rosenthal what he said about the place giving him a lot of trouble, and that he did not propose to stand for all that worry about that place, and that just as soon as his attention was called to it again that he would make a raid on it. Rosenthal said to me: "You tell Becker—"

Q. Never mind what Rosenthal said now. Go on with the next conversation with Becker after that.

The Court—Let the witness proceed in narrative form. Did you see Rosenthal after that conversation?

A. Becker told me to tell that to Rosenthal, and I told him.

Q. What did you tell to Rosenthal?

A. I told Rosenthal that Becker had told me that the place was giving Becker a lot of trouble and that the next time Becker's attention was called to that place that he was going to raid it. Rosenthal said to me: "You tell Becker he cannot raid this place unless he gets the proper evidence, and he has not a chance to get any evidence against this place, because I know every one of his men and not one of them can get in here." I reported to Becker what Rosenthal said. Becker said: "Well, that is his attitude, is it? All right, we will see. If I have to raid that place I will raid it. You tell Herman so." I went back to the place and told Herman what Becker said and Herman said: "Well, you tell Becker he better not start anything with me. I won't stand anything like that."

156

The following day, Rose testified, Becker said to him:

> Well, the trouble has started. Commissioner Waldo sent for me and told me he was informed that the place at 104 West Forty-fifth Street [Rosenthal's gambling house] was wide open and being conducted as a public gambling house, and told me to investigate it and if he found it was a fact to take the necessary steps to close the place.

Rose said Becker sent him back to Rosenthal with the bad news. Rosenthal refused to believe it. "Becker can't bluff me," he said. Rose relayed this to Becker who sent him back to try to reason with the gambler, pointing out that the raid would take the pressure off Becker, that after the raid Rosenthal could reopen and the pressure would be off him too. Rose said he summoned Rosenthal to a meeting at Burns's restaurant, across the street from the club, and tried reason.

Rosenthal's response was this:

> Tell Becker he must think I am crazy to stand for anything like that. Why, here is this place only open a short time, and I am just about building the business up. I have been around telling people that Becker is my friend, and then have him come along and raid me? Why, that is ridiculous. I might just as well take and put a torch to the place and burn it up.
>
> I met Becker the next day and told him that Herman would not stand for any friendly raid or any other kind of raid by Becker. Becker said: "Well, that place is going to be raided, and will be raided by me, and no one else, and in the next few days." I tried to get Becker—

Q. What did you say?
A. I told Becker, I said: "I will not take that message back to Rosenthal, because if I do it spells trouble," and Becker said to me: "Now, don't you worry, there will be no trouble; the only trouble in this case will be for Rosenthal." I did not take that message back to Rosenthal. A few days later I met Becker at the Union Square Hotel, and he said: "Within a week I am going to raid Rosenthal's place." I said: "Do you want me to

tell that to Rosenthal?" He said: "No, I am through with him, but I will raid it. I have got to raid it." The following week the place was raided.

Q. Did you have any conversation with Becker between the last conversation you have given and the time of the raiding of the gambling house?

A. Yes, sir, every day. Becker was telling me that he was completing his plans for the raid. I asked him what his plans were. He told me that he had a plan of the house from a visit he had made there one night with Rosenthal and me; that Steinert and White, officers attached to the strong-arm squad, would make the necessary affidavits as to having visited the place and secured the evidence against the place, and they would make the raid. Becker said: "What do you think about that?" "Why," I said, "that is awful dangerous, Charlie. You cannot get away with that on this fellow." "Oh," he said, "I will get away with it, and I want to end everything between him and I. I am going to make that raid, but I am going to pay $1,500 to make that raid, because immediately I make the raid I am going to tell Rosenthal to go and get the satisfaction papers covering the mortgage held by Donohue on the household things in that place, and that is in payment for any little damage that may be done in the making of the raid, and I am through with him."

The day after the raid, Rose said he met Becker at the Union Square Hotel and that Becker told him he had encountered Rosenthal at the police court earlier in the day. Rosenthal was openly outraged, he said, and complained: "That is a tough deal you gave me last night."

Becker said, "Well, Herman, it had to be. Now, it was a case of getting raided by me or getting raided by Costigan, and if Costigan raided you, it meant my job. Now, I just had to do it."

However, Becker assured Rosenthal that no indictments would be returned against either Rosenthal's nephew or the dealer arrested with him in the raid when the case went before the grand jury. Further, Becker promised that the policeman stationed in the house since the raid would be removed.

But Becker double-crossed Rosenthal. The grand jury indicted the two men and the policeman remained in the house, preventing Rosenthal from reopening.

Rosenthal, meanwhile, was pursuing Becker relentlessly, calling him two or three times daily on the phone, demanding that something be done about the indictments and that the policeman be removed from the house.

> Becker told Herman that he would see him, and kept putting it off from day to day. Becker then told me he had left instructions at Police Headquarters and at his home that any time Rosenthal called him on the telephone that he was not in.
>
> Soon after Becker told me that Rosenthal had begun talking around the streets about Becker's having been his partner and raided his place on framed-up evidence, and that Rosenthal was going to show him up. A few days after I again met Becker at the Union Square Hotel. He told me that Commissioner Waldo had sent for him and asked him if there was any truth in the rumors about him having been financially interested in Rosenthal's place. And Becker told me that his reply to Waldo was that he just laughed at him and said, "Why, Commissioner, kind of a new thing, isn't it, policemen giving up money? The usual thing is to have them come and say that policemen got money from them."

Waldo, said Becker, agreed the charge was absurd.

There was, however, no letup in Rosenthal's public complaints. Newspapermen, Rose said, began calling Waldo, the Mayor and various police officials, all of whom refused to comment. Suddenly Rosenthal succumbed to the infinite persuasions of Herbert Bayard Swope, the *World*'s crime expert, and he had given Swope the fatal affidavit. Word of it got around and Rose reported this to Becker who said:

"Well, I guess Rosenthal means to do what he threatened— to squeal and break me."

Becker said the papers had invited him to reply to the affidavit but that his lawyers advised against it. It was the suggestion of Deputy Police Commissioner Douglas McKay, Becker told Rose, that he obtain an original copy of the affidavit and sue Rosenthal for criminal libel.

Moss had now established all the motives—revenge, concealment, silence—and he hurried to the heart of the prosecution's case.

"Will you tell us now what other conversations you had with Becker in regard to Rosenthal prior to Rosenthal's death?"

An objection by McIntyre is aborted by Judge Goff.

"Please continue, Mr. Moss."

Moss nods to Rose who, staring straight at Becker, continues:

> They began when one day Lieutenant Becker telephoned me to my house to meet him early that morning at the Union Square Hotel. I went and met him there. Lieutenant Becker said to me, "Well, now, this fellow Rosenthal means to do all he said he would do, all he set out to do, about exposing me, and that I was his partner, and that I am a grafter, and going to show me up and try to break me." I asked him what he knew about it. Becker said that several things had been happening now. They all showed what Rosenthal's intentions were.
>
> He said, "He has started by trying to see Commissioner Waldo. He has been to Police Headquarters. He has been annoying Commissioner Waldo by telephoning to his home. The Commissioner has refused to see him or talk with him. He has tried to see Magistrate Corrigan, and he has refused to take any notice of it at all. He has tried to see Chief Magistrate McAdoo and tell him that the warrants issued against his place were secured on perjured testimony, and he has tried to see Mayor Gaynor, and Mayor Gaynor has refused to see him.
>
> "He is now directing his efforts toward the district attorney's office. If he ever gets there why it means great danger!"

Moss has done his job well. He has created an atmosphere of suspense which, despite the crowded courtroom, has caused a silence of dreadful expectation. In his testimony thus far, Rose has exceeded in infinite detail the disclosures of his printed confession, familiar now to all New York, and he gives the impression of a man who has much more to tell.

Becker has matched Rose's equanimity, but there is a terrible air of tenseness around the defendant. Perhaps it does not emanate with Becker; perhaps it emanates with the people who are staring at him. Rose resumes.

Becker said to me: "There is only one thing to do with a fellow like Rosenthal—just stop him so that he will not bother anybody any more for all time." I said: "What do you mean?" He said: "Well, there is a fellow that ought to be put off the earth." "Why," I says, "I agree with you. He is no account." He said: "Well, no use saying he is no account, and all of that, but the idea is now to do something to him." I says: "What do you mean?" and he said: "There is a fellow I would like to have croaked."

I said: "You are right, Charlie; the man is all you say he is, and I agree with you in everything; but there are other ways of handling Rosenthal." He said: "What are they?" "Why," I said, "in the first place there are some people uptown whom I can go to who will send to Rosenthal and just lay the law down to him. These men—Rosenthal will pretty near have to do whatever they ask of him. They will warn him that for the best interests of all concerned to abandon his plans of exposing you, or, as he thinks, break you."

"Why," he said, "do you think that I would ask anybody, or let you ask anybody, to go to anybody and ask Rosenthal to let up on me? You don't understand me as well as I thought you did."

I said, "All right. I will send a couple of fellows up there that will give Rosenthal a beating and warn him and tell him the reason of that beating, and if he don't stop there is something worse than a beating in store for him."

And Becker said: "I don't want him beat up. I could do that myself. I could have a warrant for any gambling house that he frequents and make a raid on that place and beat him up for resisting arrest or anything else. No beating up will fix that fellow, a dog in the eyes of myself, you, and everybody else.

Nothing for that man but taken off this earth. Have him murdered, cut his throat, dynamited, or anything."

Rose's voice mounts steadily in shrillness. His last words pierce the ear. Then his voice drops.

I said, "Charlie, don't excite yourself. This man Rosenthal isn't worth taking any such chances with." "Chances?" he says, [and Rose's voice conveys a contemptuous sneer]. "Jack, you know what I think of you, what I think of your family, and what my family thinks of you. You don't suppose for a minute I would ask you to go into anything that meant taking a chance, or meant danger to you or yours, no more than I would take myself. There is no danger to anybody that has any hand in the murder of Rosenthal. You know me, Jack. I have made good. Anything I have ever told you I would, and I will make good on this. There can't anything happen to anyone, and you know the sentiment over at Police Headquarters is so strong that the man or men that croak him would have a medal pinned on them."

I said, "All right, Charlie. I will help you. What is it you want?"

The plan, Rose said, hinged on Big Jack Zelig, then being held in the Tombs on $10,000 bail on a punitive charge of carrying concealed weapons. Rose was to go there and promise him freedom in return for assassinating Rosenthal. Rose said he took Harry Vallon with him and they talked with Zelig. The gang chieftain was not in a cooperative mood. He blamed Rose for his trouble.

"Don't ask me any favors," he shouted, "you just get me out of here. If you think you can rush me off to prison and nothing will happen you are mistaken. You will have to reckon with my friends."

Rose said he reported Zelig's refusal to Becker who said: "Well, let him rot in the Tombs then."

15. The Song of Bald Jack Rose, Part II

ZELIG, however, had reckoned without Rose's resources. ROSE offered Becker an alternative proposal.

Q. What did you say?
A. I said to Becker, "There are some friends of Zelig whom I know. I will go see them. Perhaps I could get them to act in the matter without any order from Zelig." He gave me a couple of days—I asked it of Becker, and he said: "Well, all right. Do that, and see these fellows; have a talk with them; tell them just what I have told you; nothing can happen to anybody who croaks Rosenthal. And let me know what they say." I went to Southern Boulevard to a house, and there met Lefty Louie and Whitey Lewis. I told them that I came there to warn them of the danger they were in; of the fate similar to what Zelig had met by being arrested on a charge of carrying concealed weapons; and they said, "We don't carry them any more since this trouble of Zelig's." "Well," I said, "it don't make any difference. Zelig didn't have one either. Now if you go downtown at all, you are gone." They asked me who was

doing this and I said Lieutenant Becker and the strong-arm squad.

McIntyre pounces.

"I ask that the answer be stricken as hearsay, incompetent and not in the presence of the defendant."

"Denied. Please continue."

The judge nods at Rose.

They asked me what was the cause of this and I said "Why, Herman Rosenthal." "Who is Herman Rosenthal and what had he to do with it?" they asked, and I said: "Well, he has been squealing against Lieutenant Becker, and he is trying to get to the district attorney's office, and see District Attorney Whitman and expose Becker and the workings of the strong-arm squad. Now," I said, "Becker feels, and has told me so, that all you fellows, whom, on my account he has been taking care of, owe it to him and to yourselves to see that Rosenthal does not appear and make that squeal." They said: "You mean by croaking him?" I said, "Yes." "Have you seen Zelig?" they asked me. I said: "Yes."

"What did he say about it?" "Why, I didn't talk direct to Zelig about it," I told them. "But I know that Zelig will agree to it." "Well," they said: "All right. We are willing. We will go tonight." I said: "Well, now, let us arrange it this way: You stay here, I will go to 42d Street, but just wait my arrival, and be ready at any time that I come for you to take you where Rosenthal is, and then you can do the job." They said: "We will wait."

Rose said he reported to Becker the same night, telling him that he had made all arrangements, and that Becker could expect "to wake up any morning and read the papers and find out that Rosenthal had been found murdered."

And Becker said to me, "I hope that is so. Now, tell those fellows to drop everything else. There is nothing to worry about and nothing to fear, and I will take care of anybody and everybody that has a hand in the thing." I said: "I have assured them of that, and they are on the job now."

A couple of days passed by. Lieutenant Becker called me at my house one morning and said: "Rosenthal is still at it, but I don't see those fellows at it." "Well," I said, "Charlie, I don't know. They are on the job. I will go see them again today and find out why this delay." He said: "Now, you better see that there is no further delay by them, because there won't be any delay by me."

But the days dragged on without event. Becker's irritation, Rose related, was mounting to anger.

"Either you are stalling or those fellows don't put any stock in what you say, they don't believe nothing will happen to them."

Rose said he wasn't stalling, but that maybe the last part of Becker's statement was true. It was then, Rose said, that Bridgie Webber was brought into the plot. Bridgie had money and influence and he knew the gunmen. Becker telephoned Webber and summoned him to a meeting that night.

"I went uptown to find Bridgie Webber, and I had asked Becker if I could bring along—no, I asked him what time to bring Webber, and he had said somewhere along about 9 o'clock. 'I am going up to raid a crap game up in Harlem. I can see you and Bridgie up there and meet my men up there to make this raid.'"

The Harlem murder conference seems like a key segment of the foundation of the case against Becker. It was an event attended by, and possibly witnessed by, several persons. Rose speaks now in that flat, frank tone.

I hired an automobile, accompanied by Vallon and Sam Schepps. I went to 42d Street and Sixth Avenue looking for Bridgie. Bridgie was not there. The time was coming for to keep my appointment with Becker. I left Schepps behind, telling him to wait for Webber, and immediately Webber arrived to tell him to get into a taxi and come right to 124th Street and Seventh Avenue, that I wanted to see him. Vallon and myself went uptown. We arrived at 124th Street and Seventh Avenue, and Lieutenant Becker was not there. I went into a cigar store to get some cigarettes. When I came out I found him in conversation with Harry Vallon, and I joined them.

Becker asked me where Bridgie was, and I told him I had left a man down at 42d Street to have Bridgie come up here immediately he arrived. Right then Webber arrived. We all stood at this vacant lot, sat on a board across that vacant lot, talking about Rosenthal. Becker began by telling of the efforts that Rosenthal was making to reach the district attorney.

Becker said to Webber: "Bridgie, why don't you help Jack in that thing and have that fellow croaked?" And Webber said he didn't want to lay himself liable to these fellows. "There is no laying liable to anybody or anything." That was Becker's reply to Webber. "There is nothing to happen to anybody that has any hand in the croaking of Rosenthal," he said. "I don't know whether Jack is stalling, or weakening, or what it is; or whether these fellows won't take Jack's word for it. Now you step into the thing, Bridgie, take charge of things, and see that this thing is done for me, will you?"

Bridgie said he would and Bridgie said: "Leave it to me now. The job will be done, and done quick." Then he and Becker stepped aside and held a whispered conversation, and on their return Becker called me aside, and I had some money for him that night, which I gave to him. He told me: "Now, Bridgie will be on the job to help you. Now, this thing ought to be done within a day or two." I said: "Well, with Bridgie on the job, Charlie, I think we will get some results quickly," and we left.

Webber was as good as his word. Within two days, he assembled the four killers and with Rose and Vallon, marched on the Garden Restaurant on Seventh Avenue near 44th Street, where Rosenthal was having dinner with his wife and Jack (Jacob Reich) Sullivan. They would have done it then, Rose said, but he spotted a man standing in the shadows across the street from the restaurant whom he knew to be a Burns' detective. He assumed the detective had been assigned by the district attorney to guard Rosenthal so the killing was postponed.

The next day, Rose related, Becker accosted him furiously.

"What's the matter? I see Rosenthal around every night as big as life."

Rose said the explanation about the presence of the detective preventing the assassination only enraged Becker further.

"A detective? I told you there is nothing to fear. Walk up and shoot him in front of a policeman if you want to. There ain't nothing to fear. And don't let that happen again."

Rose promised he wouldn't. Meanwhile, Becker obtained Rosenthal's affidavit as it appeared in the *World* and he assailed Rose anew.

"If you had been on the job this wouldn't have happened. I wouldn't be facing this now. Why don't you get it over and done with while there is still time."

Rose promised to act at once. He said he was going on the Sam Paul Association excursion to Far Rockaway the very next day, July 14, and that Webber and Vallon would also be there and he would get them together for a talk and make a definite plan to kill Rosenthal immediately.

"Can I depend on that?" Becker asked. Rose assured him he could.

When he returned from the Sam Paul outing Sunday night, Rose testified, he telephoned Becker and told him the gamblers' sympathies were all against Rosenthal.

Becker, Rose said, didn't seem interested in sympathy. The grand jury had issued subpoenas for all those named in Rose's confession.

> "I told you that this thing would occur if you didn't get rid of that fellow. Now, all this delay and this stalling around— you don't mean to tell me that this could not have been done all this time, croaking Rosenthal. Now, there is still time; tonight is the time, and it will just fit. It will look like the gamblers did it on account of his threatened squeal."
>
> I said, "I will try tonight."

Rose tells how he hired a red touring car and drove to Tom Sharkey's saloon on 14th Street where the car had a flat tire.

167

Rose telephoned for another car and in a few minutes the famous gray Packard arrived.

It is now one o'clock in the afternoon. Rose has been on the stand three hours and there is obviously more to tell. No one has had any lunch and Judge Goff shows no signs of adjourning. Aside from reporters silently moving in and out, with an air of thieves in a churchyard, the courtroom is tomblike.

Q. Who went into the other machine?
A. Harry Vallon, Sam Schepps and myself.
Q. Do you know who was the chauffeur on the other machine?
A. William Shapiro.
Q. Will you describe that machine, the second machine, now?
A. The only thing I remember of it is the fact that it was a gray car.
Q. Will you describe the automobile which Shapiro was driving? Will you please tell who went in that automobile when it started away from 14th Street?
A. Harry Vallon, Sam Schepps, myself, and the driver.
Q. Where did you go?
A. Up to Seventh Avenue.
Q. Who did you see there?
A. Dago Frank.
Q. Whereabouts on Seventh Avenue did you go?
A. I think the number is 2527.
Q. Who lives there, if you know, or who did at that time?
A. I don't know who lives there, but the name on the door was Baker & Harris.
Q. Had you been there before?
A. Yes, sir.
Q. How many times before had you been there?
A. Three or four times.
Q. Who had you seen when you went there?
A. At times Lefty Louie and Gyp and Frank and Whitey.
Q. The same persons that you had seen in the Southern Boulevard house?

A. Yes, sir.

Q. Did you continue to go to the Southern Boulevard house after you went to the Seventh Avenue house?

A. No, sir; they had moved to the Seventh Avenue house.

Q. Did you take that automobile direct to the house on Seventh Avenue?

A. No, sir.

Q. Where did it stop?

A. I stopped at a café two or three streets from the house; I wanted to see my brother-in-law.

Q. Where was Dago Frank found?

A. When I reached the house I asked Sam Schepps to go in and find the doorbell with the name of Baker & Harris on it, and ring the bell, and see if there was anyone at home.

Q. After he went in there did you see anybody?

A. A head popped out of the door and I recognized the face of Dago Frank.

Q. What then?

A. I beckoned him to come down.

Q. Did he come down?

A. He came down.

Q. Did you see him then?

A. I saw him and talked with him.

Q. Now please tell us the conversation you had with him.

A. I asked Frank where the rest of the crowd was and he said that he had received a message to come downtown. We started downtown.

Q. In this automobile?

A. In this automobile.

Q. When you say we, did that include Dago Frank?

A. Frank, Harry Vallon, Sam Schepps, myself and the chauffeur.

Q. How far did you proceed?

A. To 42d Street and Sixth Avenue.

Q. What did you do there?

A. Got out.

Q. Did you see anyone when you got out?

A. I did.

Q. Whom did you see?

A. I saw Bridgie Webber with Lefty Louie, Whitey Lewis and Gyp the Blood.

Q. Where were they?

A. Standing in front of Webber's place.

Q. On the sidewalk?

A. On the sidewalk.

Q. Then when you got out of the automobile, and saw the persons you have mentioned on the sidewalk, who was with you, who got out of the automobile with you, joining that party?

A. Harry Vallon, Sam Schepps and Frank.

Q. You mean Dago Frank?

A. Dago Frank.

Q. Having met, what did you do?

A. Webber asked us to come upstairs. We went up into the poker room.

Q. Who went up?

A. Frank, Gyp, Louie, Whitey, Schepps, Vallon, Webber and myself.

Q. What did you do when you got up there?

A. We sat down at a long table and refreshments were ordered for us.

Q. Did Webber remain or did he go out?

A. He went out.

Q. Are you able to say about what time it was that Webber went out?

A. No.

Q. Did he return again?

A. He did.

Q. What did he say—did he say anything when he returned, and if so what was it?

A. He said Rosenthal is around the Metropole.

Q. When Webber said that, what happened?

A. Everybody arose from the table and started for the door.

Q. Did they go out of the door?
A. Yes.
Q. Who went out; name the persons whose names you can state that you know went out of the door—the persons whom you can state first by name.
A. Lefty Louie, Gyp the Blood, Whitey Lewis, Dago Frank, Bridgie Webber, and others whom I don't know.
Q. Did you go out?
A. No.
Q. Did anyone remain with you?
A. I asked Schepps—
Q. Did Schepps remain with you?
A. Schepps remained with me.
Q. What was the next thing that occurred of which you were a witness or a hearer after they had left the poker room, as you have just told us?
A. I was standing at the couch in the place and the word came in that Herman Rosenthal had just been shot around at the Metropole.

Rose said he remained at Webber's until three o'clock in the morning, an hour after the shooting, when he went over to the Times Building and telephoned Becker at home.

" 'Hello there,' I said to him, 'did you hear the news?' 'Yes,' he said, 'and I congratulate you.' "

Rose said Becker told him he had already received a call from a newspaperman. Rose asked him if he was coming downtown and Becker said he was, that he would meet him at Webber's.

Rose said Becker arrived at daybreak and that the two of them, along with Jack Sullivan and Harry Vallon, talked together for several minutes in a doorway adjoining Webber's pool hall.

"Webber began the conversation. He said, 'Well, the job is done.'

" 'Yes,' says Becker, 'and I am glad of it.'

"I asked Becker—"

Moss gestures and Rose stops.

"I want you to use Becker's very language. Go on."

"I asked Becker what caused this long wait before his coming downtown. He said, 'I stopped over at the station house before coming here.'

"I said, 'Whom did you see over there?' He said, 'District Attorney Whitman is there.' I said, 'Well, that means danger.' 'Oh, no,' he said, 'everything will be all right; don't go exciting yourself.' I said, 'Has anything developed new?' 'They have got three or four numbers there, but neither one of them, I understand, is the correct number of the machine.' I said, 'Did you see Rosenthal?' He said, 'Yes, I went to the back room and took a look at him.' "

For the first time in his narrative there is hesitancy in Rose's voice. He shifts his hands in his lap, looks up at Goff for an instant and then at Moss.

"May I use that word?"

Moss nods in deep affirmation.

"I want you to use the very words."

"Becker said, 'It was a pleasing sight to me to look and see that squealing Jew there, and if it were not for the presence of District Attorney Whitman I would have cut out his tongue and hung it up somewheres as a warning to future squealers.' "

We have heard this remark before, but Rose's tone is snakelike and venomous and a quick massive gasp arises from the courtroom. When Rose told this in his confession, we recall, Becker had singled out the Times Building as the place to display Herman's tongue. Now it is merely "somewheres." But even a hundred such discrepancies like that would not reduce in substance the weight of this poker player's indictment. We study Becker's face and we see this omnipotent hulk beginning to collapse from within. Or do we?

Rose is not studying Becker. He is talking about going to the Lafayette Baths, then home and then to the home of a friend named Harry Pollok. It is now Tuesday afternoon and Rose says he is sick. He has gone to bed. He hears nothing about the affair until late Wednesday when Becker telephones him.

What did Becker say?

He just said "Becker." I said hello and he said, "I just saw Pollok and he told me you were there. That is a good place for you. Rest up. I hear you are not well."

I told him I was sick in mind and body and he said, "Now don't go carrying on and taking things to heart. Everything is all right. This will all be over in a day or two. Go to bed, take some quinine, brace up and don't worry."

I told him I wanted to see him and he said, "I'm very busy looking after things now, but I will try and get a chance to run up today," but he said, "I told Pollok to tell you—did you get a telephone message from Pollok?" I said I did. "Did Pollok tell you everything was all right and not to worry?" I said he did. He said, "That is just the way matters stand. Now, don't worry and get nervous." I said, "What about this fellow Shapiro, and Libby? I hear they have been arrested." He said, "Well, now, there is nothing to worry about them. Can you locate Aaron Levy?" I said, "I think I can." He said, "You try, and I will see if I can locate him, and tell him to appear for this chauffeur for me." I said, "All right, I will do that." He said, "There is nothing for you to worry about, and I know where you are, and that is a good place for you to rest up. Now, just stay right there."

Q. Is that the whole of the communication?
A. Yes.
Q. Did you have another one?
A. Yes, sir, later that day.
Q. Please give it.
A. He said, "How are you feeling?" I said, "Very badly." I said, "What is the news?" He said, "News? There is two hundred cops looking for you."
Q. For you?

A. For me.

Q. For you, Rose?

A. Yes, sir, for me.

I said, "Well, I guess I better go downtown or something."
He said, "No, you stay right where you are until you hear different from me. Now, I am doing this, don't you go jumping
at conclusions as to what you ought to do or ought not to do;
you do as I tell you. Now, don't worry, and don't get excited."
"Well," I said, "it is something to worry about, isn't it?"

"Now don't make it any worse than it is. It is nothing to
worry about. This will all blow over."

He said, "There is something else I want to talk to you about
that is more important." I said: "What is it?" He said: "Do you
know Lawyer Hart?" I said: "I do not."

"Well," he said, "I want you to go down to his office this
afternoon and get into a taxi and see him." I said: "What, with
two hundred cops looking for me, go down to Broad Street?"
"Well," he said, "I am doing this, ain't I? I wouldn't care if
the whole department was looking for you." I said: "I don't
feel well anyway."

He said: "Well, I will send Lawyer Hart to you." I said:
"Isn't that kind of risky, too?" He said: "Now, stop your worrying. I am doing this." I said: "What is he coming here for?"
"Well, I want him to get an affidavit from you saying that it
was you who advanced that $1,500 to Rosenthal and took as
collateral for it a mortgage on his household goods."

I said: "This is rather a poor time for any such things about
affidavits, or things like that, Charlie, a man murdered—and
they are already beginning to talk and pointing at you and
pointing at me, and everybody else. What is the use of affidavits
now?" "Now, this is absolutely necessary, or I would not ask it."
That was what Becker said.

"Well," I said, "I have thought—another thing is this, that
right now me coming along with an affidavit," I said, "perhaps
there will be a question about my having fifteen hundred."

He said: "Yes, I guess that is right, too." He said: "How about
Pollok? He will help you, won't he?" I said: "How?" He said:

"Get him to also give Mr. Hart an affidavit corroborating the fact that it was him loaned you the $1,500."

I said the same thing would apply to Pollok. "He is not over-burdened just now with fifteen hundred, either." Becker said: "He has got a partner, Pat Powers." I said: "Yes, that is right—all right, I will mention it to Pollok." He said: "In order that nobody else gets in on you other than Hart—You don't know Hart?" "No." "Well, I will arrange with him and he will come there, and whoever answers the doorbell he will say: 'Tell Mr. Rose that J.H. is here.' Now you admit him and give him that affidavit." I said: "All right, I will."

Hart arrived that evening with a notary, Rose said, and he and Pollok gave the requested affidavits.

Rose edges forward in the chair as though he were through and wanted to leave. Moss has taken up a sheaf of papers from the counsel table and returns to the stand.

"To go back to the day of the murder, July 16. Who paid the gunmen?"

"I did. I got the $1,000 from Webber and met Lefty Louie at 50th Street and 8th Avenue and paid him. I told him Becker said to lay low for a few days, that everything would be all right."

Moss has begun to walk back to the table. Rose rises from the chair. There is the soft sound of people shifting in chairs.

Judge Goff adjourns an hour for lunch.

16 Variations on the Theme

HELEN BECKER survived Rose's damning indictment of her husband with the same calm detachment with which she might have regarded someone else's dreams. She smiled her gentle smile for him when he returned to court with McIntyre and the embattled legal entourage, and to the few reporters calloused enough to approach this frail, feminine incongruity in Becker's life she would only say:

"I'm glad the trial has been proceeding so rapidly. There is only one way to clear up this horrible situation and to end the anxiety and the distress, and that is by a speedy trial."

McIntyre does not share her enthusiasm for speed. His only chance to save Becker is by discrediting his accusers, however long it takes. Speedy justice may be desirable in theory, but in this case speedy justice may mean Becker's execution. Juries tend to gather momentum. McIntyre's chances of turning Rose from a civic hero into a despicable liar and traitor seem fairly good. Rose's own past, with its attendant police record, is against him, and he has not benefited by his admission that he was a participant in the Rosenthal assassination. The gulf between this fact and the possible fact that he is simply escaping the electric chair by trying to put Becker in it is not so wide but that McIntyre may be able to bridge it.

At 3 P.M., Rose is back in the witness chair, as fresh and assured as he had been five hours earlier. McIntyre's eagerness to break Rose down is apparent.

"Did you not counsel, advise and supervise the murder of Herman Rosenthal?"

Whitman will not stand for this and his objection is sustained. McIntyre says he will rephrase his question.

"Do you believe you are a murderer?"

Whitman's objection, to everyone's surprise, is overruled. Rose is instructed to answer.

"I do not." His reply is demure, as though the question had been of simple propriety. (Is it true you frequent saloons?)

"Have you ever engaged in the murder of other human beings?"

Rose's denial, again in coy tones, precedes Whitman's objections.

McIntyre is also keenly aware that Rose's testimony hangs on the corroboration of Sam Schepps. He begins eating away at Schepps's innocence early. Schepps's name now seems out of place.

> At the time you signed the affidavit, in Pollok's house, regarding the $1,500 mortgage, was Sam Schepps present?
> He was.
> Was he also known at that time as Sam Franklin?
> I don't know.
> When you signed that affidavit, did you realize you were committing perjury?
> If I did, Mr. Hart and Lieutenant Becker knew I was committing perjury.
> I asked you if you knew *you* were committing perjury?
> I would have done anything Lieutenant Becker asked me to that night.
> So you would commit perjury at any time?
> That night.

McIntyre has shifted now to Rose's early life. He elicits the fact that Rose was once part owner of a hotel in Hartford, Connecticut, that he promoted prize fights there and that the man with whom he was associated in these ventures was James M. Sullivan who is now his attorney.

"Were you born in Russian Poland?"

Rose says he does not know, that it might be true.

Judge Goff leans forward.

"It is my duty to caution the witness that he may decline to answer these questions on the ground that they tend to incriminate or degrade him."

Rose accepts the advice. McIntyre is unable to obtain any more information about Connecticut or Rose's personal history. McIntyre will not give up.

"Have you ever lived with a woman not your wife?"

"Have you ever lived off a woman's wages of sin?"

"Have you ever . . ."

Whitman objects in a weary voice and he is sustained. McIntyre desists.

"What is your age?"

"Thirty-seven."

"What is your occupation?"

"I am a gambler."

Rose's history of his gambling ventures is hard to follow. His employers change frequently. Finally, he has an interest in the Hesper Club, the sacrosanct casino operated under the auspices of Big Tim Sullivan, the East Side Tammany boss. At another time, he was in business with Herman Rosenthal. In 1909, he says, he was in the theatrical business with a Mr. Harris and he boasts that he has even written a play or two himself. Once he was in the printing business. In 1911, he operated a gambling club on Second Avenue, the club which Becker raided and where the two men met.

"And what business were you in after the Second Avenue club was closed?"

"I became Lieutenant Becker's collector."

There is some subdued laughter but McIntyre conceals his annoyance.

"During the year 1910, how did you make your living?"

Judge Goff taps his gavel gently.

"The witness has acknowledged that he has been a gambler. There is nothing to gain by further inquiry."

Rose says that during the time he was in business with Rosenthal, there was never any trouble between them.

Q. Did he put you out of the gambling game in which you were jointly interested?
A. Never. I withdrew.
Q. Did you ever say that he turned you out?
A. I could not say that, because it was not so.
Q. Why did you withdraw from the gambling business in which you were jointly interested?
A. I made up my mind to give up gambling and start into legitimate business, and an opportunity presented itself that I might become associated with the late Henry Lee in the theatrical business, and for the sake of my family I gave up the gambling business and dabbled in matters theatrical.
Q. When was it that you concluded to quit the gambling business and become connected with respectable business?
A. I made that attempt on several occasions.
Q. When was that?
A. Three years ago, four years ago, six years ago, ten years ago, twenty years ago, and I will do the same again.

There is a long silence. McIntyre looks at the jury, at Whitman and at Rose. He smiles.

"Ah, then you expect to get out of jail?"

For some reason, the remark brings a scattering of gasps through the courtroom. Whitman is on his feet, moving up on the judge. Goff nods, vigorously. McIntyre rewords the

179

question several times but neither Whitman nor the judge will let it pass. Rose watches the play like a spectator. McIntyre gives up.

Q. When you had the gambling house on Second Avenue, I think it was, did Lieutenant Becker raid that gambling house?
A. He did.
Q. When he raided your gambling house were you put under arrest?
A. I was not present.
Q. How many times in all did Lieutenant Becker raid the gambling house in which you were interested in?
A. Once.
Q. Did you go into the gambling business again after the raid?
A. With Herman Rosenthal on 45th Street.
Q. After you ceased to be interested in Rosenthal's gambling house on 45th Street, were your relations with Rosenthal cordial?
A. They were not.
Q. They were not?
A. No, sir.
Q. Now, when was it that your relations ceased with Rosenthal?
A. The day following Lieutenant Becker's raid on the place.
Q. Did Rosenthal charge you with furnishing information upon which Lieutenant Becker acted when he made the raid?
A. No, sir.
Q. Did you procure information upon which the police acted in order that the raid might be made?
A. I did not.
Q. Did you procure information against any gambling houses in the city in order that the raids might be made by the strong-arm squad?
A. I never did.
Q. Were you known as a stool pigeon for the police?
A. I was known as a collector only.

Q. With regard to your alleged confession which appeared in the New York *World,* it is true, is it not, that you were paid $2,000 by the *World* for this?

A. I don't know what confession you mean.

McIntyre hands a copy of the paper to him and we wait, impatiently, for two or three minutes while Rose scans it. He returns it to McIntyre.

"That is substantially what I told the district attorney."

"You were paid $2,000 for writing it?"

"No."

A pause, and then:

"Isn't it true that Rosenthal told people your wife was a prostitute and that your children were bastards?"

Rose grips the arms of the chair and thrusts his body forward.

"No, no, no, no!"

It is the first time he has registered anger. It subsides quickly.

Q. You knew there was a plan to kill Herman Rosenthal and yet you did not warn him?

A. No.

Q. Did you warn anybody?

A. I telephoned Mrs. Rosenthal and told her that her husband was in danger.

Q. Did not your conscience prick you?

A. I did not consult my conscience.

Q. Now, you stated today that when Lieutenant Becker told you that if you did not have Rosenthal murdered that he, Becker, would have it done himself—do you remember saying that this morning?

A. I did not say that.

Q. What did you say?

A. I said that if Rosenthal was not croaked, Becker said he would do it himself.

Q. If Becker said that to you, that if it was not done, that he himself would do it, why didn't you let him do it?

A. I did not stop him.

Q. You did not stop him?

A. No.

Q. Why didn't you let him do it?

A. Well, it was entirely up to him what he did in the matter.

Q. You stated this morning that you said that if you did not have it done or do it, that he himself would do it. I want to know when he made the declaration to you why you did not let the defendant do the murder himself?

A. I was in hopes he really would.

Q. Is that the best answer you can make?

A. That is the best answer.

Q. When he told you that he would do it, why didn't you withdraw from the conspiracy and let someone else do it?

A. I was between two fires, on one side Becker, and on the other side the gang, and I thought I could handle both ends until such time as the matter straightened itself out.

Q. When you were between two fires, Becker on the one side and the gang on the other, did you go to anybody and complain and say that a foul murder was about to be done?

A. Not in that part of the world I frequented is there anybody that would have paid any attention to me.

Q. In that part of the world that you frequented no one, did you say, would pay any attention?

A. No.

McIntyre's circumlocutory questioning, the wrangles over the district attorney's objections, Rose's deliberateness in answering; all these have eaten up the hours. It is now 8:30 P.M. Five hours under cross-examination and Rose's credibility seems to have survived.

McIntyre and Hart are conferring. Rose crouches in the chair, shifting his position, his pose. It seems significant. There is something animalistic about it.

McIntyre leans wearily on the table, rubbing his brow.

"I must ask your Honor's indulgence and request that the cross-examination be continued until Monday morning. I am physically exhausted. I cannot ask another question."

Is McIntyre stalling? Judge Goff smiles.

"Go on. You are stronger than you were this morning?"

Quiet laughter.

"I have been on my feet for six hours cross-examining. I have had to go without my dinner. It is against the interests of justice to force me to go on."

His voice has risen and these last words he has addressed to the jury. Their faces suggest sympathy.

"If you have another question, put it. Otherwise the cross-examination is closed." It sounds like a firm ruling.

"Counsel does not wish it closed. Counsel states that he is unable to go on. My mind will not work as it should."

Hart is approaching the bench. Goff glares at him.

"I do not want to hear you. Sit down. One counsel at a time is enough."

Hart retreats. Goff returns to McIntyre.

"I would have acceded to your request, Mr. McIntyre, if the nature of the cross-examination for the last three hours had warranted it, but it was not apparent to me that counsel intended to finish."

McIntyre seems stunned.

"I object to the remark of the court implying that I have acted in bad faith."

Hart recovers his courage and is suddenly before the bench.

"I move for a mistrial on the grounds that your Honor's remark is uncalled for and illegal."

"Denied. The cross-examination is closed. Counsel for the prosecution may re-direct after which counsel for the defense may re-cross-examine."

"I am unable to."

Whitman and Moss confer, heads together.

"No further direct examination, your Honor."

Rose steps down from the chair and starts across the room. McIntyre springs to his feet.

"I ask that this witness be kept apart from Vallon, Schepps and Webber. I ask that your Honor have him confined in the Tombs so that he may not confer with the other three."

Goff calls the witness back.

"You are not to discuss your testimony with any other witness."

"Yes, your Honor."

McIntyre waves his arms.

"What's the use of cautioning a man like that? I demand, your Honor, that he be kept apart from the others."

"I have no authority to transfer this man to the Tombs."

McIntyre turns accusingly on Whitman.

"You took this man out of the Tombs and put him in the West Side Prison."

Color rises in Whitman's face.

"I had the power to do so." [angrily]

McIntyre returns to his seat, and tired as he is, he can still shout.

"You're not only acting as district attorney, you're acting as jailkeeper too."

The two men glare at each other. Judge Goff's gavel raps sharply on the bench.

17. When Are They Going to Croak Him?

THE LAG between the day's sensation and its appearance in the papers was doubly long over a weekend. Judge Goff had kept the Becker trial in session on Saturday and readers had something to occupy them on the Sabbath. But on Monday, barring out-of-court developments and speculation, the news seized upon such kindred events as it could. One such void was filled by publishing the names of the owners of all the disorderly houses in town. Since New York's wealthy owned slum property by the block, the list embraced segments of high society, including William Randolph Hearst. None of these owners had any idea of what their property was being used for, and some didn't even know they owned it, so the end effect was meaningless.

Promise of more substantial scandal was embodied in Bridgie Webber, the second of the squealers, when he took the stand Monday morning in the trial of Charles Becker.

What Webber lacked in self-assurance, he more than made up in eagerness to corroborate the revelations of Bald Jack Rose; that it was Rose who had introduced him to Becker; that he collected payoff money from the gamblers and gave it to

Rose for Becker; that Becker visited his own gambling house frequently but never once raided it. Moss was conducting the examination.

Q. Did you ever talk to Becker about Rosenthal?
A. Yes, at 124th Street and Seventh Avenue in the latter part of June. Jack Rose and Harry Vallon were there.
Q. Why did you go there?
A. Sam Schepps told me I was wanted there. I met Vallon, Rose and Becker there. They were talking. I stood listening. Becker said, "Well, the Jew is going all the way. He has seen McAdoo and he is trying to see Waldo and the Mayor. Now he is after Whitman. If he gets to him it is all off. When is that Jew going to be croaked?" Then he called me aside and he said, "Bridgie, why don't you speak to the boys and see that the Jew is croaked?" I said, "Charlie, that is a pretty serious thing, having a man murdered." He answered, "That Jew has got to be croaked before he gets to Whitman. I will look out for everybody." On July 10th Becker called me on the phone. I met him at 15th Street and Fourth Avenue. He asked me, "Bridgie, what are you doing about that Jew Rosenthal? He is making a lot of trouble for me. Why don't you see that he is croaked?" I told Becker that everything was being taken care of, that he was liable to read about it in the papers any day.
Q. What were you doing about croaking Rosenthal?
A. Nothing except talk to Rose. I told Rose what Becker had said and I told him to get the gunmen and bring them to my place, that if I could find Rosenthal, the job would come off. On July 15th, Rose came to my place and said Becker had told him there were subpoenas out for Abe the Rebeler, Abe Hahlo and for Rose himself. I was to see them and get them not to corroborate Rosenthal. About one o'clock in the morning, Sam Paul, Lefty Louie, Whitey Lewis and Gyp the Blood came in. They asked me where was Rose and just then Rose came in with Dago Frank, Vallon and Sam Schepps. They all sat down and had refreshments. Rose asked me where Rosenthal was. I put

186

on my hat and went to the Metropole. I seen Rosenthal sitting there. I came back and said "Rosenthal is at the Metropole." It was about one forty then. Five or six people left. I don't know who they were. I waited about five minutes and went downstairs. Then I walked over to Broadway, stayed there about ten minutes and came back to my place. Then I went back to Broadway and 43d Street and met a man named Flaherty. We rode in an open barouche over to the 47th Street station house and from there I went back to the Hotel Cadillac and stood there.

Q. Did you see the body of Herman Rosenthal that night?
A. Yes. I saw it lying in front of the Metropole.
Q. Did you see Becker that night?
A. Yes. About four o'clock in the morning in front of my place. He said to Rose and myself, "I congratulate you." Rose said, "Charlie, this is terrible. Whitman is over at the station house and has the auto number." Becker said, "No, they have the wrong number." Then he said if Whitman had not been there he would have cut out Herman's tongue. Becker told me to give Rose $1,000 to pay the boys.

Soon it is McIntyre's turn. He approaches the witness, rubbing his hands in anticipation. It is a gesture unlike him and it generates an air of expectancy.

It begins routinely but we soon discover Webber is more than just a pool hall operator. He admits he has been an opium peddler, too. He insists that he has never discussed his testimony with any of the other witnesses.

Q. Were you told that to convict Becker you must exculpate Schepps?
A. No, sir.
Q. Do you get the newspapers in prison every day?
A. I never read them. I didn't discuss the question of corroboration.
Q. Did you promise Becker that you would croak Rosenthal?

A. I said I would take care of him.

Q. Were you shocked?

A. Yes, sir.

Q. Did you communicate your feeling to anybody?

A. No, sir.

Q. You never had any trouble with Becker? He had never raided you?

A. No, sir.

Q. Yet you were asked to commit this murder? Did it prick your conscience?

A. Yes, sir.

Q. Then you said, "All right, Charlie, I will do it for you"?

A. I said I would take care of it for him.

Q. Then you weren't very much shocked?

A. No, sir.

Q. Have you murdered other people?

A. No, sir.

Q. Were you anxious to have Rosenthal slain?

A. No.

Q. He was a business rival of yourself?

A. He was not.

Q. Were you and Rosenthal friendly?

A. No. We had been unfriendly for about three years. He would borrow money and not pay it back.

Q. Did you kill him because you were unfriendly to him?

A. No.

McIntyre's sparring grows tedious. It produces only monosyllabic answers from Webber who is, however, beginning to appear uneasy. He rubs his long nose frequently and blinks his eyes which roam the courtroom.

Q. Were threats made against Rosenthal on the Sam Paul outing?

A. No.

Q. Was Rosenthal's squeal discussed?
A. Yes. Everybody discussed it but Schepps.
Q. How do you know Schepps didn't discuss it?
A. He didn't discuss it with me.
Q. You lied, didn't you, when you denied to Commissioner Dougherty that you had anything to do with the murder?
A. Yes. [*sheepishly*]
Q. What were you promised for making your confession?
A. Protection.
Q. Protection by whom?
A. The courts.

McIntyre faces the bench.

"Your Honor, I request that the immunity agreements signed between this witness, and the other prosecution witnesses, and the district attorney be read into the record and introduced as evidence."

Judge Goff rules that the agreements are not now admissible.

McIntyre shrugs. It is a gesture to say that no matter what happens, he cannot win. He returns to Webber.

Q. Did you occupy a cell in the West Side Prison with Jacob Reich, alias Jack Sullivan?
A. Yes.
Q. Did you tell Sullivan that you and Rose and Vallon had talked it over and that you would frame Waldo, the Mayor, or Becker to get out of this mess?
A. No. I never said anything like that.
Q. Did Rose say to Sullivan that self-preservation was the first law of nature, that he was going to frame Becker?
A. I never heard such a remark.
Q. Did you greet Herman Rosenthal that night?
A. Yes.
Q. You spoke to him?

A. Yes.

Q. When you said "Hello, Herman," and you knew he was going to be murdered, did your conscience prick you?

Webber looks down, does not answer.

Q. When you returned to your poker room and all the men rushed out, did you try to restrain them?
A. No.
Q. Did you know they were going to the Metropole to shoot him to death?
A. Yes.
Q. You have testified that Schepps was never present during discussions of the murder of Rosenthal. Are you saying that to prevent him from being an accomplice?
A. No.
Q. Before you made your confession, did you say in the presence of Jack Sullivan in the Tombs, "My God, how badly do they want Becker? I can't stand this any longer. We will give them Becker."?
A. No.
Q. Did you promise Sullivan, in the presence of his brother, that you would give him $25,000 to go into business if he would not be a witness for Becker?
A. No.

The impact of Webber's testimony is dulled by the fact that everyone is hungry. Webber has been on the stand eight hours during which Judge Goff has refused to adjourn for lunch. It is now 6 P.M. He refuses again and orders the next witness. It is Harry Vallon, the third man. He is restless in the chair, continually runs his finger around his neck inside his high starched collar.

Moss takes him over the same ground and he tells the same story, varied only by the sound of his voice. He gives us one new fact: A young Negro boy had witnessed the Harlem conference the night Becker urged Webber to proceed with the assassination. Schepps, he adds, was not present but standing down the street. Nor does McIntyre enliven the testimony which lasts three hours. Still, Goff has not had enough and he orders one more witness. It is 9 P.M. Eleven unrelieved hours of testimony.

The last witness is Winfred R. Sheehan, an energetic, brusque man who identifies himself as secretary to Police Commissioner Rhinelander Waldo. Moss hands him a voluminous stack of oddly assorted papers which he spends several minutes examining. These papers, he tells the court, are complaints received against Police Lieutenant Charles Becker. Most of them were written anonymously, he adds, although a great many are signed.

"These were received by the Commissioner's office?"

"Yes."

"And what was done with them?"

"Complaints of this kind are turned over to the appropriate department for investigation."

"Even anonymous ones?"

"Oh, yes."

"And to whom were these complaints against the defendant given for investigation?"

"To Lieutenant Becker."

A murmur rumbles through the court.

Sheehan is asked to read two or three. They all accuse Becker of various graft devices. To each complaint Becker has affixed his report: "Signer unknown."

One letter recommends, "Investigate Becker quietly. He is making more than Devery ever did."

This reference is to the infamous Big Bill Devery, a recent ex-chief of police who amassed an enviable personal fortune from gambling halls and brothels.

On Tuesday, we realize that the confession of an accomplice in a crime cannot be admitted as evidence, under New York State Law, unless it can be corroborated. Whitman's entire case

191

against Becker—plastered together of the melodramatic recitations of Bald Jack Rose, Bridgie Webber and Harry Vallon—would collapse of its own weight unless Sam Schepps, the loquacious little gambler from Hot Springs, his legal purity preserved thus far, confirmed everything. He strutted across the courtroom, took the oath and heaved himself into the chair with a rude air that obviously antagonized the jury whose powers of belief would soon be taxed by an incredible story. They would be asked to believe that Schepps had been privy to every step of Rosenthal's murder, but a participant to none; that he had heard only enough of the plot to prove it existed, but not enough to know what it was all about. Moss took Schepps along this tightrope with debatable success.

Schepps was not so much confident as arrogant and as the testimony wore on, Moss became increasingly apprehensive with each question. Schepps testified that he was present at the famous Harlem conference when Becker allegedly asked Webber to take over arrangements for the assassination. Schepps said he rode in the gray murder car with Webber and Rose when it picked up Dago Frank, one of the gunmen, and brought him to Webber's gambling hall. He was present in the gambling hall when Webber went out in search of Rosenthal, and returned to report the victim at the Metropole. Schepps said he saw all the gunmen rush out and he wondered where everybody was going. He was on hand when Rose paid $1,000 to Lefty Louie after the job was done and he had ridden in numberless automobiles with Rose and Webber during discussions of the plot but he really hadn't heard what was said at any time. Schepps said he was at Pollok's house when Rose signed the affidavit concealing Becker's part in the so-called loan to Rosenthal, and he even carried messages from Rose to Becker after the killing without knowing what it was all about. In short, when Moss had finished, Schepps was a man who had heard and seen only what he was supposed to have seen and heard. The quality of his testimony, which would have classified him

192

as unusually dense, conflicted somewhat with his reputation as an alert Broadway character. The jury was not unaware of this.

When McIntyre finally got to Schepps, therefore, it was with no little anticipation. McIntyre might better have looked forward to a day of insolence and evasion. Schepps greeted McIntyre's approach with a sneer which never altogether left his face.

As *The New York Times* observed, "Schepps had little respect for the court in which he sat and less for Mr. McIntyre."

McIntyre determined that Schepps was thirty-six years old, and Austro-Hungarian by birth, and a man with a checkered past.

Q. Did you ever sell fake jewelry as gold?
A. No.
Q. What other businesses have you been in?
A. None.
Q. Did you ever smuggle opium across the Canadian border?
A. Yes.
Q. How long were you engaged in smuggling opium?
A. Two days. [*Smirking*]
Q. Are you now a fugitive from justice?
A. No.

During the Sam Paul outing on the Sunday preceding the murder, Schepps said, everybody was talking about Rosenthal's squeal but he didn't hear anybody mention murder. McIntyre's temper is rising.

Q. Who gave the gunmen the $1,000?
A. Jack Rose. He paid it to Lefty Louie at 50th Street and Eighth Avenue.
Q. Isn't it true that you were all alone and that you in fact were the paymaster for the murder?
A. [*Hotly, loudly*] If you say that you lie!

The judge blinks in astonishment. "The witness will use proper language in addressing the court."

"I'm sorry, I apologize." Schepps lowers his head.

McIntyre raises his.

"I want no apology from that thing. I would not lower myself to accept an apology from such a groveling specimen of humanity."

Whitman bounds to his feet, pointing his arm malevolently at McIntyre.

"He apologized to the court, not to you. And I object to counsel's belligerent manner."

McIntyre shakes with anger. A roll of fat that rims his shirt collar along the back and the sides of his neck reddens furiously.

"And I object to the insolence of the witness and the insolence of the district attorney."

Judge Goff's gavel assaults the bench and his voice thunders the two men into silence. Schepps is grinning. He is seated well back in the chair, his upper body thrust forward, his elbows on the arms of the chair. His hands dangle. Nor does he stop grinning when McIntyre confronts him anew. First, the night of July 15, the eve of the murder, when Vallon and Rose and Schepps had dinner at Luchow's.

"Have you been told to say Rose never discussed anything with you?"

"No."

"Well, what did you talk about?"

"The weather."

[Sarcastically] "Oh, the sun came up and the clouds were in the sky and things like that?"

"No."

[Shouting] "Well, what did you say?"

"That it was a nice day."

Laughter.

McIntyre moves on to later the same night when Schepps,

194

Rose and Vallon went to the home of Rosenthal's ex-wife to obtain an affidavit reflecting on Rosenthal's morals.

"Why did you go to the house?"

Schepps stares defiantly at McIntyre, hesitating several seconds.

"For the pleasure of the ride."

"Why did you go inside the house?"

[*Registering astonishment*] "You wouldn't want me to wait outside, would you?"

Schepps's insolence, amusing at the outset, is beginning to take on weight. There is no laughter this time.

McIntyre moves on. Schepps admits going with Rose and Vallon to Tom Sharkey's saloon where, at Rose's request, he ordered the murder car by telephone. Rose wanted a car, said Schepps; he didn't know what it was to be used for. Nor did he gather any indication of the intent when he rode in the car with Rose and Vallon to pick up Dago Frank.

"Had you heard of Rosenthal's complaints to the District Attorney?"

"I read in the paper that he was going to make some disclosures."

"How did you become acquainted with Dago Frank, Whitey Lewis, Lefty Louie and Gyp the Blood?"

"I was introduced by Rose."

He met them in April, he said. Asked under what circumstances, Schepps replied:

"Under no circumstances. Rose and I were walking along 14th Street when we saw these men and Rose introduced me."

"How did he introduce you?"

Schepps stares blankly at McIntyre. Then he extends his left hand, looks at it and says, "This is Gyp." Then he extends his right hand, looks at it and says, "This is Mr. Schepps."

After the laughter subsides, Schepps grins, adding:

"That's how. You know how people are introduced."

McIntyre cannot altogether suppress his anger.

"Yes, I know that and I know a lot of other things about you, too."

"Well, tell them then."

McIntyre had less trouble with Schepps after lunch. Whitman and Moss lectured the witness and he returned to the stand a relative model of restraint and courtesy.

Schepps confirmed that he was present in Webber's when the proprietor went out in search of Rosenthal.

Q. Didn't you know that he was going out to locate the victim?
A. I did not.
Q. Did you hear any of the gunmen say anything then?
A. I did not.
Q. Coming down in the automobile with Dago Frank, was anything said?
A. I didn't hear anything.
Q. Did you hear Webber when he came back and said "Rosenthal is at the Metropole"?
A. Yes.
Q. And were you not suspicious?
A. Suspicious of what? No.
Q. After the gunmen went out, did you ask why?
A. No. I started to leave and Rose stopped me.
Q. Did you ask Rose what Webber had meant when he said Rosenthal was at the Metropole?
A. No.
Q. Weren't you curious?
A. No.

The courtroom seethes gently with whispers. It seems incredible that a gambler who lives by his wits could have seen and heard all he said he had seen and heard without knowing what it was about.

Schepps admitted meeting Vallon after the shooting and the

next day visiting the four gunmen in their Seventh Avenue flat to deliver a message from Rose.

Q. You knew then that these men were the murderers and that Webber and Rose had arranged the murder?
A. I did not.

Schepps told of taking another message from Rose to the home of Lt. Becker. The message was that Rose was sick and worried and on the point of committing suicide. Becker told Schepps to reassure Rose, that everything would be all right. This was the second day after the killing.

Q. Whom did you see at Becker's home?
A. Mrs. Becker, the houseboy and Lieutenant Becker.
Q. You saw Mrs. Becker?
A. No, I made a mistake. Just Lieutenant Becker.
Q. Are you changing your answer because you know I could call Mrs. Becker to the stand and prove you were lying?
A. No. I just made a mistake.

All eyes are now on Mrs. Becker. Her expression remains benign. She gives no sign that she has heard the exchange containing her name.

Asked to describe Becker's apartment, Schepps said he couldn't because it was at night and Becker would not turn on the lights.

"I started to light a match to light my cigarette and Becker said 'Don't do that. Someone might see you from the street and get suspicious. They've been tailing me all day.' "

When Rose surrendered to the police, despite Schepps's protest that it was not necessary, Schepps left town arriving in Hot Springs on July 25, nine days after the murder.

"Did you see a lawyer there named James L. Graham?"
"I did not."

"Did you say that the reason for killing Rosenthal was that he peached on the gang after he had been given $5,000 by Rose and the others to leave town . . . ?"

Whitman's objections were too late. McIntyre had been able to bring Becker's line of defense into the testimony of a hostile witness. Schepps did not answer the question but the seed had been planted in the jury's mind. Becker was going to attempt to show that Rosenthal was the victim of a gamblers' revenge framed on a police lieutenant.

"Did you frame-up on Becker in the West Side Prison?"

Schepps looked at the judge as though for help, then at the district attorney.

"Answer me!"

Schepps glared at McIntyre. His jaw clenched.

"My answer," he burst forth, "is no!"

"Did the district attorney in consideration of your testimony promise you immunity?"

"He did not."

"Did you sign something?"

"I don't care what I signed. I had no fear."

"Did you sign something, I ask you?"

"I signed a paper."

"What kind of paper?"

"I don't know. The only thing I agreed to do was to tell the truth."

"Who has the paper?"

"My attorney, Bernard H. Sandler."

"Will you waive your privileges and permit me to bring Mr. Sandler before the court?"

"I will not."

McIntyre asked Schepps if he had said, as quoted in the newspapers, that Rosenthal was killed because he was a "dirty cur." Schepps denied making the remark. Whitman objected and the court sustained him.

Abruptly, McIntyre pulled Schepps back to the time of the murder.

"You testified that you left Webber's shortly after the gunmen and went to the Times Building drugstore where you had a soda, that you heard the shots and ran to the Metropole?"

No answer.

"How did you know the shots came from the Metropole?"

"I saw the crowd running there."

"Did you see Rosenthal's body?"

"An outline of it."

"When you saw the police at the Metropole did you tell them what Webber had said about Rosenthal being at the Metropole and give them a clew?"

"I did not."

"When you visited the four gunmen on Seventh Avenue, how long were you there?"

"Ten minutes."

"Did they ask you if Jack Rose said everything was all right?"

"No."

"Think again, Mr. Schepps."

"I don't have to think very hard to answer your questions."

McIntyre goes back further, to the Harlem conference.

"You say you stood a block away while Webber, Vallon, Rose and Becker conferred?"

"Yes."

"Don't you know you are trying to save yourself by swearing you were not in that conference?"

"I'm not trying to save myself. I was not there."

"Do you mean you could see Becker from a block away?"

"Yes. I saw Becker, Rose, Webber and Vallon there."

Schepps said he left with Webber and Vallon and rode downtown with them. They were in the back seat whispering, he said, and he could not hear a word.

"Why did you go to the meeting at all?"

"To accompany Webber."

"What did you say to Rose in trying to prevent him from turning himself in?"

"I told him I thought Becker would attend to everything.

199

Rose said, 'No, it looks like they are trying to get me and I am going to make a clean breast of it.' "

McIntyre turns from the witness to the judge. His voice is hoarse and weary. He asks for an adjournment until tomorrow. He is exhausted. He has been at Schepps four hours.

"The cross-examination must be completed today, Mr. Mc-Intyre."

Hart, McIntyre's dark, dapper assistant, confronts the bench. He will continue. Goff has refused before to allow it but this time he consents.

Hart is fresh and spirited.

"Did you tell Postmaster Johnson in Hot Springs that Rosenthal was hated because he interfered with pimps outside his own district?"

"Never."

Wednesday's parade of prosecution witnesses moved swiftly across the jury's fatigued perceptions. The trial was now in its ninth day and Whitman appeared to be rushing his case as though to build up a pile of evidence to obscure the doubtful impact of the incredible Schepps, his key witness the day before.

Mrs. Lillian Rosenthal, widow of the slain gambler, her motherly obesity swathed in black with two strands of imitation pearls around her neck, lumbered across the room and struggled into the chair. She dabbed at her nose with a handkerchief throughout her testimony which was familiar to everybody; Becker's friendship for her late husband, Becker's loan to Rosenthal, Becker's installation of Rose in the club, Becker's raid and his promise to wipe out the $1,500 loan.

Those were promising days, she said. Now it was bleak. She didn't even have enough money to bury her husband although Bridgie Webber, she added in mock irony, sent her fifty dollars "in sympathy."

What Mrs. Rosenthal did not tell the court was that the four months' rent past due on the 45th Street brownstone had been paid, that she had been moved into a comfortable apartment in the West 60's, and that bank drafts turned up regularly in the mail box. She could not have identified her donor, however, other than to say this windfall came from "friends of Big Tim Sullivan," the Tammany sachem.

She denied that the gamblers had offered her late husband $25,000 to leave town.

"It ain't true," she sniffed. "Beansy never got a cent."

Next was Otto Aversi, lanky, phlegmatic chauffeur employed by Col. Henry Sternberger, commander of the National Guard, a stockbroker and boon companion to Becker and various other police officials. It was Sternberger's car Becker had used the night of the murder and Aversi confirmed Becker's own story. His value as a prosecution witness seemed doubtful. He said he drove Becker, Jacob Reich and Deacon Terry, the *American* reporter, to the fights at Madison Square Garden. Afterward, they all went to the Prince George Hotel on East 28th Street where they had a few drinks; then to 33rd and Sixth Avenue where Terry caught the subway for New Jersey. Then to the World Building where Becker and Reich remained for about twenty minutes, then he delivered Reich to the corner of 42nd Street and Sixth Avenue and took Becker home to the Bronx, arriving about 2 A.M.

Then came Harry Pollok, a nervous, tense little man who recoiled whenever he was asked a question. He told how Rose sent him to police headquarters to let Becker know where he was hiding. Becker, Pollok said, was pleased.

"That's a good place for him to stay." He said Becker took the phone number and promised to call Rose.

Bernard Rudiger, a waiter at the Union Square Hotel, testified that Becker and Rose met three or four times a week in the restaurant, talked at length together, and that he saw Rose give Becker money on several occasions.

Then a short stream of disembodied characters testifying that Becker visited Rose frequently at home; a maid, somebody's sister-in-law, a nurse, a gambler.

A disbarred lawyer and convict named James E. Hallen, brought to the court in chains from Sing Sing, testified that he overheard Becker, after his arrest, tell a Tombs visitor, "The people will give me a pension for doing away with that squealer Rosenthal. No one is going to convict us on the testimony of criminals."

Hallen read his testimony from a scrap of paper held in his hand. He said he thought the exchange was important and he had written it down at the time.

McIntyre attempted on cross-examination to have Hallen's twenty-year record of arrests for swindling and larceny read into the record but Goff ruled against him. Hallen himself, however, had no objections. Laughing, he told McIntyre:

"You ought to know my pedigree. You defended me last time."

Three officials of police: Chief Clerk William Kip, Chief Inspector Max Schmittberger and Deputy Commissioner George Dougherty, testified as to the nature of Becker's duties as strong-arm squad commander and as to his salary of $2,250 a year.

Isaac D. White, legal reporter for the *World,* said Becker came to his office to obtain a certified copy of Rosenthal's published affidavit against him. He told White he was suing Rosenthal for criminal libel.

Carrie Pollok, wife of the man who gave Rose refuge after the killing, admitted under cross-examination that she never saw Schepps at her house at either of the two times he claimed to have been there—when Rose signed the affidavit for Becker and when Rose left to surrender to police.

Mrs. Pollok made no lasting impression on the jury but her testimony made a lasting impression on Pollok. Carrie was not his wife. She was Mary Anderson, a chorus girl whose real name was Caroline Hockscheter. This was revealed two days later when the real Mrs. Pollok, Mary Emma Kattor, taking care of Pollok's house and two children in Freeport in the belief her husband was laboring bravely in the city, was brought up-to-date by the newspapers and filed suit for divorce.

John Carney, operator of the telephone booth at the Times Building, produced records showing that Rose telephoned Becker at 2:57 A.M. on July 16, about an hour after the murder. McIntyre did not cross-examine.

Daniel A. Bentian, thin and formal, identified himself as clerk in charge of signature cards at the Franklin Savings Bank.

Moss was able to ask only one question.

"Did the defendant open an account in your bank in April of 1912?"

McIntyre stopped the witness and, after ten minutes of debate with Moss, he won his point. Goff ruled that Becker's bank accounts, unless it could be shown that they contained money taken from Rosenthal, were irrelevant and inadmissible. They might show Becker was a grafter but they had nothing to do with murder. It was a blow to Whitman.

Max Margolies, twenty-two, sallow-faced and raucous-voiced, testified that he overheard Becker describe the interior of Rosenthal's gambling house to members of his staff so they could obtain warrants for the raid. None of them had ever been inside the place and the affidavits for the warrants, therefore, were falsified.

As the prosecution rested its case, the furnishings of the late Herman Rosenthal's gambling casino went on auction at the Broadway Art Galleries. A carved Cathedral Oak dining room suite, consisting of six chairs covered with red Spanish leather, a table and a crystal cabinet, went on the block first and brought $475. Altogether, the first day, the sale took in $6,300.

18. The Diabolical Plot

BECKER had come through his denunciation far better than the press wanted to admit. Reporters watched for signs of collapse and when they could not find them they marveled at what they described as Becker's stoicism. Becker was neither on the brink of moral disintegration nor was he inwardly passive. He was painfully harassed, like a bear set upon by hornets. Whatever emotion he suppressed in the courtroom, he let loose upon McIntyre and Hart.

"Between that judge and your inability to stop the DA," he stormed at McIntyre, "I'm going to fry! I could have done better by myself."

Accustomed to the frustrated fury of criminal defendants, McIntyre only smiled.

"The judge could not be more helpful," he said. "As long as he continues to prejudice the case against us it doesn't matter what the jury does. No conviction will ever survive an appeal."

"I don't want to appeal," Becker snarled. "That costs money.

I want an acquittal. You better put me on the stand. I'll tell that jury what the story is."

McIntyre's eyes flashed.

"The minute you get in that witness chair Whitman can start asking you about why you have so much money. And if he convinces the jury that you're taking payoffs you won't have a chance. Don't you understand? This city is fed up with grafting cops."

On Friday, October 18, the eleventh day of the trial, Becker's attorneys began his defense. If the witnesses for the prosecution were a seamy lot, those offered by the defense failed to contribute anything to Becker's character.

John W. Hart, junior counsel for Becker and his long-time friend and attorney, began with a thirty-minute speech. Hart lacked the oratorical command of McIntyre but his voice rang with earnestness and sincerity.

". . . The defense will show that Webber and Rose, with Vallon and Schepps, conspired to kill Rosenthal entirely apart from Becker and each with an independent motive. . . .

"Months before the murder of Rosenthal, Becker knew that an attempt would be made sooner or later to job him and he repeatedly asked his superiors to transfer him from the strong-arm squad. . . .

"Rosenthal could not be trusted by any of his associates in the gambling business, as Rose himself swore. There was every palpable reason for them to get rid of him; for Becker there was none. . . .

"When Sam Schepps was brought to New York he was put into the same cell with Jack Rose. . . . We shall prove these men made statements that Becker was not implicated—they were confessing to save themselves. There was then going on a public bidding that if anyone would come forward to implicate Becker immunity would be given. As the evidence coiled about these men, they determined to deliver Becker to save themselves. . . .

"The two greatest disturbers of the gambling element were

Herman Rosenthal, the informer, and Charles Becker, the raider. They have gotten rid of Rosenthal and now they are trying to get rid of their worst enemy, Charles Becker."

Hart's last points had a certain validity. Rosenthal was, however, a lesser menace, for his revelations, like the revelations of dozens of informers before him, would mean at the worst a temporary shutdown. But Becker, whether he was a rigid enforcer of the law or the lord of the Tenderloin, controlled the destinies of hundreds of criminals.

The first defense witness was William Travers Jerome, a former New York district attorney whose integrity no one had ever challenged. He was asked to repeat a telephone conversation made in his presence from the club rooms of the New York Bar Association on July 17, the day after the murder, by Lt. Becker to Jack Rose. He was to have testified that Becker told Rose there were 200 policemen looking for him and that he had better give himself up. Whitman objected to the question as hearsay and Judge Goff would not allow Jerome to answer.

Next came Police Commissioner Rhinelander Waldo who said that all orders for gambling raids were made by his office to Inspector Cornelius Hayes who in turn would direct Becker. Hayes had recently been suspended from the force by Waldo for telling the Curran inquiry that Waldo never gave any raiding orders other than to instruct him to maintain "outward order and decency" in keeping with the Mayor's policy. Nor was Waldo allowed to tell whether Becker had actually requested a transfer.

Alexander Luban, brother of Morris Luban who swore he overheard Becker and Rose plot the murder in the Lafayette Baths, testified that his brother was a chronic liar and that he, personally, would not believe him under oath.

Luban had also claimed to have been in the Metropole the night of the murder and that he saw Rosenthal shot down. The next witness, Samuel Goodman, a flower manufacturer, said Morris Luban was with him the night of the murder and could not possibly have been a witness to it.

Frederick Hawley, the *Sun* police reporter who telephoned Becker to tell him Rosenthal had been slain, said he was with Becker from 3:30 A.M., when Becker arrived downtown, until after eight o'clock in the morning and that the conference with Rose and Webber could not have been held as the prosecution claimed. Whitman cross-examined him.

"Did you report what you have said here to the police?"

"No."

"Did you tell anybody?"

"I told the city editor and one or two men at the office."

"Did you write about it?"

"No. I didn't think it had anything to do with Rosenthal. At no time did I suspect Becker of being involved."

"Why didn't you tell the district attorney before this trial?"

"I didn't like his attitude."

Hawley was fired the next day by the *Sun*.

McIntyre called the district attorney to the stand and tried unsuccessfully to get him to fix the span of time he had confronted Becker in the 47th Street station house after the shooting. Whitman admitted he had seen Becker only once about 4 A.M. but that he did not see Hawley.

Police Lieutenant Patrick Shea, a robust Irishman with steel-gray hair and pink cheeks, testified that he and his wife were at Becker's home at the hour and date Schepps claimed to have delivered the message from Rose and that Schepps was not there.

Robert Smith, a hoarse-voiced, tweedy man who identified himself as a trainer of race horses and a frequenter of the Metropole, said he had often heard Webber threaten to kill Rosenthal. On cross-examination, Whitman attempted to indicate that Smith's wife was a prostitute and Smith angrily refused to answer any questions about her.

Matthew Ryan, warden of the West Side Prison, was no help to Becker. Sustaining Whitman's objections, Judge Goff refused to allow Ryan to tell to what extent Rose, Webber, Vallon and Schepps met together except that their cells adjoined one another.

Louis Plitt, sallow-faced brother of Charles Plitt, Becker's erstwhile press agent, said he visited Rose in the West Side Prison and that Rose got down on his knees and swore "On the grave of my mother, Becker had nothing to do with Rosenthal . . ."

Becker's only substantial gain appeared to come with the testimony of Jacob Reich, alias Jack Sullivan, "the king of the newsboys" who was also under indictment for the Rosenthal murder. Sullivan took the stand with the presence of a messiah, albeit with a Bowery accent.

"The most remarkable thing about Sullivan," said the *Tribune*, "is that he lives in Washington Heights. His accent bespeaks another locale."

Sullivan, who had once been a bodyguard to William Randolph Hearst, was stocky, jaunty with the face of a worn prize fighter. He wore a loose blue suit and a gray bow tie. He appeared impressed by no one and when Judge Goff advised him that because he was under indictment he need not answer questions which might tend to incriminate him, he retorted with a snort:

"I'll answer any question you got."

Throughout his two hours in the witness chair he remained, as the *Tribune* reported, "vehement, picturesque and irrepressible."

Sullivan told how he was in the Cohan Theater soda fountain when someone came running in with the news that Rosenthal had been shot. He went immediately to the hotel, saw Rosenthal and bent over him to see if he was dead. This, he said, was at least ten minutes after the shooting. He went around to Webber's about 2:40 A.M., half an hour later, and talked with Vallon and Webber. He was not allowed to repeat the conversation.

Q. Did Rose, Webber or Vallon ask you to connect the defendant with the murder?

Objection sustained.

Q. What did Rose say to you about Rosenthal's death?

Objection sustained.

Q. What did Vallon say?

Objection sustained.

Annoyed at the objections, Sullivan turned and shouted at Goff.

"Judge, if you'll let me talk for ten minutes in my own way, I'll tell you the whole story. I been here an hour arreddy and I ain't been able to say anything."

Sullivan was, however, allowed to tell that on July 29 he met with Rose, Webber, Vallon and all their attorneys in the counsel room of the Tombs and that Rose said to him "The only way for us to beat the chair is by implicating Becker."

Sullivan said he shouted at Rose, "You bald-headed old bastard—are you up to your old game again?"

Q. Did you say to Webber, "Bridgie, for God's sake do not frame up." And did Bridgie say, "I am going along on the band wagon; Rose, Vallon and I have talked it over and we would frame anyone."?
A. Yes, sir.
Q. When you moved to the West Side Prison did you ask Webber why you were moved and did he say it was Mr. Whitman's idea so that you could all get together?
A. Yes, sir.
Q. And did Vallon say to you that if you did not corroborate

them, they would never get out and that Whitman would indict you for murder?

A. Yes, sir. Before I was indicted, Webber said "You better come in with us and get immunity." Why, I knew for six weeks I would be indicted. About three days before Rosenthal was murdered, I was in the Garden Restaurant with him and Mrs. Rosenthal. If they had killed him that night, they would have killed me too.

Q. Did Bridgie say that if you would stick with him he would invest $25,000 in a hotel and give you half interest?

A. Yes, sir. And a thousand dollars right away. Name my price, he said.

Q. Did you receive a message recently from the district attorney?

A. Yes, sir. Last night. He . . . (Objection sustained.)

Cross-examined by Moss, Sullivan responded to virtually every question with a rampage.

"You framed-up an indictment on me—don't try to put another frame around me. You got me wrong—got me mixed up with some other guy."

Admonished to answer the questions in the interests of justice, Sullivan snapped:

"Justice? There ain't no justice or I wouldn't be in jail."

When Goff dismissed him, Sullivan appeared incredulous.

"What? No more questions? Why the court don't know nothing yet!"

Goff waved him off the stand.

On Saturday, Becker's attorney put Jack Rose's newspaper confession into evidence in a dubious effort to point up discrepancies between it and his testimony in court. McIntyre also had read into the record the immunity agreements signed between the district attorney and Rose, Vallon, Webber and Schepps. The agreements provided simply that if the four men fulfilled their promise to testify truthfully against Becker, if they did not fire a shot into the body of Herman Rosenthal, and if they agreed to remain in custody until the Becker case was disposed of, that they would not be prosecuted for the murder.

Judge Goff adjourned court at 1 P.M. so that the members of the jury could register to vote in the forthcoming municipal elections. The twelve men, escorted by seven guards, were taken in three cars to their respective precincts. Two more cars filled with reporters followed the caravan and everywhere they stopped a crowd gathered.

On Monday morning, October 21, McIntyre succumbed to his client's demands and announced that Becker would testify at the risk of being branded a grafter. "He will deny any part in the murder."

McIntyre's announcement triggered rumors that Becker at last would expose the entire system of police graft. And there were other rumors that Shapiro, the chauffeur, stirring in the Tombs, was going to kill Whitman's case by testifying that Schepps was in the murder car as it sped away from the Metropole.

Neither happened. Becker did not testify and Shapiro's bombshell was of another sort.

The timid chauffeur sent into court an affidavit saying that neither Vallon nor Schepps had been in the murder car "although Jack Sullivan urged me to say that they were."

Shapiro also recalled more clearly than ever that as he drove away from Rosenthal's bullet-punctured body, one of the gunmen declared, "Becker has the cops fixed. It'll be a clean getaway."

Altogether this day, the defense pushed through a total of twenty-one witnesses, half of whom were businessmen and neighbors of Becker who testified uniformly that as far as they knew, Becker was of good character, "peaceful and quiet." This phrase recurred with such frequency that for more than an hour the atmosphere suggested a trial for disorderly conduct.

There was also the treasurer from Hammerstein's Victoria

Theater who said the theater was closed July 15, further refuting Morris Luban's testimony that he saw Rosenthal shot after attending a performance at the Victoria.

Police Lieutenant William Duggan told the court that in November of 1909 Bridgie Webber reported both a holdup and a broken jaw and accused Rosenthal of having it done. He said Webber swore he would get even with Rosenthal.

The trial was now into its third week and there was no longer any need to speculate about Becker's physical stamina. It was giving way. He slept poorly if at all and his appetite had declined. He looked haggard, his eyes sunken in hollows of faint purple. He was less meticulous about his dress and this indifference to his appearance extended as well to his hands. "His fingernails," *The New York Times* reported, "were dirty."

Meanwhile, Thomas Coupe, the desk clerk who had fled to England after watching the assassination from the doorway of the Elks Club, arrive in New York on the *Mauretania*. It was too late for anyone to care, but Whitman announced he was more interested in Coupe's help in cleaning up New York generally than he was in having his testimony in the Becker case specifically. Coupe was not called to testify. Assistant District Attorney William A. DeFord, who had escorted him back from London, spirited the scrawny young Englishman off to an East 60's rooming house and posted a guard of special officers around the building. Whitman paid tribute to Coupe's courage in "risking his life" by returning and admitted that the County of New York had been obliged to pay Coupe's passage and to put him on a per diem handout as long as he was in New York.

On Tuesday, McIntyre had read into evidence depositions taken from Schepps's acquaintances in Hot Springs and the jury heard again how Schepps allegedly boasted of his role in the murder. Postmaster Fred Johnson had testified that Schepps said, "I don't want you to think the fellow we killed was of any account. He was a dirty cur."

More significant was the testimony of Thomas Pettit, Mayor

of Hot Springs and manager of the Hotel Marquette where Schepps was confined.

"Schepps told me after he was arrested that he would not say anything to anyone until after he had talked to Whitman. He said, 'It is up to me to make the best bargain I can. One man confesses, another corroborates, but it takes the third man to make the case against the fourth man. I'm the third man.'"

Douglas Hotchkiss, Hot Springs correspondent for the *American,* said Schepps boasted that he was "the keynote to the whole situation in New York."

Police Lieutenant Ernest Von Deizelska of the 47th Street station was a puzzling witness. Asked to pinpoint the time Becker arrived at the stationhouse to view Rosenthal's body, the lieutenant produced the station blotter and pointed to an entry showing Becker arrived at 4:25 A.M. instead of 3:30 as the defense had claimed. He was not cross-examined.

John B. Maher, round, gray and balding, a theatrical producer, testified that on the night of July 6 he and the defendant had dinner in a restaurant on 23rd Street. This was the night Rose testified that he and Webber had dinner with Becker in Luchow's.

Charles E. Foye, a detective with Becker's squad, testified that on July 12 at the corner of Second Avenue and 29th Street at three-thirty in the morning (all policemen have a good memory for the time of day) Rose said to him, "You're a friend of Rosenthal's so tell him to shut his mouth or I will shut it for him so it will stay shut."

Cross-examined by Moss, Foye said he did not relate this threat to the district attorney's office "because I thought the district attorney was trying to make it out that all policemen were parties to the murder of Rosenthal."

Charles Reich, younger brother of Jack Sullivan, confirmed Sullivan's report of the frame-up proposition put to him by Webber and Rose.

Q. Did Bridgie Webber, while in the West Side Prison, say that he would put up $25,000 for your brother to go into the hotel business if Jack would listen to reason and join him and Rose?
A. Yes, he said just that and he made the offer in my presence.

Aaron J. Levy, the Tammany lawyer representing Shapiro, the chauffeur, testified that Becker had nothing to do with his taking the case. Rose intimated in his confession Becker had hired Levy.

Judge Goff recalled Sullivan to the stand to clarify questions he had evaded or ignored during his testimony. Moss, acting as an officer of the court, read the questions which had been prepared by Judge Goff.

Among them was this:

Q. What did Webber say to you in the West Side Prison about giving you your freedom?
A. He said, "There is only one way you can get out—and the district attorney knows you are as innocent as a baby—but he wants you to corroborate us that Becker was with us in 42d Street after the murder. If you don't, you'll spend six months in jail." I answered, "I don't care if I spend six years in jail. I won't swear any man's life away for you liars."
Q. What did Webber say after that?
A. Webber said to me, "I had you brought here so that nobody could get to you in the Tombs. We're all in bad. We've got to help each other. Becker is a Dutch son of a bitch. Everything depends on you. If you say you didn't see Becker there in front of my place after the murder, we're all in bad. If you say you did see Becker, we're in good. If you do as we want, I'll give you $25,000 to set you up in business after we get out. If you want $1,000 now, just ask for it or any sum you want—just name your price, but for God's sake corroborate us!"

There is no one else to be heard. Is it possible that somewhere in this ten-day deluge of contradictory accusation, con-

214

fession, passion, dispassion and legal rhetoric, confined with the labyrinthine structure of the law, lies the truth? It all seems to be a case of one man's word against another man's word.

Was Becker really the gang lord, so deluded by self-assessments of his power, that he ordered a clumsy assassination to prove them? Or was he really no more nor less than a policeman, as corrupt or as honest as the area in which he operated, trapped by his own inadequacies into being punished for a murder committed by more clever and ruthless associates?

There was a third possibility of which such people as Whitman and the omnipotent newsman Swope were not unaware: Becker was too powerful; he had usurped authority and control from its traditional wielders and it was necessary to get rid of him.

No matter how persuasive Becker's story, nothing could erase the universal knowledge that he had profited privately by his job. His bank accounts were not admissible as evidence, but they had been published in the newspapers and everybody, including members of the jury, knew about them. They impeached Becker's integrity. Had he testified, his stalwart manner and bearing might have helped him. But McIntyre had calculated the risks and refused, under threat of resigning, to allow Becker to expose himself to further exploration before the jury. His explanation for Becker's silence was lame and the heat with which he delivered it to reporters did not redeem it.

"Lieutenant Becker did not testify because the State has failed to make its case. The only testimony against Lieutenant Becker is that of the accomplices to a murder and two convicts."

19. A Conspiracy Hatched in Yonder Prison

MCINTYRE was not well, but Goff would not be convinced of this. His consistent refusals to allow the exhausted McIntyre to carry cross-examinations of witnesses over to the next day indicated disbelief and revealed a hard legal stratagem outside the province of a judge. McIntyre had suffered for several years from an undiagnosed heart condition and his physicians kept him going during the trial. Although he slept fitfully, the doctors hesitated to give him sedatives because of his heart. Finally, McIntyre reluctantly submitted to the judge an affidavit signed by his doctors and Goff's treatment of him softened. He adjourned court in midafternoon on Tuesday, after decreeing that prosecution and defense would be allowed three hours each for summation the following day.

We have seen McIntyre plead for time, and we wonder at its validity, too, for McIntyre has a powerful and dynamic voice; it seems to gather itself from throughout his heavy frame, and his words have a relentless momentum, a mesmeric force. He throws them at the jury with thrusts of his arms and hands and shoulders. Every eye in the jury box is fixed on him as he begins his heroic defense of Becker.

"The defendant has endured the pelting of a merciless storm from a conspiracy hatched in yonder prison. The prosecution has partaken too much of the nature of a private proceeding."

We had not expected him to attack the district attorney, but perhaps it is what we have been waiting for. Perhaps some fragment of truth lies buried within this crusading prosecutor.

. . . by your verdict this defendant will live or die. No other determination can be made. I am defending an American, not a murderer; and his accusers are vile creatures, not lovers of the flag or the institutions under which we live, but a lawless and degenerate set, reeking with infamy. . . .

The district attorney has been misled—perhaps deceived—it may be he is actuated by ambition, and ambition often beclouds good judgment, to the end that he has fathered a prosecution framed by crooks. This trial had its birth in the hearts of four murderers—Rose, Webber, Vallon and Schepps—self-confessed assassins all of whom, when it is over, will be free to walk the streets of the city and murder again if they please."

There is a subtle, instantaneous shift of attention from McIntyre to Whitman. Then the mass of eyes falls back on the thundering voice.

Rose, as the evidence shows, cherished animosity toward Rosenthal and, as I will show, his feeling toward him was more bitter than gall. . . . He connived at Rosenthal's murder and, when detected, a link had to be forged to someone higher up. The public mind had been inflamed. Public clamor was rampant. The evidence shows that the district attorney didn't want small fry, to use his own words, he wanted the big fish. Rose saw his opportunity.

Whenever Whitman's name is mentioned now, the eyes move to where he sits, composed, at the counsel table, his mind intent, his consciousness divorced from the harangue.

Is it not extraordinary that we find Charles Becker here today charged with murder and yet the four gunmen remain untried?

217

You are asked to find Becker guilty; yet in three months, these four men may be found innocent. You have Becker in the death house and these four men free. Why weren't they tried first? Is it because the district attorney knows he could not convict them? Then he never would have been able to convict Becker. Isn't there legal jugglery in this case?

If these four men did not kill Rosenthal, the case against Becker collapses because these are the men he is charged with having forced to do the killing. . . .

McIntyre's pattern of persuasion changes now. The rolling force of his argument becomes a succession of blows.

Now, how do you attempt to establish the gunmen as the murderers? There is no connection here that Becker ever saw one of these men in his life—except that Jack Rose says so. . . .

Jack Rose is a self-confessed murderer. Rose, Vallon, Webber and Schepps are the cold-blooded assassins; if their testimony stood alone, there would be no question of fact for you to pass on.

Now what does the district attorney of this county do? Does he bring you men of credulity, integrity, honesty? He does not.

He brings Morris Luban—a murderer at heart—an eighteen-karat crook, a forger and a thief. He comes into court manacled and shackled from prison in the state of New Jersey. What is his motive? Mr. Whitman says he will try to keep him out of his troubles abroad.

Luban never saw Becker but once before in his life and in street clothes. Yet he recognizes him naked in a room full of steam. He is willing to swear away a man's life to get out of jail.

Oh, God forbid that such testimony as this shall ever be heard again in a courtroom. . . .

. . . the district attorney also brings us Hallen, another felon. Am I not justified in saying the district attorney is misled by ambition?

The office of the district attorney is a great office. I was there for years. The community stands in dread of it, yet it is the district attorney's duty to protect the accused as well as to prosecute. It is his duty to ascertain the truth and if he steps one jot beyond that line he debauches his office.

Whitman is leaning over whispering to Moss. There is no sign he hears himself brushed with a charge of debauchery.

Now, gentlemen. The State is going to talk about those meetings between Rose and the defendant in the Union Square Hotel. These meetings are as consistent with innocence as they are with guilt, and if there is any doubt in your mind the law requires you to acquit. . . .

The State will say that because Rosenthal went to the *World* and published an affidavit charging Becker was his partner, that this provides the motive for murder. Now you know what kind of a man Rosenthal was; a bad man, a lawbreaker, a man without moral sense, living and working in the dark. And the State wants you to believe that Becker plotted and planned to murder him. Think of a policeman instigating so clumsy a job . . . sending a numbered car to a public hotel, calling the victim out and shooting him down in front of witnesses . . .

They will tell you that Becker knew where Rose was hiding and that he kept this from the police. That's not true. Rose was not wanted by the police until two days after the murder—a day after Rose perjured himself by signing that chattel mortgage affidavit. . . .

. . . bear in mind that Rose admitted he perjured himself when he signed that affidavit. . . . Would he not commit perjury then a thousand times if his own neck was in danger?

Why has McIntyre mentioned this? Rose could only have signed such an affidavit at Becker's order.

Rose, Vallon, Schepps and Webber are not indicted in this murder, yet they participated. . . . You've got articles of agreement like a bargain sale between the murderers and the district attorney . . . and by this agreement the district attorney wants you to look upon this miserable thing, Schepps, as a Sunday School representative. . . . Yet you heard testimony taken in Hot Springs that Schepps admits he is one of the murderers. . . .

. . . Rose told you he telephoned Becker from the Times Building. See his shrewdness. He made the call from a public switchboard so there would be a record of it . . . if he was so intimate with Becker why didn't he know Becker's private number? Hawley knew it and Hawley was only a newspaper reporter.

. . . Rose swears he met Becker on 42d Street after the murder and that Jack Sullivan, Vallon, Webber and Schepps were there. Jack Sullivan says Becker was not there. The only people who saw Becker there are the people who are accusing him. . . .

Seemingly without interrupting his momentum, McIntyre steps to the counsel table, takes a drink of water and returns to confront the jury which waits, their expressions registering what could be hope.

. . . Rose is the hell of the jugglers; the hell of the assassins, the hell of the robbers who boil and kill; the infernal tool of the deceitful; the hell of the revengeful, and every thought of that monster comes to his associates as a magnetizer, and each thought of his has been imparted to his fellow murderers.

Rose is responsible for the whole frame-up. When I approached him under the light and looked in his face for the first time, I beheld a cold-blooded murderer. . . .

Are you going to let these murderers go and send this man to the chair, or are you going to let this man go and demand of the district attorney that he send these bloody murderers to the chair?

Are you going to convict an innocent man and turn out a parcel of villains and murderers?

Are you willing to say their testimony has been corroborated as the law contemplates?

Now, you have one of the most solemn duties to perform. This man's life is in your hands. The verdict is life or death. The charge is murder, not graft or extortion. When the time comes he will answer those other charges. But differentiate between murder and graft.

In a moment I close. We have done the best we could. If there be shortcomings in his defense, blame him not, blame his counsel. Remember that to say he is guilty is to say he must die. There is no midway. It is murder or it is nothing. Remember, too, that it is the filth of the earth that accuses him. . . .

Judge Goff recessed the court for an hour. Reporters raced to the phone but aside from that the talk and motion in the corridors was subdued. Becker remained at the counsel table, his eyes moist and swollen at the intent of McIntyre's words. He wiped his eyes as the guards came for him and he followed docilely as he was led to the prisoner's pen on the second floor where he had lunch of a chicken sandwich and coffee. Mrs. Becker, accompanied by Becker's brother, waited in the ante-room off Judge Goff's chambers. Mrs. Becker was not hungry. Her face, which had borne for so long an air of patient suffering, was white and drawn. She stared into space and waited.

We are aware that McIntyre's last gesture for his client has been a plea or an accusation; there is still no explanation. If this does not suggest direct concealment of fact, there is the impression that Becker has allowed sweeping omissions. There are too many questions that have not been answered. Becker's failure to take the stand cannot be held against him, for the oldest principle of our legal freedom is the assurance given the accused that he need not testify against himself. Still, it is hard to separate principle from the hunger to know what happened. McIntyre has not told the full story. We must rely now on the prosecution.

First Assistant District Attorney Frank Moss takes it up without preamble as court reconvenes. He speaks with characteristic earnestness, an almost irresistible earnestness. He is no orator, but he seems to mean what he says.

> . . . the men behind the guns were the four gunmen. The men behind the gunmen were Rose, Webber, and Vallon. But the will, the brain behind the whole conspiracy was Charles Becker, and he is as guilty—more guilty—than the men who fired the fatal shots; for it was he who directed the shots.
> . . . the defense has told you that Becker will go to the chair and that you will walk shoulder to shoulder on Broadway with the informers—Rose, Webber, and Vallon. No one knows better than the counsel for the defense that those men will never walk free on Broadway. You know what those men gave

up when they took the witness stand. You know those four men would never dare walk free on Broadway—the friends of the gunmen would take care of them if they did. Had there been no confession, no squeal, had these informers not confessed, it would have been called a gamblers' war and everybody would have gone free.

The defense has sought to becloud the issue and throw dust in the eyes of the jury by referring to the immunity stipulations. What are they? You have heard them read and you know that in them all four men waive immunity if it can be proven that any one of them fired a shot. We had to make those stipulations to get at the facts and the truth regarding this crime.

. . . are we to be blamed for the character of the witnesses? Are we to be blamed for not having genteel characters? They were Becker's associates. . . .

The faces of the jury, which had registered hope for McIntyre, now register expectation.

Again and again an alleged conspiracy by the gamblers to do away with Herman Rosenthal was referred to by the defense. . . . Suppose those men did hate Rosenthal, does that let Becker out?

. . . Jack Sullivan testified for the defense that Rose day after day put himself in Sullivan's power by saying it was all a conspiracy against Becker. Is Rose a fool? I ask you to consider the improbability of that. . . .

Schepps had no connection with any part of this situation. He knew *after* the murder . . . and was an accessory after the fact. This is a separate crime. Murder in the first degree requires premeditation. . . . Schepps knew about it afterward and that is where he became a criminal. . . .

The corroboration rests on Schepps only up to the point where he became an accessory. After that it rests on Luban and the others and on the circumstantial evidence. . . .

Moss takes us laboriously through the prosecution's narrative, from Rose's becoming Becker's collector, to Becker's alleged partnership with Rosenthal and the $1,500 loan, to the raid by which Becker closed Rosenthal's house, to Rosenthal's squeal in the pages of the *World,* his confession to the district attorney, to the affidavit obtained from Dora Gilbert, Rosenthal's ex-wife, exposing Rosenthal's alleged moral lapses.

You see that Becker was the center, and step by step this plan unfolds and it does not help the defendant that his hands did not extend from the auto, touch the gunmen, or pull the trigger. He worked on Rose, Vallon and Webber.

Who was the person interested in the affidavit of Rosenthal? Whose friends were Dora Gilbert's friends? Who got them to go there? In whose interest was the affidavit obtained? In whose interest was the trip to the gunmen's house? They did not go for Sam Paul or any other gambler. Who were they going for? In whose interest? Who was in danger? How was it that action followed action, and followed immediately and close? Who else but Becker?

Although Lefty, Gyp, Whitey, and Dago Frank fired the shots; although Rose, Webber, and Vallon are participants, the man who is responsible is the man who urged the murder—the man who prostituted himself as a policeman is the man to be tried first, and not the gunmen. To get a verdict we must have all of you twelve men. If we lose one—if you through sympathy, through some idea of fraternalizing (*sic*), hold out, you block the administration of law and order.

If, when a crime is proved, a jury breaks down through temptation, pressure or any circumstance, all the work of the police, the judge and the prosecution is for nothing.

Do not shirk your duty to render a verdict as you find it, but take the manly stand. If you acquit, that is your prerogative.

But if you think it is proper to hold him accountable for this awful crime, then in God's name, in the country's name, do your duty. The district attorney submits this case to you, asking for a verdict of murder in the first degree.

It is over. The rustle of departure spreads through the court as we hear Judge Goff say that he will deliver his instructions to the jury tomorrow. There is a sudden sense of impatience. The tension which should have grown steadily through the trial has not. Instead, it blossoms in full now and we wish everything were over. The press has gone and the remainder of the crowd funnels itself through the door. Becker is led back to the Tombs. At the prisoner's exit he and his guards stop. Mrs. Becker is coming toward him, her eyes half closed with tears which glisten in ragged smears on her cheeks. She leans across the balustrade, her body bent awkwardly, her head against Becker's chest. He surrounds her with his arm. His head is down and he talks gently to her. Abruptly, she pulls away, wiping her face with a handkerchief. She is smiling thinly and there is an air of apology about her. Becker hugs her quickly once more and leaves.

Judge Goff's instructions to the jury lasted three and a half hours. He reviewed the case minutely, using as the basis of his narrative the prosecution's contentions as to how and why Rosenthal was slain. He restated the prosecution's case.

It seems almost biased. He added, however, these directives to the jury:

> The defendant is not called upon to establish his innocence. The burden of proving his guilt rests upon the prosecution.
>
> The defendant was at liberty to take the stand in his own behalf and his failure to avail himself of that privilege must not be taken to his prejudice.
>
> If you believe a witness has testified falsely in any particular, you are not on that account to reject the whole of his testimony.
>
> The charge against the defendant is first degree murder . . . and in first degree murder there must be deliberate and premeditated design to kill. . . . The elements of premeditation and deliberation are mental operations. Frequently, they are confined to a knowledge of the person himself . . . it is the duty of the jury to infer this from facts and circumstance. . . .
>
> If it be true that Becker instructed Rose to kill Rosenthal, I instruct you that Becker constituted Rose his agent and instrument in the carrying out of the design; whatever Rose did, Becker in the eyes of the law did . . .
>
> It is not my purpose to comment on the facts of the case; that

belongs to you; upon your shoulders rests the responsibility for its determination.

. . . the testimony which the People relied upon came in greater part from the lips of the witness Jacob Rose . . .

This skeleton of the case as I have described it . . . in considering it you will also consider all testimony that contradicts it or detracts from it.

It is apparent from this testimony that the main witnesses against the defendant Becker are what are called accomplices. There is no doubt that Rose, Webber, and Vallon are accomplices.

There is a question about Schepps being an accomplice. I must say that I am in doubt, and to such an extent am I in doubt, that I decline as a matter of law to instruct you that he was an accomplice.

If my recollection serves me right, there is no direct testimony that before the commission of the crime Schepps had any knowledge of the contemplated crime or took any hand in the preliminary preparation and had any participation in the crime itself or with any of the men who did the physical act of killing. His relations with the men might generate suspicion but mere suspicion is not proof, and even though he may have had a suspicion of what was in contemplation . . . that suspicion would not be legally sufficient to impute guilty participation. . . .

It is a rule of law that one accomplice cannot corroborate another . . . a conviction cannot be had upon the testimony of an accomplice unless he be corroborated by such other evidence as tends to connect the defendant with the commission of the crime.

The character of such other evidence is not defined in the code . . . the application of that rule must depend upon the judgment and the conscience of each juror. It is sufficient for the judge who presided to pass on whether there is evidence which tends to connect the defendant with the crime . . . and I have so decided. . . .

Reference has been made to motive. Motive is not necessary where proof of crime is direct. Where the proof becomes circumstantial in its nature, proof of motive becomes very important.

The motive that it is alleged the defendant was governed by, was that of dread or apprehension of exposure of his relation with Rosenthal. . . .

I have spoken of circumstantial evidence. It is the rule of law in considering circumstantial evidence, if such evidence be susceptible of two constructions, one tending to the guilt of the defendant, the other tending to his innocence, that construction most favorable to the innocence of the defendant must be given.

In considering the testimony of the witnesses Rose, Vallon, Webber, and Schepps, you must consider the motive they had and the fact that they have been promised immunity from prosecution for a crime of which they are concededly guilty.

The defendant is on trial for a specific crime. He must be tried for that crime and no other. . . .

If this man is innocent the State cannot recognize or expect a conviction. If this man be guilty, justice will not permit his acquittal. I submit the case to you.

As suddenly as it began it has ended. The judge rises, swirls about and leaves. The jury sits for a moment as though stunned by the abruptness of the judge's departure. It recovers as the bailiffs approach and beckon. The jurors rise and file out, heads down, eyes averted from the inquiring stares of the crowd.

The tension has, in a strange way, subsided. There is the feeling that it is over, that whatever the jury may decide will be in measure anticlimactic. The question of Becker's guilt, it seems from all that has been heard, may never be known, that the jury's verdict will at best be an arbitrary one.

It is 4 P.M. Becker is permitted to pause at the exit for a few words with his wife and then to the reporters pressing against the railing he says, in a firm voice that does not seem to come really from this strain-streaked and weary face:

"I have no fear of the outcome for I cannot conceive that any New York jury would fail to see that the case was a frame-up. I confidently expect to be acquitted."

20. One Down, Four to Go

BECKER waited alone for the outcome. He sat on a bench in the prisoners' pen adjoining the Bridge of Sighs on the second floor of the courthouse, his body erect, his back pressed against the wall. Twice he leaned forward, as though to rest, his elbows on his knees, his head in his hands.

Mrs. Becker returned to the anteroom for her vigil. With her were her sister, Susie Lynch, younger and even more demure; Becker's brothers, Police Lieutenant John Becker and Jackson Becker, the stock broker; Charles Reich and Charles Plitt. It was a silent gathering, silent with terror. Mrs. Becker wore a dark blue wool dress with a white ruffled collar, a dark blue coat hung about her shoulders. Her face was chalk white, her eyes red from crying. Her lips drawn and quivering.

At 5 P.M., the jury sent out for copies of Rose's testimony. When Mrs. Becker heard the call to convene, she arose unsteadily to her feet and stood motionless, trembling. John Becker stepped over and put his arm around her. She did not go into the court, but sat down again as though her legs would not support her.

At 6 P.M., the jury sent out for its supper. Judge Goff went to a restaurant on Canal Street and ate alone. Becker ate half a chicken sandwich and drank three cups of coffee. His wife shook her head savagely when John Becker asked her if she would not eat something.

At 8 P.M., the jury sent out for copies of the immunity agreements. At nine o'clock, they asked for the Hot Springs depositions.

After that, there was no word. Judge Goff went out for a walk, accompanied by two bailiffs, and returned to his chambers an hour later.

Becker now began to pace his cell, not hurriedly from anxiety but slowly as from despair.

The crowd in the courthouse began to thin after 10 P.M. as the heat in the building mysteriously went out. Reporters and the remaining spectators rapidly put on their overcoats and stood in disconsolate little groups, shivering as the building grew increasingly colder.

Although the courthouse throng had lessened, it was not so in the streets. Centre Street in front of the entrance was choked with people, staring alternately at the court and at the Tombs opposite.

Inside the Tombs, not a prisoner slept. They too were waiting to hear Becker's fate. And in the 23d District Democratic Club, the Tammany hierarchy gathered in melancholy silence, waiting. One could not be sure which they feared most—his conviction or his acquittal. Either way, it seemed, the system stood to suffer.

At five minutes before midnight the jury came in. Becker's keepers misunderstood the message from the court and it was ten minutes before Becker was brought in. The court waited in silence. The jury bravely kept its pose of sober contemplation, resisting the efforts of all to read their minds. There was nothing to suggest their verdict. It is said that a jury with a guilty verdict moves slowly, somberly, weighed down with reluctance and regret. These twelve men were merely there, harborers of a solemn trust, a pledge not to reveal until directed to reveal.

Becker is suddenly before the bench, McIntyre beside him, a bailiff poised behind. The judge speaks to the jury.

"Have you reached a verdict?"

Harold Skinner, heavy-set, swarthy, the foreman, rises slowly.

"We have, your Honor."

His voice is low and yet without hint of what he will say next.

"And how do you find the defendant, guilty or not guilty?"

"Guilty, your Honor."

There is no sound. Becker does not flinch. Judge Goff stares at him for an instant. The clerk is asked to poll the jury and we hear this phrase repeated 12 times:

"You find the defendant guilty of murder in the first degree, so say you?"

And twelve times we hear the answer. "Yes."

The noise of the stampeding newsmen drowns out the remaining formality. The court clerk is asking Becker for his true name, his age, his nationality, the names of his parents, whether or not they are still living, his address. Judge Goff rises wearily.

"The defendant is remanded to the custody of the sheriff until Wednesday next at ten o'clock in the morning when the defendant shall be returned to this court for imposition of sentence."

In the anteroom, meanwhile, Mrs. Becker remains fixed in her fearful wait. She does not know. The sound of footsteps running in the corridor penetrates her thoughts. She blinks. Then she hears the word, shouted from excited mouth after excited mouth and she knows. She rises to her feet, her eyes wide in fright. Her hands clutch her breast and she falls to the floor before John Becker can reach her. He picks her up, carries her to a room on the second floor, through the scurrying throngs who stare in embarrassment and sympathy. A doctor is sent for. She revives, sits up on the couch.

"It's terrible. A terrible shock. I can't believe it. It will be reversed. He is an innocent man. Oh, this is too horrible."

John Becker sits next to her, his arm supporting her. There is nothing to be said. Sobs shake her and she retires convulsively into her grief.

When she is taken to the prisoners' pen to see her husband, she throws herself into his arms, her sobs ringing with fresh strength. Becker folds her to him. The guards, his friends, all look away. At last, taking her from him and pressing her shoulders in his hands, as one would support a doll, he studies her tragic face. His voice, husky but firm, seems to reach her. She opens her eyes.

"It will come out all right in the end. Don't worry for me, little woman."

Her arms sweep around his neck and she is kissing him, quickly, hard, desperately, again and again and again. With a wrench, he leaves. At the side entrance to the Criminal Courts building on White Street, Mrs. Becker sits in a chair, surrounded by her friends, waiting for a taxi. Her sister is bathing her temples with a moist handkerchief. Whitman and Moss stride out the door and past the little group of whom they take no notice.

In the Tombs, the news of Becker's doom had swept into every cell. Muffled words of sympathy and encouragement follow his dreary, rhythmic march through the cold and shadowy corridors. He does not acknowledge his supporters but he hears them and even in his cell he hears other sentiments hissed through the bars into the darkness, epithets for Rose the Squealer, who, in some eyes, had become Rose the Arbiter of Justice.

21. "To Do Execution upon You . . ."

THERE WAS an element of incredibility in Becker's conviction and, therefore, a certain skepticism underlying the eagerness of the crowd which jammed Judge Goff's courtroom on the morning of October 30, 1912, to hear the omnipotent Tenderloin baron sentenced to his death.

Becker and his attorneys had already prepared a battery of motions for a new trial as well as a persuasive appeal to the higher courts and his sentence of death Becker appeared to regard with almost bored detachment. Flanked by Hart and McIntyre, Becker stood easily, his hands clasped in front of him, his head cocked to one side, as Goff read from the code this stark and ageless judicial prose:

> The judgment of this court is that you, Charles Becker, for the murder in the first degree of Herman Rosenthal, whereof you are convicted, be and you are hereby sentenced to the punishment of death, and it is ordered that within ten days after this day's session of the Court, a sheriff of the County of New York deliver you together with the Warden of this court to the agent and Warden of Sing Sing where you shall be kept in solitary confinement until the week beginning Monday, the

9th day of December, 1912, and on some day within the week so appointed the said agent or Warden of the State Prison of the State of New York at Sing Sing is commanded to do execution upon you, Charles Becker, in the mode and manner prescribed by the law of the State of New York.

The newspapers of New York were almost unanimous in praise of this exercise of speedy justice and their enthusiasm intensified the bitterness of Becker's words when, on the day before he was sentenced, he granted an interview to the press.

"The newspapers cannot be too emphatic in saying that I denounce my conviction as legal butchery."

"Some of the papers say that my defense has cost me $25,000. That is untrue. The sum named is at least $2,000 more than my wife and I ever had at one time in our lives. After all the years I worked as a police officer and after the seventeen years in which she taught school it would be strange if we had not saved something."

Becker's defense had been costly. McIntyre's fee, paid by Tammany, was $13,000. But there were other expenses.

"Lieutenant," a reporter asked, "did you talk to Rose over the telephone about the murder of Rosenthal that night?"

"So help me God, no!"

"Do you think that Rose, being Rosenthal's enemy, took this particular time, when there was an affidavit out accusing you, and the public was beginning to comment about your conduct, to bump off Rosenthal?"

"I do, yes. That's exactly what I believe."

"Do you think that Jack Rose is so vicious he is capable of such an act?"

"I didn't think he was vicious when I first knew him. But when Jack Rose got on the stand and admitted he felt no regret at Herman Rosenthal's death, or his share in it, and felt no pangs of conscience, I certainly did learn to believe he was utterly vicious and capable of anything."

Becker always was a man to be believed. His voice rose in tone.

232

"Does any reasonable man believe Jack Rose—a man of the world, accustomed to living by his wits—when he says he felt obliged to do my bidding? A mere police lieutenant? Why didn't he go to Bridgie Webber and have Webber go to his friend, Jim Smith, in the district attorney's office and tell him about this order? Why didn't he go to the district attorney? Why didn't he tell Commissioner Waldo what I had asked him to do? He could have tied me hand and foot and what did he have to fear from me in vengeance if he failed to do as I ordered him?

"Schepps told a tissue of lies. He was the murder paymaster. I'm certain of that. He was the biggest liar of all that bunch of lying rats yet it was his story I'm certain convinced the jury that this awful charge against me was true."

Becker could never verbally cross the chasm between his origins and the image of social respectability to which he aspired. His language either lapsed into East Side colloquialisms or reached for incongruous words or expressions. To hear him describe the predicament as an "awful" one made you flinch. One could accept the word "terrible" from Charlie Becker, or even "horrible" but not "awful." He might as well have called it "dastardly."

The day after he opened his heart to the press, Becker found himself assailed by McIntyre.

"If you open your mouth again when I'm not around," raged the lawyer, brandishing a copy of the New York *Press* in his client's face, "you can get another attorney. You keep your mouth shut. I'm trying to keep you out of the electric chair but you seem determined to put yourself in it. If you have anything to say in your defense you tell it to me and I'll tell it to the courts, not the newspapers."

Becker accepted the reprimand docilely.

Nor was McIntyre the only person concerned about Becker's loquaciousness. Charlie Murphy, Tom Foley, the Sullivan kin and all the rest of the Tammany hierarchy watched the papers each day with mounting apprehension. It was not that they expected Becker to tell all, it was simply that their fear symbolized their dilemma.

As an overlord of commercial vice, Becker was through. In fact, all policemen were through being underworld monarchs. They might still serve the cause of gambling, prostitution, narcotics and whatever, but they could no longer direct it. Becker had shown that policemen were too vulnerable on one hand and too powerful on the other. He had shown that crime must be separated from its source of protection by a buffer, a middleman who could be expendable. Policemen who dealt directly with the underworld could not help but know too much. At the same time, these policemen were also in a position to do what Becker had done. This power must be concentrated elsewhere. Policemen must be given limited authority. The theory of organized crime as it operates today had been established. It would take modifications and perfections, but it was there in its essentials.

In time, the first great middleman of crime was selected. He was, it was said, Arnold Rothstein, the insatiably ambitious gambler and bankroller of all manner of profitable perfidy. He became the expediter, the executive secretary, who arranged for the distribution of the commodities of crime but spared the principals of crime from knowing each other. He was a one-man clearing house for the financial requirements of gambling, prostitution, narcotics and, thanks to prohibition, bootlegging. He made arrangements for nameless purveyors to buy protection from nameless police officials and nameless politicians. If anyone was caught, it went no further than Arnold Rothstein and he never broke the law. Like Becker, Rothstein could not remain forever in control of a business whose rate of expansion almost equaled that of oil or real estate development. Whomsoever other ambitious men could not outsmart, they were apt to do in. Rothstein's career was cut short by bullets and his empire fragmented into specialized provinces. He thus had many heirs. Some of them, like Frank Costello, Lucky Luciano, Albert Anastasia, Joe Masseria and Dutch

Schultz, were well known; others never shared their gory notoriety, but they were no less important in the scheme of things. To flourish, crime requires both customers and protection. As long as it has the former, it will probably also have the latter.

In the meantime, however, there was still no answer to the problem of what to do about Becker. Broadway bookies were giving 8 to 5 that he would one day be a free man. What then? By some miracle, or perhaps simply by the expectation of liberty and exoneration, Becker had kept the pledge of silence. He knew enough and could prove enough, to send at least half of Tammany's bosses to prison. Suppose the odds on his ultimate freedom dropped? Becker was only human. What would he do to keep himself from being electrocuted? On this imponderable, the decision was made. Becker was to receive all the help he needed. Becker's hopes were to be sustained with money, with lying witnesses, with whatever would ease Becker's apprehensions about being executed. If Becker was to be done away with, it must not be at the hands of the State. But time enough to worry about that. For the moment, Becker's silence was easily obtained.

This attitude, however, was not shared by the components of Becker's now enfeebled empire. A majority of the gamblers, brothel keepers, pimps and footpads whose destinies he had long controlled were glad to be rid of him. True, their business had all but ceased with his arrest, but Mother Sin had ruled New York for too long to allow her profitable progeny to wither altogether. Some of the gamblers, however, found it awkward to get started on their own. Precinct captains were suddenly reluctant to take the familiar payoff. They couldn't really guarantee protection because nobody was in charge. And they knew that policemen who accepted graft and then failed to deliver had always been marked men with poor prospects for old age. There seemed to be nothing to do but wait. Sooner or later someone with ambition and imagination would take these frayed strands of crime and weave them into an orderly pattern. It had to be done. The demand for the product had not lessened, yet it was hard at times to find even a floating crap game. Brothels reduced their overhead by reducing their staffs who went into the streets to compete with the thousands of free-lance prostitutes working in concert with a few bold, if jittery, saloonkeepers and hotel desk clerks. Patrolmen hesitated to harass them because of the inconsistent attitudes displayed by the various precinct commands.

Was Becker really the key? Speculation about his role in the underworld complex began to decline a week after the trial when he was chained to a pair of deputy sheriffs, escorted by ten more, and taken to Sing Sing prison at Ossining, an hour's train ride up the Hudson. A passive crowd estimated at slightly upwards of 2,000 filled the street and pressed against the portals of the Tombs, for Becker's departure had been announced in advance. A wedge of deputies pushed through the throng followed by Becker and his guards and behind them Mrs. Becker, her head held high, her eyes fixed on her husband's back. She was chicly dressed in a flowing dark blue dress with a white lace collar tight about her tiny throat, and an immense flapping hat which she demurely held in place with one hand. As the little group reached the curb and the car which was to take them to the train, a woman lunged from the crowd and grasped Mrs. Becker by the arm. The woman's wrinkled face was distorted in a grimace of exaggerated concern. Mrs. Becker stopped and confronted her. "We believe in you," the woman said and withdrew into the crowd before Mrs. Becker could answer her. Mrs. Becker was allowed to sit next to her husband in the train and, embarrassed by the cordon of guards around them, they talked self-consciously and impersonally.

"It seems," said Mrs. Becker, "that the suffragettes are making great gains."

"Women should be allowed to vote," said Becker, patting his wife's hand.

At Ossining, the crowd clogging the railway platform was more curious than decided, as though greeting a celebrity whose

236

status had not yet been established. The courtesy of Sing Sing guards who left Becker and his wife alone for more than the hour provided, as Mrs. Becker later said, the last opportunity for her to kiss her husband in nearly a year and a half. Their visits would henceforth be confined to an hour and a half a week, separated by two wire gratings and four feet of space. Mrs. Becker would write every day, long maddeningly cheery letters which Becker was allowed to answer at the rate of not more than three times a week. When Becker's attorneys finally filed the appeal, the urgency of Mrs. Becker's visits to the prison abated for it automatically postponed the date of execution for six months. News of the appeal was popularly greeted with disapproval although a large segment of the New York Bar Association was inclined to agree with the points McIntyre raised. He charged Goff with prejudicial conduct generally and specifically; that Goff had failed in his instructions to the jury to review the defense's case; that he had failed to cite the hostility of all the prosecution witnesses toward Rosenthal, the victim; that he had virtually directed the jury to return a guilty verdict. McIntyre also charged that the testimony of Rose, Webber, and Vallon had not been corroborated because Schepps was an accomplice; that the State had failed to prove that the gunmen Becker was accused of hiring were in fact guilty; that the immunity granted the State's star witnesses was basis in itself for bias if not outright perjury; that the proof of the pre-murder meetings between Becker and Rose in the Union Square Hotel stemmed from the circumstantial observations of two waiters and was therefore not competent. Finally, McIntyre declared, there was no hope for a fair trial because of the public clamor raised by Whitman's dramatic conduct of the investigation.

At least one of Becker's points of defense was near to being resolved. The four young gunmen, assuming the appearance and manners of Bowery waifs rather than that of the killer roles they had coveted, began moving onto the front pages of the newspapers as their trial neared. All had lost weight on the

Tombs' diet and their young faces, once prematurely puffed with the fruits of their licentious life, now seemed pathetically shrunken. They were all in their early twenties, but they looked like emaciated teen-agers. They were making a conscious effort, on instructions from their counsel, to soften the *d*'s in their language and to listen more respectfully to their elders. Gyp the Blood, who not long ago had admitted in an offhand way to police that he had demolished a saloon and maimed several of its occupants with a home-made bomb " 'cuz I likes ta hear da noise," taxed the credulity of the press by addressing several of its representatives as "Sir" and by lamenting, in halting but acceptable English, the recent attempt to assassinate Teddy Roosevelt. Furthermore, he said, he was studying the guitar and he dismissed as preposterous his reputation as a back breaker.

"Aw, you don't believe that, do you?" he coyly asked one newsman with the effrontery to bring it up.

Like his fellow defendants, Gyp was blithely confident of an acquittal. They were all, in fact, preparing for freedom. Lefty Louie was applying the dexterity developed by years of picking pockets to the building of a model dirigible, a machine whose revolutionary potential, he said, intrigued him. One could have easily inferred that he was thinking of becoming an aviator.

Dago Frank, whom the noted detective Valentine O'Farrell had acknowledged to be "the toughest man in the world," was being visited regularly by a priest and was studying earnestly to be worthy of readmittance to the Faith. He did not greet reporters with a Bible under his arm, but he did manage to intrude a comment about Christ's trial before Pontius Pilate. "They framed Jesus on account of public clamor," he said, sniffing delicately. The analogy was not lost on the press and several reporters gagged.

Whitey Lewis, his only experience in life having been in the use of blackjack and pistol, was the sole exception to this manifest uplift movement. He sat in a corner of the Tombs' visitors room, discreetly silent until reporters questioned him directly. He was looking forward, he said softly, to his release and his return to a fictional calling as a garment factory push boy.

"When did you last work at that?" a reporter asked.

"Oh, I been outta work fer some time. I'm keen to get back at it."

Their attorney, Charles F. G. Wahle, a former police court magistrate and Tammany grass roots spokesman, hovered in the background like a prodigal sire, his big, heavy-jowled face beaming through a haze of self-generated cigar smoke. There had been some suggestion that Tammany was taking care of his fee in the case and he took pains to dispel the notion.

"I want you to know," he said during a well-timed lull in the conversation, "that these boys [a gesture embracing them] have paid my fee out of their own savings. Of course, I'm representing all of them and I know that no other lawyer would handle the case, so I have adjusted the fee within their reach." He pulled his pince-nez delicately off his large nose and wiped the glass with his handkerchief.

Savings? The implications of virtuous thrift seemed to stun the reporters and they relayed the news without comment. Challenging the assertion that one had savings seemed tantamount to questioning a man's declared love for his mother.

Virtue was even visited upon them. Copies of the New Testament were mailed to each of them by the Rev. Thomas Chalmers, a Brooklyn zealot to whom Mayor Gaynor had once refused a permit for a street-corner campaign to convert Manhattan's Jews to Christianity.

Several New York clergymen, as though in concert, began attacking Mayor Gaynor from the pulpit. The city was in the grip of a vicious crime wave, they charged, and it was all Gaynor's fault with his hypocritical policies of "outward order and decency." One clergyman, commenting on the Becker case to the titillation of his congregation, noted with anguished irony that Judge Goff's 1894 exposures of evil, as counsel for the famous Lexow Committee, had been in vain. Things were much worse today. However, Christianity appeared to be hard pressed everywhere. In Constantinople, the heart of Turkey's defense against the assaults of the Bulgarian and Greek armies, in the preludes to the First World War, the Moslems had declared a blood purge of all Christians and even now the slaughter had begun.

But on November 6, 1912, Woodrow Wilson won the Presidency from Taft and Teddy Roosevelt, by a landslide. The same election put Tammany's William Sulzer in as governor of New York State, a hollow triumph for he was soon unjustly impeached (Tammany giveth and Tammany taketh away). In five states where suffrage was on the ballot, only in Wisconsin did it fail to pass. Through it all, Vincent Astor and the indulgent heart of America were celebrating the young scion's twenty-first birthday which meant his automatic inheritance of sixty-seven million dollars.

On the morning of November 8, a Friday, the four young gangsters, brandishing their new images of innocence, minced into Judge Goff's gloomy courtroom. They were confident, they said, of being acquitted. Everybody was confident. It was the prevailing attitude. Lawyer Wahle, who had been adamant in demanding that each of the four be tried separately, consented without explanation to the district attorney's motion for a mass trial. Actually, the proceedings were delayed until almost noon while Goff, in an adjoining courtroom, finished charging the jury in the trial of a Queens carpenter accused of killing his lawyer.

Even with the late start, Wahle and Whitman had agreed on five jurors at day's end. They were all older men, as the four defendants had requested, and they were all equipped with either voluminous mustaches or beards which was said to be a coincidence.

Lefty met the press as court adjourned for the weekend. His companions stood behind him, nodding in benign approval of his remarks.

"If we can get seven more jurors like these five, we'll be sat-

240

isfied. All we want is a square deal. Any reasonable jury will have to acquit us on the testimony that will be brought out. We are sure of acquittal. We'll be out of here by Thanksgiving. Come and have a drink with us then. We'll be ready for one by that time."

What kind of testimony did Lefty have in mind that would mean acquittal, reporters asked? Wahle heaved his bulk in front of his client, adjusting his pince-nez.

"We will call twenty witnesses. We will prove that Vallon was on the murder car as it left the Metropole and we will prove that he was not drunk in the Lafayette Baths as he has claimed. In short, we will tell the true story of the Rosenthal murder for the first time."

In other words, as Monday's proceedings revealed, Wahle and his clients were crying frame-up too.

On Sunday night 20,000 suffragettes, each carrying a lantern, marched down Fifth Avenue. An awed reporter for *The New York Times* described it as a "river of fire," doubtless a figurative impression as well.

On Monday, the four young thugs, their spirits buoyed by a weekend full of strategy meetings with Wahle, swaggered into court and, surrounded by deputy sheriffs, arrayed themselves at the counsel table. They smiled and waved to members of the press who, with the prospective jurors, were the only spectators in the court. Goff had also closed this trial to the public.

It was 7 P.M. before Wahle and Whitman had agreed on the remaining seven members of the jury, a selection in which the four defendants had been, to Wahle, annoyingly active. Like the first five, they too were older men. Wahle's reasoning was that male maturity would be less offended by the base language and the seamy disclosures of his clients and their witnesses.

From the newsstand-sales viewpoint of New York's editors, the trial was something of an anticlimax and they gave it far less space and attention than that of Becker. And, in its major aspects, the trial was a repetition of Becker's. Rose told his interminable story, unshaken by Wahle's cross-examination. Nor could Wahle ruffle the testimony of the other prosecution witnesses left over from Becker's trial. Wahle made a small gain with Giovanni Stanish, the testy inventor who had identified Gyp the Blood in the Becker trial as one of the killers he had seen in action in front of the Metropole. This time, he picked Dago Frank. Judge Goff ordered his testimony stricken. But there was Louis Krese, the unemployed waiter, and Jacob Hecht, the waiter at the Metropole. Their identifications could not be shaken.

Shapiro the chauffeur was the star witness. Terrified almost out of his wits, his appearance was a telling one. He shook with fright, his voice broke repeatedly and his face was soaked with sweat. Whitman conducted the examination.

"Were you threatened to prevent you from testifying here?"

"No, but I would not be here if Big Jack Zelig was still alive. These are his boys."

Goff ordered him to step down, to identify each of the defendants by name. Shapiro inched out of the chair, his knees threatening to give way beneath him. Slowly he walked over to the long table, the four young men glaring at him, half rising from their chairs like enraged dogs straining at their leashes.

Shapiro raised his hand to point. His eyes wide, his face frozen. There is a pause between each word. One wonders if he can speak.

"Gyp.

"Lefty.

"Whitey.

"Dago."

His last piece of testimony is an echo from the Becker trial.

"Dago Frank said to the others, 'There are no cops around. Becker said so. Everything is OK.' "

Wahle's cross-examination of him only makes matters worse. Wahle tried to pick discrepancies out of Shapiro's various stories. Shapiro readily admits he lied at first.

"If I had told the truth I would have been killed." He added that he might not have talked even now, but his mother nagged him into it.

Wahle opened his defense on Thursday with a sentimental address, begging for sympathy.

"These are not monsters in human form, but simply four young men, one of them scarcely more than a boy (Lefty had just turned twenty-one). They are bad without question, wicked without question, each of them, but far, very far, from such depths of crime as might culminate in the commission of a murder." His clients watch him reverently, their eyes swelling with tears.

"Gyp here. He was never known as Gyp the Blood. That's a fiction, the invention of an imaginative reporter. This boy is the victim of evil companions. Oh, he is bad, they are all bad, but they have never been convicted of anything approaching murder. . . ."

Goff's hand is in the air, waving back and forth in agitation.

"Mr. Wahle. These men are not on trial for being bad. Will you confine your remarks to the question of murder."

We hear no more of wayward youth. We hear Wahle's story of how Rosenthal was killed. Rose, knowing that Big Jack Zelig blamed him for his arrest on the weapons charge, sought out Zelig's men to persuade them that he, Rose, had had nothing to do with it. Through Dago Frank, he arranged to have a meeting at Webber's poker rooms with the two detectives who had arrested Zelig and who, Rose swore, would exonerate him. Dago and his three companions, Lefty, Whitey and Gyp, arrived at Webber's but the detectives were not there. In the meantime, Wahle said, Rose, Webber, and Vallon had hatched the plot to kill Rosenthal, having retained as the assassin a mysterious underworld gunman known only as Itzky who just happened to be at Webber's when Dago and the boys arrived. Rose, Webber, and Vallon saw the opportunity to frame the four and lured them to the Metropole on the pretext that the missing detectives were there.

But only three of the accused succumbed. Dago remained at Webber's for a few minutes and then went home. The three gunmen, accompanied by Rose, Webber, Vallon and Itzky, walked to the Metropole. Vallon went inside returning a moment later with Rosenthal. As Vallon and the gambler appeared in the doorway, Itzky drew a gun from inside his coat. Vallon jumped aside, drawing his own gun, and the two men shot Rosenthal down. Whitey, Lefty and Gyp, who had not even been armed, watched in amazement for an instant and then turned and fled.

Wahle buttressed his story with the testimony of the four defendants themselves, and the same witnesses on whose testimony Becker's defense had been based. But it was no use. On Tuesday, November 19, 1912, Judge Goff charged the jury, pointing to the flaw in the defense's story.

If the gunmen were lured to the Metropole to make them victims of a plot, why also make them witnesses to a killing?

It took the jury just twenty minutes to agree on a verdict of guilty of murder in the first degree. Dago threw himself across the counsel table, his body quivering convulsively with sobs. Gyp fell back into his chair, slumping forward to cradle his head in his hands. Whitey and Lefty stood paralyzed with terror, their faces ashen, frozen. For New York's most fearful gangsters, the pendulum had swung the other way.

To Whitman, it was more meaningful. "The conviction of these four killers," he said, "means the end of gang rule in New York." This broad, panacean interpretation of the case, however, was not Whitman's alone. Newspapers and magazines took up the theme and Whitman's stature grew. In *Collier's,* Richard Harding Davis reviewed the Becker case under the title, "Defeat of the Underworld." The underworld smiled its wry little smile.

On November 21, Rose, Webber, Schepps and Vallon were freed from the West Side Prison. They refused to talk to reporters as they hurried down the broad stairs, each climbing into a separate taxi and each going his separate way. Rose, however, announced soon afterward that he had written a book during his incarceration. He had titled it "Twenty Years in the Underworld," and he was looking for a publisher. He never found one. After that, Rose said, he was going on a lecture tour, preaching against the evils of crime. Webber and his wife took a boat for Havana. Schepps signed a vaudeville contract and began a tour of the Far West. Vallon went back to dealing cards but he didn't announce it.

On November 22, the forces of reform gave a testimonial dinner at the Aldine Club for the valiant district attorney. All political overtones were denied but it appeared that the next mayor of New York City or the next governor of New York State would be Charles Seymour Whitman.

22. Whitman for Mayor, Governor and ____?

THERE WERE two distinct schools of thought attendant on District Attorney Charles Seymour Whitman. One, and by far the largest and most pervasive, ascribed to him almost messianic qualities and capacities. His good friend and supporter, the venerable Reverend Dr. Lyman Abbott, enjoyed articulating Whitman's heroic stature in the pages of *Outlook,* the wholesome monthly which he edited. In its Christmas issue for 1912, with Becker and the four convicted assassins contained on Sing Sing's death row, *Outlook* proclaimed Whitman editorially as "The Next Mayor of New York" and described him as the man "who is today, more than any other one man on the continent, perhaps, the champion of Civilization, of law and order and decency, against the criminality and graft and vice of the metropolis banded together and supported by crooked police officials and crooked political leaders . . ."

The other, minority attitude about Charles Seymour Whitman did not find such succinct expression until later. But it was there, forming itself in the minds of people less given to political passions. Franklin P. Adams finally stated it in his Plutarchian column in *Harper's Weekly*: "For always a man's job is a greater thing that he, and in Whitman's mind, it seemeth to me, lurketh the conviction that he is greater than the job . . ."

Whatever Whitman's thoughts at the time, he took no immediate part in the burgeoning campaign to put him in City Hall, a campaign conducted by the Reverend Dr. Abbott and the wealthy little corps of businessmen and financiers who were more interested in Whitman's independent clarity of mind than in his demonstrations of virtue. The remaining members of New York's political potential, except for Mayor Gaynor who was too quixotically independent, were enmeshed in political machinery. If Whitman's backers could not control him, at least they could be confident that nobody else could either.

Whitman's passive role in his own political progress was only temporary. He may simply have been too busy. He had been responsible for the Curran inquiry, which had resumed after the Becker trial and which was turning up a goodly number of lesser scoundrels for Whitman to prosecute. For a time it appeared that New York might really undergo a cleanup after all. Whitman plunged his office into a tenacious investigation of police graft and by the spring of 1913 had forced the dismissal of dozens of cops and officers, ignited repeated district shake-ups, and sent four police inspectors to prison. He was looking into the machinations of a municipal monopoly known familiarly as the ice trust and he was beginning to travel about the countryside, delivering restrained addresses on idealism in government in such sober surroundings as his old alma mater, Amherst, and at Fordham University and at New York University which gave him an honorary Doctorate of Law as well as a thundering ovation as New York's next mayor. Well, if that was what the people wanted . . .

Whitman also spoke now at the YMCA and at church gatherings. Anticipating his political ascendancy, Whitman told a starry-eyed gathering of the Young Repulican Club what they must do to keep the New York district attorney's office out of politics. It had the ring of authoritative hindsight. "The man who is influenced in the conduct of the great office of district attorney, and in the prosecution of crime by motives political or selfish, is violating the law of the land, in spirit at least, as truly as does the criminal. . . ." And, as always, Whitman paid tribute to the press as the conscience of the public whose vigilance, he said, was the only lasting assurance of honesty in high office.

Whitman's failure to get into City Hall that year was not altogether his own fault, but more the flowering of a number of conflicting forces which suggested to him, and to his backers, that he would do better going after the governorship the following year.

Becker was still thrashing in the courts, with appeals and new trial motions and, while Whitman might have liked to let somebody else cope with Becker in the obviously long and bitter struggle that lay between the deposed gang lord and the electric chair, he was a fighter and there were indications this was one battle in which default would have been distasteful.

Another factor was William Randolph Hearst, now thoroughly rejected as both king and a maker of kings, who had returned to New York for one last dabble. With his efforts to launch a fusion ticket into City Hall, Hearst seriously splintered the reform elements, both publicly and privately. There was some doubt that Whitman could rally an independent majority and with the Republican organizaton in New York split between pro-trust and anti-trust there was even greater doubt.

And the office of mayor was wide open. Gaynor, his health undermined by a bullet wound inflicted months earlier by a disgruntled and deranged city docks employee who had been dismissed from his job, sailed for Europe and died of a heart attack off the coast of Ireland.

Another giant had fallen, too. The ailing Big Tim Sullivan, his voice, if not the power of his name, long since muted as the roar of Tammany, escaped from his male nurses in the Bronx and was apparently run over by a New Haven Railroad train.

248

His body lay in the morgue unidentified for thirteen days before a policeman recognized it.

In the end, Whitman let the Independent League nomination for mayor go to another reformer, thirty-five-year-old John Purroy Mitchel, a sterling figure who had all of Gaynor's fire but considerably less cynicism and who, after being elected, made the greatest cleanup strides of all. Whitman ran for another term as district attorney and even the endorsement of Tammany Hall, in one of its spasmodic gestures to convert its growl to a purr, failed to handicap him.

Whitman expanded his horizons now, his mind set on taking the Republican nomination for governor in the summer of 1914. He eased up on his probe of the police in favor of broader exposures and began uncovering kickbacks to city officials from private contractors of various kinds. Tammany made a vast amount of money in this area and if there were any lingering doubts as to why he had received Tammany's support he wanted to dispel them. This inquiry led into exposures of similar grafts in Albany, among them an alleged $50,000 shakedown by a state official in awarding a contract for $1,500,000 section of aquaduct at Niagara. This prompted a knot of Republican state legislators to propose that Whitman be appointed a special deputy attorney general with state-wide authority. Governor Martin H. Glynn, the Tammany lieutenant governor who had succeeded the impeached William Sulzer, angrily rejected the proposal. He knew Whitman would be running against him in 1914.

No matter, Whitman could reach into Blackwell's Island, site of the infamous city institution for the insane, the aged, and the indigent, rich in exposures of sadism, neglect and, of course, graft. In later years, Whitman bitterly assailed the state's prison system and became a prime mover in its reform. He called the progress of penology "slow and grudging" and voiced, perhaps for the first time, the now familiar belief that the purpose of prisons is "reform and reclamation, rather than punishment and retribution."

The new expansion of his public concerns was indicated when Bald Jack Rose, still lecturing on evil and trying with doubtful success to operate a truck farm near Danbury, Connecticut, called at Whitman's office, trailing a few disinterested reporters, and offered his services in the great crusade against vice. It was the first encounter between Whitman and the man who had helped make him a hero since the Becker trial but Whitman gave his star witness a cold reception. Afterward, Whitman told reporters, "It is hard for me to figure out what he wants. If he has any evidence, I welcome it, but I'm not interested in helping him punish someone in his own interest."

Whitman's attitudes were consistent with the coming age of enlightenment. After all, the automobile self-starter had been invented for a year now. It was not popular, but there was no doubt that inevitably all cars would have them. The same forces of reaction which clung to the horse were also clinging to the crank. And the ill-fated *Lusitania,* the princess of the Atlantic, made a record crossing in four days and eighteen hours. It had to churn a steady incredible twenty-eight knots to do it and nearly everyone aboard was seasick but it was progress.

If Rose was rebuffed by Whitman, he was warmly applauded when he addressed a dinner meeting of the Twilight Club, sharing the speaker's table with Whitman's chief aide, Frank Moss, Judge Ben Lindsey, the founder of the juvenile court, and with two clergymen and a criminologist. Rose said nothing about the Becker case, to everyone's disappointment, but instead paid heavy tribute to Judge Lindsey. "If there had been juvenile courts when I was a boy," he said, "my life would not have been misspent." He explained that typhoid had rendered him hairless as a boy, that the taunts of his playmates had driven him to truancy which led to reform school where he met gamblers and criminals who did not tease him about his baldness and among whom he found compassion and sympathy. He had learned the error of his ways, he said, but the lesson had been bitter.

If comment on the Becker trial would not come from Rose's lips, there was no silence in other quarters. Some aspect of the case appeared almost daily in the papers. Sam Schepps, the great corroborator, had found he was no asset to vaudeville and his contract had been broken. He appealed in court for a reduction in alimony payments to his ex-wife on grounds his services to the State of New York in the Becker affair had rendered him unemployable. He was not successful. Schepps turned up in London toward the end of the year, his presence revealed by a cable he sent Mrs. Becker offering to provide new facts about her husband which would free him. All he asked, he said, was $10,000. Mrs. Becker did not respond.

Charles Plitt, Becker's erstwhile press agent, was stewing in the Tombs again, this time on a perjury charge, and in an hysterical effort to free himself he sent Whitman a lengthy account of Becker's graft operations which Whitman publicly dismissed as a work of fiction.

Becker's first motion for a new trial, on grounds the verdict had not been in accordance with the evidence, had been summarily rejected by Judge Goff. In the meantime, John McIntyre had withdrawn from the case for reasons he did not announce and John Hart, Becker's attorney friend, filed a second motion for a new trial on grounds of new evidence. The motion went first before Justice James Gerard who promptly referred it to Judge Goff for a decision.

The new evidence offered by Hart was embodied in affidavits signed by Harry Cohen and Isadore Schoenhaus, the two cab drivers whom Rose, Vallon, Schepps, and Webber swore had driven them to the famous Harlem murder conference. Both men had been in Whitman's custody during the trial but had not been called to testify. In the affidavits accompanying Hart's motion, Cohen and Schoenhaus denied that they had ever taken Rose, Vallon, Schepps, or Webber into Harlem at any time for any reason.

Judge Goff denied the motion. His ruling was based partly on the fact that Becker's appeal had yet to be heard by the Court of Appeals but he gave these grounds for denying the motion: That the affidavits merely contradicted evidence given at the trial but did not invalidate it, that the evidence was not new but available at the time of the trial, and finally that the evidence itself would not result in a different verdict if a new trial were granted. There were other affidavits: Two reporters who interviewed Bridgie Webber on his return from Cuba swore the dandy little gambler told them Rose's confession was as much a surprise to him as it was to anybody; that he had no choice but to go along with it.

There were times when Whitman must have felt he had launched himself upon a sea of perjury.

Becker's case, meanwhile, was still before the Court of Appeals, a swashbuckling document which raised nearly 4,000 points of law. The appeal had been filed at a time when Mrs. Becker feared she might not be present when Hart argued it before the justices in Albany. She had paid one last visit to her husband and had come away laden with despondency. The death house aura had stunned her, suddenly, as though she were really seeing it for the first time. "A horrible place," she recalled, with shudders of revulsion. "The dark stone corridors, the iron doors with the narrow slits and all those eyes looking at me." The eyes of death, she felt. Her horror was apparent to Becker for he could not speak. He seemed overcome with shame that his gentle wife should have to see him in these surroundings. "I have never seen such agony on anyone's face," she said, "and for a moment I wished that he had died instead."

Returning to New York, Helen Becker slipped quietly into the Women's Hospital on 110th Street where she remained for six weeks of frustration, fear, and hopelessness. Her baby was more than two weeks past due and it was finally delivered by Caesarean section. The doctor told her as they wheeled her into surgery that he could not promise to save both her and the child. Numb with pain and drugs, her face drawn and deathlike, she replied, "Then you better save me. The baby's no help to Charlie."

252

They had wanted a son whom they planned to name after his father. If it was a girl, she would be called Ruth. It was a girl. Helen Becker awakened the next morning, a Sunday, to find sunlight filling her pale white room with almost blinding intensity. Soon the infant was brought to her and she later told how her hopes were suddenly restored. The tiny child seemed well and normal, if quiet in manner, but when it was returned to the nursery later in the day, Helen Becker could not suppress a vague uneasiness. The doctor was standing by her bed when she awoke in the morning and she knew.

"I'm sorry, Mrs. Becker," he said simply, "but your little girl died during the night."

Well, she could bear it, she thought. But she did not know how to explain it to her husband.

Five days before Christmas of 1913, Becker's mother died. The eighty-five-year-old invalid, who had been blind for several years, never knew about her son. For the year between his trial and her death, Becker's brothers maintained a kind deceit, explaining that Becker had been called to the Far West on police business. Becker wrote her regularly, however, and his brothers read the letters to her, ascribing to them a fictitious postmark such as Los Angeles or Seattle. Becker had been attentive to her over the years and his long absence puzzled her. As she lay dying in her tiny apartment on Greenwich Avenue, just north of Washington Square, she seemed troubled that Charlie should remain away so long. Lt. John Becker made the trip to Sing Sing to tell Charlie his mother had died.

In Albany, the Court of Appeals took Becker's formidable petition under submission after hearing three hours of argument by attorney John W. Hart and an equal amount of rebuttal from Assistant District Attorney Frank Moss. Ten days later it did the same for the four assassins. Their attorney, Charles F. G. Wahle, argued the case eloquently, although he had less to argue about. His points of appeal were that Judge Goff had erred in his instructions to the jury, that the prosecution's use of such nicknames as Gyp the Blood and Dago Frank had inflamed the jury and prejudiced its reasoning. Goff's hasty conduct of the trial was also cited.

Early in February, 1914, the Court of Appeals sustained the conviction of the four young gunmen. It could find no errors of law in Judge Goff's conduct, it said, and as far as the names of the defendants inflaming the jury, were these not in fact the names the defendants had chosen for themselves and by which they had always been called?

Two weeks later, the Court rendered its judgment on Becker. It set aside his conviction and ordered a new trial. In a scathing, unanimous decision, the Court charged Judge Goff with gross misconduct, both in matters of law and discretion, and attacked virtually every salient of the prosecution's case. It lumped the State's four star witnesses under the heading "dangerous and degenerate," and said that this fact alone should have motivated Judge Goff to make sure he did not err. Moreover, he expressed open hostility to the defendant and his counsel and rendered a fair trial impossible.

The Court said that on its face, Bald Jack Rose's story taxed human credibility, with or without corroboration. And as far as Schepps providing corroboration, the Court suggested, his tale was totally beyond belief and that therefore he was an accomplice.

The ruling cited the failure, or refusal, of the prosecution to call to testify the two cab drivers who allegedly drove the conspirators to the Harlem conference, a conference, incidentally, which the Court said it doubted seriously had ever occurred.

The Court also criticized the manner in which the four chief prosecution witnesses were confined. "These four men (Rose, Vallon, Webber and Schepps) were engaged in a common undertaking of attempting to save their own lives by placing in forfeit that of Becker." The court's refusal to permit the defense to cross-examine the four men minutely on their opportunities for "fashioning a harmony of evidence by which they sought to convict him" was a grievous error.

In his instructions to the jury, the ruling noted, Judge Goff was scrupulous in defining the principles of law which govern the jury, but in his review of the case he outlined only the prosecution's claims, leaving to the jury's unaided memory the chore of recalling to what extent the defense had refuted them. Judge Goff made no reference, the Court concluded, to the defense's charge that the prosecution witnesses had, by their "harmony of evidence," revealed the perfection of their conspiracy rather than the extent of their truth.

Becker was taken from Sing Sing's death row, amid the hoarse cheers of his fellows in doom, and returned to the Tombs to await his second trial. Helen Becker was permitted to accompany him on the train. They were as happy as lovers on a picnic for they knew now it was only a matter of time before they could resume their lives.

"You've lost weight," she told him, crossly, her hand gently probing the hollows of his cheeks.

"You'll fatten me up," he replied, solemnly. Then he took her hand and kissed it.

23. Sabotage in the Electric Chair

IT WAS Warden James J. Clancy who took the news to Frank Cirofici, Jacob Seidensheiner, Louis Rosenberg and Harry Horowitz, who no longer wished to be called Dago Frank, Whitey Lewis, Lefty Louis and Gyp the Blood. Warden Clancy hated prisons and was so strongly opposed to the death penalty that he escaped attending an execution whenever he could. And when he could not, he was physically ill for days afterward; Warden Clancy was always resigning only to succumb to idealistic persuasions that he should remain in order to make Sing Sing a better place.

Warden Clancy left his office, his hands in his pockets, and walked disconsolately across the prison yard to the square rocklike structure of death row; the death house, it was called around the prison, a term which really referred to the smaller box-shaped appendage at the rear of the building containing the recently-invented electric chair. There were sixteen men in the death house now and Warden Clancy morosely reviewed the odds against any of them being spared by virtue of appeal, reprieve, commutation or some other miraculous avenue. The guard admitted him, softly wishing him good morning, and again at the inner door, another deferential greeting. He straightened his shoulders and quickened his pace, heading for the last four tiny cells in the row. Clancy stood on the far side of the corridor, midway in the row of cells, so that all four could see him.

"I'm sorry, boys," he said, looking down, "but the Court of Appeals has upheld your conviction."

He waited, bracing himself inwardly for a response. Instead, a run of sighs, a chain of stirrings behind the four heavy doors. It was strange how those doors were impervious even to sound, how they distorted it.

"That's all right," said Lefty, who was closest to him. "That's all right. We're not through yet." Clancy was somewhat reassured.

With its decision, the Court of Appeals had set a new execution date, April 13, 1914, Easter Monday. It was now the middle of February. Two more months of life.

Attorney Wahle, his eyes swollen with crying, visited his clients two days later. He had not exhausted all the possibilities; even now he was considering an appeal to the Federal courts on grounds his clients' constitutional rights had been violated. He was purposefully vague on this point, for it had just occurred to him. Lefty and Gyp tried to cheer him up, but it was hard. Wahle had not been able to escape from the families of the four youths. They descended on him almost daily, filling his office with crying young women and elderly men with cracking voices, and exhausted his time with pointless suggestions.

Whatever hopes the four doomed youths themselves nurtured, they were alone. Rabbi Jacob Goldstein, the Jewish chaplain, increased the frequency of his visits to Gyp, Lefty and Whitey, and Father William Cashin, the Catholic chaplain, was urgently redeeming Dago Frank to the fold. "He was born a Catholic," said Father Cashin emphatically, "and he'll die a Catholic."

During March, Wahle made two more futile appeals to the

courts, and the aura of doom settled more heavily on the chaplains and even the guards at Sing Sing. The four assassins had developed a likeable, cheery manner and they won considerable support and sympathy among prison officials. Their attitude was not one of bravado, but that of innocent men wronged who had the good grace to accept the perversities of fate.

On April 1, Wahle had an idea. Becker's second trial had been set for May 6, 1914, and if Becker were acquitted this time, it was not inconceivable that the case against Gyp, Dago, Lefty and Whitey would collapse too. He formally petitioned Governor Martin Glynn for a stay of execution pending the outcome of the Becker trial. Whitman raced to Albany to protest. The Becker case had nothing to do, legally, with that of the gunmen and a reprieve would imply official doubt to the minds of the public from which the Becker jury would be chosen. A reprieve would be prejudicial to justice. Not only that but, if Becker were acquitted this time, it might be politically ruinous to then insist the gunmen be executed.

Anticipating that Glynn would refuse the petition, Whitman sent Shapiro, the chauffeur, and Krese, the waiter, to Sing Sing to reidentify the four gunmen so that they could testify at Becker's trial that the four men executed had been the killers of Rosenthal. The stratagem was a notorious failure and it backfired. Lefty had been lying on his bed when Shapiro and Krese arrived. As the door of his cell was pulled open, Lefty looked up and saw Shapiro who had not yet focused into the cell. Lefty pulled a pillow over his head and warned the others. "It's that goddam chauffeur," he cried. An aide from Whitman's office, who had accompanied the two witnesses, dedemanded that Warden Clancy force Lefty to be identified. Clancy refused. Nor did he force Whitey from under his blanket, Dago from behind his bed, or Gyp from his embryonic crouch in the corner of the cell.

Wahle was outraged. He accused Whitman of exceeding by all rational bounds the authority of his office and he attacked

Warden Clancy for permitting the four youths to be subjected to "this cruel torture."

Clancy was stung by Wahle's words. "I have been a friend to these boys," he protested. "I did not force them to be identified. The district attorney's request, as presented to me, was not out of order."

Wahle did not forgive him, but the boys did. "Forget it," said Dago, generously, reaching through the door slit to pat Clancy on the shoulder.

Whitman struck back. He permitted the press to interview a new star witness, heretofore a secret one. He was a twenty-four-year-old East Side salesman, Jacob Goldman, who said he had been present with Jacob Luban in the Lafayette Baths and had heard Rose and Becker discussing Rosenthal's demise. He said that Becker's friends had kidnaped him during the trial and kept him prisoner in a hotel room to prevent him from testifying. Further, he declared, they had paid him fifty dollars a day to still his subsequent indignation. Vallon and Schepps joined in, too. They told reporters that Becker's agents made repeated attempts to bribe them not to testify.

On April 8, five days before the scheduled execution of Gyp, Lefty, Whitey and Dago, Governor Glynn refused to grant a stay.

Rabbi Goldstein hurried to the death house to comfort the boys. Father Cashin came soon afterward. Warden Clancy had already told them the news and then disappeared for two days. When he returned to the prison, he submitted his resignation again.

With all hope seemingly gone, a trainful of New York reporters came jogging up the Hudson to see how the boys were taking it. Rabbi Goldstein was glad to see them.

"I have spent the afternoon with these boys," he said, "and I am convinced they are innocent. In all my years as a prison chaplain, I have never seen such consistent claims of innocence. Instead of weakening their resolve, the approach of death only makes it stronger. I said to Louis Rosenberg (Lefty), 'Is

there anything you want to tell me before the time comes?'
And he said, 'Yes, Dr. Goldstein, there is. I am not guilty.' "

The following day, Rabbi Goldstein and four other rabbis,
all officials of the Union of Orthodox Jewish Congregations
in America, went to Albany to plead with Governor Glynn to
grant executive clemency.

Glynn, a portly, earnest man, received them in a sweat. He
paled and trembled as they opened their appeal by bowing
their heads in prayer. He fidgeted with a button on his vest as
they implored him to be merciful. He let the tears roll down
his ample cheeks, but he shook his head firmly.

"If I were to do what my heart tells me to do, I would stop
this execution. But it is not my heart to which I must listen, it
is the law. My nights are sleepless because of the knowledge
that I stand between these boys and death. But there is nothing I can do. It is the law."

"But there is new evidence," pleaded Rabbi Goldstein.

"Where is it?" cried the Governor in an agonized voice.
"Show it to me!"

"It will come out at the Becker trial," Goldstein replied.

Glynn shook his head again, wiped his eyes with a handkerchief and left the room. He retired to his own quarters in the
executive mansion and refused to see anyone for the remainder
of the day. When the sisters and mothers of Whitey and Frank
arrived for an audience, he would not see them. The number
of anonymous letters threatening him with death or worse if
he did not spare the young gunmen began to increase and Glynn
had the guard around the capitol doubled.

Glynn had also rejected Rabbi Goldstein's plea that the execution be postponed until after Passover so plans were made
for a private Passover feast on death row on Easter, the day preceding the execution. Dago had been invited but he declined.
He planned to take Communion on his way to the electric chair
the next morning and he would fast on Sunday.

On Friday morning, Lefty, Whitey and Gyp summoned Warden Clancy. They were prepared to "confess," they said, with

260

one condition: Dago was to be freed because he had not even been at the scene of the crime. Clancy relayed this offer to Governor Glynn who did not answer it.

On Friday evening, Attorney Wahle called at the home of Judge Goff at 310 West 104th Street with a motion for a new trial. He had affidavits from three witnesses, he said, two of whom had seen the Rosenthal murder and could identify the real killers, and a third man who had been at Dago Frank's home at 2:30 A.M. the day of the killing, and had seen Dago there, thus establishing that he could not have been at the Metropole. Judge Goff ordered a hearing for Saturday morning and summoned Whitman to show cause why a new trial should not be granted. He declined, however, to stay the execution.

The four gunmen let out shrieks of joy when Clancy brought them the news. They made no response when Clancy, moving the next morning on leaden feet, told them that Goff had denied Wahle's motion and dismissed the three witnesses as liars.

Lefty, the most literate of the four, was commissioned to pen a joint statement to the Governor, a direct plea.

"We know," Lefty wrote, "that the second Becker trial will prove that Vallon and Webber did it. You are the only human one who has the power on God's earth to listen to our plea. . . ."

Wahle, meanwhile, was doing what he could to comfort the sisters, brothers, mothers and fathers, all assembled in his office, weeping. At midnight, he caught a train for the prison.

At about the same time, a guard making his rounds of the death house, unlocked the door of the execution chamber and peered inside, drawn by morbid ruminations, apparently, for he had never checked it before. Spread over the floor of the chamber were the shattered pieces of the dynamo which created the lethal charge. There would be no execution as scheduled. The dynamo had been built especially for the prison and was the only one in existence. Warden Clancy put out a call for Edward C. Davis, the electrician for the State of

Massachusetts, the man who had invented the electric chair and Sing Sing's official executioner. He was finally found Sunday morning in New York. Informed by phone of the damage, he said it would take several days to repair. But shortly after noon he turned up at the prison with the parts to assemble a dynamo and by midnight he had built a new one. It was even better than the original. When he tested it he was pleased to discover it delivered in excess of the required 2500-volt charge swiftly and smoothly. The last obstacle had been removed. The wrecker of the dynamo, however, was never known. There were some who suspected the Warden.

On Saturday morning, the Reverend Burton Lee, an Episcopalian who was the prison's Protestant chaplain, arrived at the death house staggering under the weight of a gramophone and a selection of recordings, among them "Nearer, My God To Thee," and "Home Sweet Home" and "The Rosary." After less than a bar into the first tinny hymn, the Reverend Mr. Lee began to sing in a wavering baritone. Dago Frank, who had a clear tenor voice, drowned him out. Then the other three boys began to sing, too, and midway in the last chorus of "Home Sweet Home" three Chinese, waiting execution for killing a fellow countryman in a fan-tan dispute, had succumbed to the spiritual ground swell and had joined in. Then the Reverend Mr. Lee led a prayer service, suggesting that all the prisoners take part and fervent mumbling soon rumbled through the building. Looking about, the now over-wrought clergyman saw the guards standing in the background, ill at ease. He gestured them frantically to their knees. As he left the death house, the Reverend Mr. Lee heaved a soulful sigh and a sob or two. "It was a great hour," he said, when he had found his voice.

On Saturday afternoon, two Franciscan nuns from New York arrived and requested permission to see the boys. Warden Clancy let them in. Only one of the nuns spoke. "We came," she said, "to do what we could to help you. But there is more that you can do to help yourselves. Remember to let your deaths atone for all your sins." Then together the nuns sang three choruses of "Whispering Hope," in faltering harmony, and quietly departed. The objects of their comfort sobbed piteously.

On Sunday morning, Rabbi Goldstein presided at the special Passover Feast which had been prepared by a hotel at nearby Ossining. It consisted of:

Hudson River bass (stuffed)
Chicken soup and macaroons
Roast chicken
Mashed turnips
Matzos
Hard boiled eggs
Peaches

The three men ate slowly as though with each mouthful they were consuming time as well. Rabbi Goldstein bravely stuck it out to the end and then collapsed in tears in the Warden's office.

Meanwhile, the four youths had been taken from their cells to a shower room at the far end of the building. Whispers of encouragement issued from each cell as they shuffled past. Their clothes were taken from them and they were instructed to scrub themselves with laundry soap. In their absence, their cells were stripped of everything except beds. Emerging from the shower, they were given their death suits, dungarees and slip-over jackets, collarless, of a coarse black material. Their cells had been disinfected and they had to cope with the stench of creosote as well as the shock of losing, without warning, all their personal effects. The imminence of death hit.

Late in the afternoon, Warden Clancy came with the gramophone and recordings by a famous Warsaw cantor, G. Sirota. From their naked, smelly cells, the four boys stared dazedly at the spinning gramophone.

As Clancy turned to go, Dago called to him. Clancy went inside the cell, and sat on the bed next to him. Clancy announced the next day that Dago Frank had confessed. Dago himself had

263

had no part in the killing. He had not even been there. Rosenthal had been shot by Vallon and Gyp. Becker had nothing to do with it.

His composure regained, Rabbi Goldstein returned and spent the remainder of the day praying, comforting, listening to the mounting fears. Lefty showed him an anonymous letter, written in Yiddish, which he had received several days previously. It asked, "Why are you protecting Becker?"

"Are you?" asked the Rabbi.

"No, no," Lefty cried. "We're not guilty, not guilty. The truth is in the record of our trial."

To the Rabbi, each man uttered his last observations and sentiments.

"We are ready," said Lefty.

"Tell my Mama she is not the mother of a murderer," said Whitey.

"We don't expect any mercy from Goff or Whitman," said Gyp.

Dago said nothing.

Rabbi Goldstein, challenged by this vast impasse, pressed Lefty to confess. The only confession he got was a request that he relay to all youths of the East Side the admonition that they mind their parents and go to the Synagogue.

Throughout all New York that day, death in the electric chair had been the sermon subject of countless clergymen who denounced it, denounced Whitman, denounced Goff, denounced the Governor and declared that a "theistical" government was the only hope for mankind.

As night came, Goldstein left the death house, promising to return early in the morning. His vigil was taken up by Rabbi Koppstein, his assistant, and by Father Cashin, both of whom spent the night.

In Manhattan, 500 members of the East Side Peddler's Association met in wild and anguished session and amid hysterical fits of weeping adopted a resolution calling for a telegraphed plea of mercy to Governor Glynn. It arrived in Albany in a deluge of hundreds of others just like it.

Warden Clancy, on the verge of hysteria himself, left the prison and caught a train for New York, turning his duties over to Deputy Warden Charles Johnson who had yet to become emotionally embroiled.

Judge Goff had left town and could not be reached. Whitman, however, announced that he would keep a phone line open to the Warden's office at Sing Sing throughout the night.

Shortly after midnight, the forty-eight witnesses—twelve for each execution, as required by law—began to arrive along with four doctors who were not identified and who would perform the autopsies. The boys' brains were to be preserved for the advancement of science, it was solemnly announced. And, at the same time, guards noiselessly stacked the four plain pine coffins outside the death house door. Lefty's father, an aged, bearded little man in a black overcoat, arrived about 1 A.M., was taken to see his son. He faltered and collapsed at the death house entrance. "I can't go in there again," he wailed.

At 5:35 A.M., four guards came for Lefty who was to go first. When Dago heard them coming, he began to scream. They took him first, carrying him the length of the death house and on into the chamber, slitting his trouser leg and strapping him into the chair. He did not resist, but he seemed hysterically oblivious. Father Cashin had followed him all the way, his voice strident in prayer.

Lefty went next, stumbling but unaided. Whitey followed and Gyp came last. Whitey collapsed at the chamber entrance and had to be helped into the chair. In thirty-nine minutes, all four were dead.

The funerals for Gyp and Lefty were big and prolonged, in the traditions of the lower East Side. For three days, until the last body had been buried, the East Side teemed with people, milling aimlessly with an air of bewilderment and disbelief, strangers conducting wakes in numberless saloons. So heavy were the crowds outside the 184th Street home of Mrs. Cirofici, where her son lay in flower-enshrined grandeur for three days, that a squad of mounted policemen was dispatched to maintain order.

That same week, a Jewish magazine, *The American Hebrew*, assailed Rabbi Goldstein and his colleagues for meddling with justice, noting that the Catholics had organized no gubernatorial plea for Dago Frank. "If Jews are to demand equal rights in other matters, they must accept equal rights to punishment."

24. Give Becker a Fair Trial

BECKER'S SECOND TRIAL was set for May 2, three months after his first conviction had been reversed by the Court of Appeals. But no matter how much time he had, Whitman could never eliminate the one ugly defect in his case: the mercurial character of his witnesses. The legal flaws, minutely detailed by the Court of Appeals, were inherent in the nature of those upon whose testimony he must depend. Bald Jack Rose was the cornerstone of the case, yet his testimony was ripe with hatred. Vallon and Webber had been denounced by the court, by implication at least, as conspirators whose motives were clearly those of survival. Schepps could never be used again. Whitman knew now that the most compelling motives in the complex jungle of Broadway were survival and money and that in between there lay a dense fabric of expedient loyalties and relative truths; that objective truth as Whitman understood it did not exist.

Whitman did the only thing he could do in the late winter of 1914. He began to buy his witnesses. To reinforce the loyalties he could purchase he applied the consummate pressure of his office to judges, magistrates, policemen, politicians. He made lots of promises; promises he might not be able to keep unless he was elected governor. He accepted fresh donations from his friends and from the Society for the Prevention of Crime, the organization formed in the 1890's by the crusading reformer, the Reverend Dr. Charles Parkhurst. The society was the funnel through which private funds flowed into his office. Whitman played his witnesses as with a hand of poker. He arranged to have some of them released from jail, others put in jail, sentences suspended, revoked, postponed, and even lengthened. He dropped anyone even vaguely connected with the case into a complicated pressure cooker situation of his own making and when all else failed, he put them on his payroll as "confidential investigators." In this latter category were Sam Schepps (if he could not testify, he could still inform); Jacob and Morris Luban (the Court of Appeals had branded them perjurers but they possessed a vast amount of underworld knowledge); Harry Cohen, the taxi driver who denied the Harlem conference (at least the defense couldn't use him); Harry Pollok, in whose home Rose had hidden following the murder; J. L. Goldman, otherwise known as "Jake the Brick" because of his unruly red hair, the witness to the Lafayette Baths conference, the man who claimed Becker's friends had kidnaped him during the first trial; Louis Krese, the waiter, and three other men whose roles were never explained, who never testified, whose participation was revealed only by the appearance of their names on the expense vouchers Whitman submitted to the county for payment.

Whitman's claim on all these people became a proprietary one. In addition to paying them about $25.00 a week plus expenses, he also bought their clothes and paid their doctor bills —or, rather, the County of New York did, in sums totaling approximately $10,000. Whatever he thought about the ethics of this, Whitman did not keep it a secret. However, he also received substantial funds for investigation from the Society for the Prevention of Crime. One official estimated that the society had relayed to Whitman amounts which, over a period of five years, must have approached $200,000. Much of this went to William J. Burns and his squad of private eyes.

It was apparent that the forces of reform were united behind Whitman and that they all regarded the Becker case as the goal of the great crusade. Becker's second trial, in fact, was Whitman's last chance. His campaign for governor was gathering momentum and to lose Becker could be to lose it all. At the outset, the odds were against him. The Court of Appeals had excoriated the character of his witnesses, making them even less palatable to a jury. Becker's position was not much better from this standpoint, but his strategy of defense had been plotted for him by the Court's ruling. Further, public outrage had ebbed considerably in the sixteen months since the first trial and the spectacle of the gunmen's execution had served to some extent to satiate whatever popular lust there was for blood.

These factors were a subject of intense speculation and appraisal not only by Whitman, and Becker, but by all the forces the case symbolized. Whatever happened, the age of the freewheeling gunman was gone. Their exposure as a result of Becker had made them an object of hatred and politicians hesitated to use them henceforth. The body of corruption was still alive in the police department, but the word was out that the gangster was not to benefit thereby. Mayor Mitchel had revoked the famous dictum, issued by Mayor Gaynor to whom police brutality was repugnant above all else, that policemen were not to use their billy clubs unless in deadly peril. Mitchel freed the billy from this restraint and gangsters' heads were being split all over the East Side. Between the politicians' rejection and the resurgence of the billy, the gunman was driven back into the slums to await a fresh call for his talent. However, this did not eliminate the element of fear that still influenced the behavior of prosecution witnesses.

Whitman decided, in the end, to cling to his original formula of prosecution. His reason was both expedient and logical. It was familiar to everyone and he had endowed it with his own beliefs in its validity. All it needed was a substitution of ingredients. As the corroborator of the murder plot, he would use a witness obviously clear of all entanglements. His name was James Marshall, a 22-year-old Negro tap dancer of doubtful talent. He had once served Becker as a stoolie and that accounted for his presence at, and observations of, the Harlem conference. He turned out to be one of the worst witnesses but Whitman knew the risks and, anyway, he had no choice. The Harlem conference was the key link in the conspiracy to rub out Herman Rosenthal. The Court of Appeals had termed it the foundation of the State's case.

As soon as Becker had been returned to the Tombs, the district attorney maintained a profound silence, although there were obvious leaks. The newspapers, alert to the drama of a bad man fighting twice for his life, pressed Whitman relentlessly for official comment and when it was not forthcoming they made their own. For days, stories about the Tenderloin being assessed to raise Becker's new defense fund filled the front pages. They were only partly true. The underworld was not assessed directly. The Tammany hierarchy paid the bills and then went about recovering the investment. The effect was bad either way. It renewed Becker's link with organized evil.

Becker was also interviewed. He sat on the edge of his bunk in his old cell at the Tombs, merrily puffing a cigar. He was pale, thin and gaunt, but irrepressibly elated.

"I feel like a free man already," he said. "I know I'll win this time. There is no case against me. And when I am free, the first thing I'm going to do is hunt down the real murderers. The man who actually did the killing is Vallon. I'm sure of that."

Helen Becker was with him every day. They gave the appearance of a young couple planning a honeymoon, instead of a half-doomed man mapping a fight for life. The school had given Mrs. Becker a leave of absence until after the trial.

To defend Becker, McIntyre had neither the strength nor the desire. And Becker didn't really want him. Further, it had been decided that his reappearance was bad strategy. His successor was chosen after agonizing debates between Becker, his wife, his faithful old attorney John Hart, and a nameless minion of Tammany who would hurry back to Tom Foley and Florrie Sullivan and report the sentiment. The ultimate choice was a good one. W. Bourke Cockran, an ex-judge, a vigorous, hulking man with highly developed talents as a spellbinder. He was close enough to Tammany to understand the complexities of his assignment, but far enough away to avoid the taint. He had, however, the misfortune to have paid tribute earlier to Whitman, in an unguarded public utterance, as the saviour of New York.

Judge Goff was out of the picture. Whitman was afraid the angry old jurist, if he tried the case again, would remain a hazard to a legally supportable conviction. The case was assigned to Justice Samuel Seabury whose background in exposing crime rivalled that of Goff, but who was by nature a more temperate man. He had been chief counsel for a 1904 legislative probe of New York and the scandal-scouring inquiry came to bear his name.

The trial opened on May 2, 1914, in the same setting with the same general cast of characters. Judge Seabury had summoned 500 prospective jurors and it was four days before Cockran and Whitman could agree to twelve men who conceivably hadn't made up their minds. On the last day, the New York Globe, impatient to capture a scoop, took a chance and prematurely printed an extra that the jury had been selected. Newsboys were hawking it outside the courtroom while the struggle to find the last juror was still going on. Worse, the paper had printed Whitman's opening remarks to the jury, an address he had had the foresight to distribute to the press in advance. Cockran cried for a mistrial but Judge Seabury refused. Instead he fined the Globe, its managing editor, city editor and a reporter $250 each for contempt of court.

Cockran had also moved for dismissal on grounds the evidence was insufficient to support the indictment, and when that was denied he asked for a change of venue, contending an im-

271

partial jury could not, in all reality, be found in the City of New York. Judge Seabury denied that too and the trial finally began.

Someone else was missing, too; Frank Moss, the bearded, brilliant young inquisitor who had borne the weight of courtroom drudgery in the first trial. He and Whitman had had personal differences, it was said, and Moss had resigned. Neither would dicuss this sudden separation but Moss's friends said he could no longer accept Whitman's relentless preoccupation with Becker.

Seabury had no fear of the pathetic sight of the faded Helen Becker corroding the jury's good judgment and she sat in the first row of the gallery, immediately behind her husband with whom she exchanged urgent, affectionate glances. The courtroom, as before, was occupied largely by newspapermen, city officials and off-duty policemen, all of whom were admitted before the public was allowed to take the few remaining seats. One additional seat became available as Whitman began his opening remarks to the jury. A tall, young man seated near the rear, later identified as a municipal clerk, arose quickly, shook his fist at Whitman and shouted, "It's a frame-up. Whitman will never be elected governor with a case like this." He was removed with unnecessary force by two husky bailiffs.

If Whitman had been driven by ruthless determination at the first trial, he was now ruthlessly methodical. No ambivalence would be permitted to develop in the jury's minds, there would be no more legal vagaries. It was a simple case.

Yet, to the optimistic Becker as he watched the furrowed faces in the jury box and heard the sonorous pronouncements of the district attorney, there was something hopefully repetitious about it all.

". . . the real murderer of Herman Rosenthal, the real criminal of them all, is the man who on the 16th of July in the year 1912 was a lieutenant of police in the city of New York.

". . . This assassination was planned by the defendant to

halt the arm of the law in the uncovering of criminal conditions in this city . . .

"I don't represent Rosenthal's heirs. I represent the people of New York County. *They* are my clients. And the people of New York claim that this defendant *Becker* [he spat the name out, like a distasteful oath], notwithstanding that he was not at the murder scene and notwithstanding that Rose, Webber and Vallon, too, were guilty, is the real murderer of Herman Rosenthal."

Well, that was what he said before, and he had lost. What was new about this trial? The chain of witnesses was the same; the ambulance surgeon, the police medical examiner, Louis Krese, the waiter who said he had seen the killing, who had identified three of the gunmen. Cockran did not cross-examine. There was no reason to. Krese had not implicated Becker. He had only testified that a man had been shot and killed in front of the Hotel Metropole at about 1:50 A.M. on July 16, 1912. The defense would concede that. Smiles of confidence broke at day's end on the faces of Cockran and Becker and the rest of the defense staff, John Johnstone, a promising young criminal lawyer and Martin Manton, a colleague of Hart's who had stepped in to assist Cockran at the last minute. There was another lawyer at the defense table and his presence carried uncertain connotations; Hartford T. Marshall who had once been Bridgie Webber's lawyer. There were frowns of concern the next morning when Whitman summoned chauffeur Shapiro to testify. He had been kept out of the first trial for fear, Whitman had explained, that he would be rubbed out. Now there was no fear. Shapiro was uncomfortable, his eyes shifting constantly in an effort to escape Becker's stares. But after half an hour, Shapiro had made ony one new revelation. Was it a mistake? He said that Schepps rode to the Metropole from Webber's poker parlor. Whitman let it pass.

"What, if anything, did you hear said in the car as you were driving to the Metropole?"

"I heard them say, 'Becker has the cops fixed; everything is all right.' "

Manton cross-examines. A man of dignity and restraint. His questions are dispassionately delivered, a contrast that quickens the jury's attention.

"Do you remember when you testified during the gunmen's trial that you said it was Frank [Dago Frank] who said, 'Becker has the cops fixed?' Now you say you don't know who it was. Just somebody in the car."

Shapiro blinks and shrugs.

"I don't remember what I said at the trial."

"How is that? If you cannot remember what happened a few months ago at the trial, how can you remember what happened the night of the murder?"

No answer.

"Do you remember saying to Mr. Marshall, one of the counsel for the defense, when he spoke to you in the West Side Prison, that it was Vallon who struck you on the head with a gun?"

"That's not true. Mr. Marshall wanted me to say that."

The score at this point, Becker tells Cockran, is still no better than fifty-fifty.

Another performance by Bald Jack Rose is inescapable. He takes the stand, groomed to perfection, his skull as pale as ever, but his manner is detached. He gives no sign that he had ever seen or heard Becker before. His testimony has a distant quality, as though he were no longer involved. As he is sworn in, he gives his occupation as that of "lecturer." There are snickers around the courtroom.

The story sounds the same. He is led into it by Whitman and, with Judge Seabury's consent, and over Cockran's objections, he is allowed to deliver, virtually without interruption, the whole narrative. It sounds the same, but it also sounds different; especially the part about when Becker sent him to Rosenthal to collect $1,500 for the defense of the press agent, Plitt. Didn't he say the first time that the amount sought was $500?

Now it is $1,500. Then, too, there is the part about Harry Cohen, the chauffeur, who allegedly drove him to the Harlem conference. He had not mentioned Cohen's name at the first trial. He shrugs at this discrepancy and at his failure during the first trial to testify that James Marshall, the colored boy, came up and spoke to Becker at the Harlem meeting. Had Mr. Whitman instructed him to change his testimony? Manton asks.

Rose admits readily, almost wearily, that he has known Zelig's gunmen for years, that they frequented the clubs in which he was interested, that he often employed them. He does not evade when Manton asks about his confinement in the West Side Prison together with Vallon and Webber and, later, Schepps. They were together constantly, Rose says, they were given freedom of the jail, except at night when they were locked in separate cells. Manton asks:

"Do you remember waiting for your lawyer in the counsel room, with Jack Sullivan, and Sullivan asked you what you were going to do and you said, 'Whitman doesn't want us, he wants Becker. I'm going to give him Becker.' Do you remember that?"

"No."

"And then your lawyers came in and Sullivan was still swearing at you; he called you 'a bald-headed SOB.' Do you remember?"

"It never happened."

There has been some variety in his testimony, but it is hard to assess its effect on the jury. Rose is no longer in danger of prosecution himself, perhaps some of his incentive is gone. Becker's fate is meaningless to him now, he has only his vanity to consider.

Bridgie Webber and Harry Vallon testified the same day. They had been bitter enemies for several months and would not acknowledge each other's presence in court. It was said they had had a dispute about money matters and that Vallon had attempted to foreclose a mortgage on an upstate farm owned by one Charles Webber, Bridgie's brother.

Webber told the court he was now manufacturing paper boxes in Passaic, New Jersey. His testimony otherwise was tediously familiar until Manton cross-examined him.

Q. Did you not think you were doing a terrible thing when you told the gunmen Rosenthal was at the Metropole?
A. Yes, sir. I didn't stop to think.
Q. After Becker's last trial, you became remorseful?
A. I have been remorseful ever since.
Q. You would not have come from New Jersey if Mr. Whitman had not gone over to persuade you?
A. I wanted to forget about the Becker case.

Vallon and Webber passed each other midway in the court-room floor. They did not speak, or nod. Whatever their animosity for each other, Webber had given the defense no chance to drive a wedge between them.

Vallon's story bore no apparent changes. The only hope for fresh revelation was with Manton's cross-examination.

Q. When you got to Webber's the night of the murder, did you know Rosenthal was to be killed?
A. No. Not that night.
Q. Were you perfectly sober?
A. Oh, yes.
Q. Didn't you tell Commissioner Dougherty when you were arrested that you were drunk the night of the murder?
A. I don't remember.
Q. You went to the Metropole first, didn't you?
A. No.
Q. Didn't you ask Commodore Dutch to look in the window and see if Rosenthal was there?
A. No.
Q. Didn't you see Beebe there and ask the same of him? And didn't Beebe tell you to get your own messenger boy?
A. I wasn't there.

Manton poked around in Vallon's background, but all it produced were Vallon's denials that he knew people named Sheeney Mike, Sheeney Sarah, Flabby Annie or Viola, or that he had a team of pickpockets working Madison Avenue.

Commissioner Dougherty testified that on July 18, 1912, Becker denied having seen Rose for five days.

"Did you tell Becker you were trying to find Rose?" Manton asked him.

Dougherty dropped his eyes for a moment.

"No," he said.

George Young, a phlegmatic, hefty man, secretary to Dougherty, said Becker told him on July 18 where Rose was hiding.

And so the trial went, a series of inconclusive contradictions.

The most uncomfortable witness was Otto Aversi, ex-chauffeur for Becker's friend, Col. Otto Sternberger, who testified to having driven Becker home from Madison Square Garden the night of the murder. Manton asked him:

"Did Whitman or his assistants threaten you with an indictment in another matter if you refused to testify that you drove Becker through 43d Street the night of the murder?"

Aversi searches for Whitman's eyes, but they are not available.

"Yes, sir."

"Did he also ask you to testify that Becker said if he saw Rosenthal he would shoot him himself?"

"He asked me in a way, yes, sir."

Charles Plitt may have been Becker's press agent once, but he took the stand for the State. He saw Becker in the police station the day after the murder. Becker, he said, asked him, "What the hell was the matter with that bunch? Were they all cockeyed drunk? The way they pulled that trick you'd think they were setting the stage for a motion picture show."

In the train to Sing Sing, Plitt testified he talked to Becker alone in the men's room and gave him a drink of whiskey. "We both clasped arms in tears. He asked me to kill Rose if anything happened to him."

Plitt had not testified in the first trial. Manton pursued this.

"You were under indictment for perjury in the civil suit brought against you in connection with the killing of Waverly Carter in a raid by Becker. What happened to that indictment?"

"It was dismissed."

"Why?"

"I don't know."

"Isn't it true that Mr. Whitman's office had it dismissed in return for your testimony here?"

"No."

"Do you remember testifying before the grand jury?"

"I think so."

There is a sheaf of papers in Mr. Manton's hand.

"Is this your testimony?"

"I think so."

It is allowed as evidence and Manton reads it, a long and awkward document. In it, Plitt accuses the New York *World* of being responsible for Becker's plight and he accuses the district attorney's office of bribing witnesses against Becker. Whitman, he describes as "that old fizzle and jury fixer."

"How much money did the district attorney's office pay you?"

"Thirty dollars."

"Just thirty dollars?"

"Thirty dollars a week."

"For how long?"

"Ten weeks."

The last link in the chain Whitman was forging to shackle Becker to the Rosenthal killing was the Harlem conference. It was the key. It was the only evidence that Becker had ever met with the three conspirators before the killing. There was the Lafayette Baths meeting, when Becker was supposed to have nagged Rose about the delay in the assassination, but the Court of Appeals had branded as perjury the only testimony Whitman had to corroborate Rose, that of Morris Luban. Jake Goldman, alias Jake the Brick, whose alleged presence at the bath huddle had been widely publicized, was not called to testify. There was no explanation, except that the defense could easily link Goldman with Luban. They were known to be friends. It was the Harlem meeting or nothing. To prove this conspiracy, Whitman had only the testimony of James Marshall, the twenty-two-year-old Negro dancer who had worked for Becker three months as a stool pigeon. A tall and gangly boy, whose face was a variety of expressions—sleepy mouth, dancing eyes— shuffled onto the stand as the last witness for the State.

He told of his work for Becker and how, on that June night, he had been given money by Becker to enter a poker game in Harlem. He was to leave the game when it was at its peak and meet Becker as the signal for the raid.

Whitman conducted the examination.

Q. You saw Becker before the raid?
A. Yes, sir. At Seventh Avenue and 124th Street. On the corner by a vacant lot.
Q. Was he alone?
A. No, sir. There was a man speaking with him and a man standing a little way off from him.
Q. Have you seen the man you say was talking with him since?
A. Yes, sir.
Q. Who was the man you saw talking with Lieutenant Becker?
A. Jack Rose.
Q. How close were you to Jack Rose?
A. I touched his sleeve.
Q. What did you do then?
A. I went to meet Officers Steinhart and White who were going to make the raid.
Q. Who were the other officers with them?
A. Shepherd and Rice.

It was quick, positive and convincing. Manton cross-examined.

Q. Did you know it was Jack Rose that night?
A. No. Not until I seen his picture in the paper.
Q. Have you seen him since?
A. Only once. When Officer Maxwell took me to identify him.
Q. You have only seen Rose once before in your life, then. That night in Harlem?
A. Yes, sir.

Cockran tried to gauge the effect of Marshall's story. It was either a failure or it was a deft piece of legal surgery that had laid open a sweeping wound in the defense's case; a wound that would continue to enlarge itself in the jury's mind. Neither Marshall's face nor his manner had revealed anything. He could be telling the truth, or he could be lying. One had the feeling it was all the same to Marshall.

Becker made a feeble plea to Cockran to be allowed to take the stand himself. Cockran brushed the suggestion aside. His reasoning was the same as McIntyre's had been. Graft had not been mentioned. If Becker testified, Whitman could ask him almost anything. Legally, Becker's silence did not prejudice him. It may have been a bad decision, but it seemed to Cockran like the lesser of two inescapable hazards.

The blustery Jacob Reich, alias Jack Sullivan, King of the Newsboys, remained Becker's star witness. Outraged, expansive and angry, Sullivan shouted his charges that Rose, Webber, and Vallon had staged a dirty frame-up to save their own hides, and he added one new bit of nasty information. When he met Webber several hours after the murder, Webber was elated to the point of glee. "I am the happiest man in the world," he quoted Webber as saying. "That sonofabitch Rosenthal is dead."

Q. Were you also indicted for the Rosenthal murder?
A. Yes. I sure was. They framed me too.
Q. What happened to the indictment?
A. I don't know.

Q. Have you been tried?

A. No.

Q. Are you still in jail?

A. No. I spent eight and a half months in jail and they never tried me and they never dismissed the indictment.

Sullivan said he spoke to Webber after being released from jail and that Webber said he was going down to his lawyer and sign an affidavit that Becker was innocent. He met Webber several days later and the gambler was downcast. Sullivan said Webber told him:

"My lawyer told me I am a self-confessed murderer and that my affidavit wouldn't be worth the paper it was written on. I wish I was dead. My wife keeps hounding me. She calls me a murderer."

Cross-examined by Whitman, Sullivan was testy, impudent and evasive.

"Isn't it true that for many years you have provided bail bonds for prostitutes who are arrested?" (Whitman was speaking from experience.)

"You would ask me that!"

For the rest, the defense pounded away with witnesses like Isadore Fishman, a bankrupt leather goods manufacturer, Broadway character and friend of the three informers. "Vallon told me afterward that they were sorry for Becker but they had to do it to save themselves."

Then there was Charles Reich, brother of Jack Sullivan, a composing room foreman on the *Globe*. He said that when he went to the West Side Prison to visit his brother, Rose urged him to persuade Sullivan to corroborate them.

Morris Beecher, a gray, gravel-voiced lawyer, testified that it was at his office at 301 Broadway that Webber admitted to Sullivan they had framed Becker and that he would like to undo it all.

Roslyn Whytock of the *World* and James Rooney of the *Globe* testified Webber told them in a shipboard interview on

281

his return from Havana that Becker had nothing to do with the murder. (When this appeared in print, Webber had gone immediately to Whitman's office where he signed an affidavit denying it.)

Whitman cross-examined Whytock and after several minutes, it became apparent that discrepancies between several newsmen's versions of an interview do not constitute evidence.

For each blow the defense scored, Whitman was able to soften it; as in the testimony of James Moloney, a Tombs jailer, who swore Shapiro confided to him that it was Vallon and Schepps who rode away from the Metropole on the getaway. Whitman asked him:

Q. How many conversations did you have with Shapiro?
A. Just one.
Q. The one to which you have just testified?
A. That's right.
Q. Do you expect the jury to believe that Shapiro confided in you to that extent in just one conversation?
A. I guess so.

Fred Hawley, the reporter who was fired by the *Sun* for his testimony in the first trial, repeated it. He had been with Becker from 3 A.M. to 7 A.M. the morning of the killing and there had been no meeting with Jack Rose or Bridgie Webber.

Two attorneys testified in quick succession. They were Michael Delagi and Lewis Abrams, both of whom had defended press agent Plitt in his murder trial, the trial for which Rose claimed Becker was raising a defense fund. The two lawyers said they had been appointed by the court to defend the penniless Plitt, that the only fee they received was $500, which was paid by the State. Becker, they said, paid them nothing.

Police officers Joseph Shepherd, John Shields and Francis Rice testified to the Harlem poker raid. Marshall was there, all right, they said, and he did talk with Becker. But there was no sign of Jack Rose or anybody else. (Will one working cop always stand behind another working cop?)

Deputy Sheriffs Kearn Carroll and Thomas Winters, who escorted Becker to Sing Sing, testified they were with Becker constantly, that he was never alone in the men's room, that there was no conversation with Plitt, as Plitt had testified.

Cockran sought to introduce as evidence the pre-execution confession of Dago Frank to Father Cashin, the Sing Sing chaplain, that Becker was innocent. Judge Seabury refused to admit it. Such a statement, he ruled, did not qualify under the laws of evidence as a "dying declaration."

Dollar John Langer, the saloonkeeper who hated Becker, found it safe to return from Canada but he never came near the trial. Reporters sought him out in his saloon one otherwise desultory afternoon and chatted with him about the case. Langer's sentiment for Becker was widely known and because of it reporters thought his comments were especially newsworthy if, as it turned out, puzzling.

"It's strange," said Dollar John, "that they don't get the real killer of Rosenthal. He's walking around a free man. There are at least eight men in New York who know who he is."

As the last day of the trial neared, the defense decided that Manton's performance had earned him the right to sum up, to weave the pieces of rebuttal together clearly and logically, to help the jury separate the valid denial from the spurious accusation.

Manton lowered his voice to command attention and concentration and he began.

"Rose," he whispered, "the obvious liar. In the first trial, he said it was $500 he was instructed to collect from Rosenthal to defend Plitt. This time, it is $1,500. Why did he change? Because of the prosecution's remembering that the lawyers who defended Plitt were available to testify that Becker paid them nothing!"

For the rest, Manton's summation is a series of well-aimed punches.

"Marshall, the colored boy. He had never seen Rose before in his life, he did not speak to him, he only came near him in the dark of night, his mind on something else. He has never seen him since except when the district attorney arranged an identification meeting. On the face of his testimony, and that of three self-confessed murderers, you are asked to condemn the word of three police officers whose pasts, you can be sure, were raked from birth by the district attorney in an effort to discredit them.

"Why was Marshall clothed, fed and housed in a fine hotel at the State's expense?

"Why wasn't Moe Levy, or Harry Cohen, the cab driver, produced? He can testify as to whether he ever drove Rose or Webber or Vallon to the Harlem meeting. Is it because he will deny it?

"Jack Sullivan. Why did he stick to the truth? Confronted with the greatest temptation. Indicted for murder, he is offered freedom and money to lie. Why did he refuse? Because he is a truthful man.

"Please recall Plitt's testimony. He was Becker's friend until he got into trouble and he could save himself only by becoming Becker's enemy. Can you believe that those deputy sheriffs would allow a doomed man to go to the washroom alone?

"Remember this, gentlemen of the jury, the men who accuse Lieutenant Becker would be on trial for muder had they not accused Lieutenant Becker. And the only corroboration of their desperate testimony comes from a little colored boy whose only motive is that he was paid, fed, clothed and housed by the district attorney; a little colored boy who was once a police informer, a man who betrays others for pay."

Whitman fired the State's last salvo himself. He reached deep into his heart for his words and no one could doubt that he spoke the truth.

"They told a great many lies, the defense did, but when they

284

said that I wanted Becker they did not lie. Of course I wanted Becker. I did not want the little chap, I wanted the man who is really responsible for crime. . . .

"Rosenthal was in a position to give us information which would have led to the indictment and conviction of Becker. To Becker and to no one else was the death of Rosenthal of prime importance, outweighing all else. No one else had any real motive to kill Rosenthal. A gambler's war? Did they show it? The gamblers did not fear Rosenthal, there was nothing he could do to them. The only thing the gamblers fear is the ill-will of the policeman who allows them to exist. By murdering Rosenthal, Becker fulfilled his obligation to the criminals to whom he was giving protection and he eliminated the only threat to his own power and success. . . .

"Do not ask me why he arranged a murder in such a clumsy fashion. I can only say that Becker's power had reached such proportions that he felt he could do anything. . . .

"James Marshall would have testified at the first trial if we could have found him. We knew only that a little colored boy had witnessed the Harlem meeting. We didn't know who he was. And when we found him, he was Becker's own stool pigeon. Is that a frame-up?"

Cockran, prior to beginning the defense, had submitted a motion for dismissal for lack of evidence. It was denied. Now he submitted a motion for a directed verdict of acquittal for the same reason. It was denied. The next day, May 22, 1914, Judge Seabury instructed the jury. He skillfully avoided the pitfalls into which Judge Goff had fallen and his admonitions were minimal. The jury went out immediately after lunch and returned in exactly one hour and fifty minutes. Becker and the defense had not left the court. The accused man spent most of the time talking to his wife, patting her hands, and reassuring her. Cockran said he did not see how the jury could convict. But as the jury filed in, it was obvious from their heavy tread and downcast expressions that they had.

Mrs. Becker fainted. Becker himself was stunned. He was

285

remanded to the sheriff pending sentencing a week later and hustled over the Bridge of Sighs to the Tombs. He was sentenced to die the week of July 6, 1914, and taken to Sing Sing the same day by car. Mrs. Becker was not permitted to accompany him. She stood at the heavily guarded Tombs doorway and watched her husband, shackled and handcuffed, as guards half-carried him to the waiting car. There was no crowd this time.

Within days, Cockran withdrew from the case. Mrs. Becker had no more money with which to continue to retain him. To Manton, she gave Becker's house in Queens in lieu of his fee. Most of Becker's funds were exhausted and Mrs. Becker knew she would need every penny that remained.

As the doomed Becker faded from the front pages, Whitman emerged upon them. The press hailed his reconviction of Becker and followed the district attorney attentively as he stumped the state with restraint in the prelude to his campaign for the governorship. His fervor for gangbusting and graft exposing was bound to suffer and spasmodic complaints about his sudden indifference to evil began to appear in letters-to-the-editor columns. Whitman had not lost his zeal for righteousness, he had simply rechanneled it. Now he was attacking the immorality of political campaign expenses; the man who had the most money to spend, he said, stood the best chance of winning. He proposed in speeches at Dartmouth, at the convention of the League for Religious Education, that campaign expenses of candidates be borne by the state, with candidates limited to a predetermined budget. He also said he would run for governor with or without the support of the Republican Party. At about the same time that Mrs. Becker gave her Queens real estate to her attorney, Whitman acquired a modest summer home at Newport. It, too, was a gift; from New York socialite Arthur Curtiss James.

Whitman's speechmaking increased in tempo and variety; from the Alumni dinner at Amherst, to a Republican fund-raising dinner; from the Friendly Sons of St. Patrick banquet to the laying of a YMCA cornerstone in Brooklyn; from preach-

ing the evils of civil service regulations to the members of the
Lotos Club to warning of the evils of military politics to members of the National Guard Convention. To those attending the
annual dinner of New York's Hungarian Republican Club,
Whitman lamented the annoyances of coping with patronage
seekers. It was a chore, he said, that the officeholder's political
party could help render. Actually, Whitman had little trouble
finding rostrums; he was, after all, a national celebrity. Whitman gave his support to women's suffrage, too, and when the
Republicans began looking about for their candidate they
really couldn't see anybody but Whitman, and as their hero, he
swept them all into Albany on November 3, 1914. Whitman's
own victory was a landslide. He defeated the incumbent Governor Martin Glynn of Tammany, by more than 130,000 votes.
Crowds jammed the street outside Whitman's home at 37
Madison Avenue and at 7 P.M., his victory assured, the new
governor and his wife emerged sedately into the throng of cele-
brants, stepped into a taxi and jogged leisurely uptown to dinner.

Times Square was a solid mass of people, cheering the election of a hero. Police banned all auto and horse traffic from the
Square (none could get through anyway) and issued dizzying
estimates to the press as to the size of the crowd. Women and
elderly men were fainting on the sidewalk in front of the
Times Building where the continual posting of election returns attracted the densest crowd. As each new return was
hung, and Whitman's winning margin widened, a deafening
cheer went up. Pinned in this human crush, and yet oblivious
of it, was a knot of Belgian and French refugees. They were
standing at an adjoining window, reading the flow of bulletins
describing the progress of the German juggernaut through
Belgium and France. There was a war on.

Whitman's only comment on his triumph was, "The election speaks for itself."

Generally, the press interpreted it as a firm rebuke to Tammany, to the selfishly ambitious Hearst, to Teddy Roosevelt

and the anachronistic Bull Moose philosophy, and even to President Woodrow Wilson for accepting the support of Tammany.

"The Democrats have been beaten," declared an editorial in the *World*, "because they have tolerated Charlie Murphy as their boss. Murphyism has broken the back of the Democratic Party in New York State."

The other papers, except for Hearst's, echoed this in varying forms, all of them hailing "the restoration of Republicanism." As far as Tammany's rejection was concerned, there was some obvious truth in it. William Sulzer, the impeached Tammany governor, had run on his own behalf and polled almost 100,000 votes. He trailed the field, but to him this support was pure vindication of his unjust ejection two years earlier from Albany.

Charlie Murphy read the editorial judgments and when reporters sought him out, he shrugged. "The people have spoken," he said. "They will doubtless speak again."

25. The Character of an Innocent Man

ON FEBRUARY 12, 1915, nine months after Becker's conviction, James Marshall, the key corroborating witness, was dragged into a Philadelphia police station after being arrested for beating his wife. The woman's angry denunciations of her husband to the desk sergeant attracted the attention of two reporters, one from the Philadelphia *Ledger*, the other from the *Telegraph*. Mrs. Marshall turned on them.

"You know my husband," she shouted. "He's the man what told all them lies about that policeman in New York."

The reporters, James Fenerty and James McGovern, looked at each other.

"What's your name?" Fenerty asked Marshall, who told him.

"Were you a witness in the Becker case?"

Marshall admitted he was.

"Your wife says you lied on the stand."

Marshall nodded.

"I only did what the district attorney made me do."

Fenerty phoned his city editor who promptly wired Manton's office. Manton sent his associate, Philip Johnstone, to Philadelphia and, accompanied by the two reporters, took

Marshall before U. S. Commissioner Howard Long. In the meantime, his admission of perjury was the lead story on the front page of the *Ledger* now on the street.

To Commissioner Long, Marshall gave a long and wordy affidavit in which he said that Whitman's men had tracked him down in Washington, D. C., had shown him false gambling affidavits he had given as a stoolie for Becker and threatened to jail him for perjury if he did not testify as requested against Becker. Marshall said he did as he was told; that he was kept in the custody of the district attorney's men who moved him from New York to Philadelphia to Washington to Richmond to keep him away from Becker's agents. Altogether, he swore, the district attorney's office paid him $250 plus all his expenses from April 11, 1914, until the trial ended on May 22. He said he did not know who was talking to Becker that night in Harlem, that he never noticed.

Marshall was anxious to get to New York to get away from his wife, to see his mother, and to get some new bookings from his agent. He readily accepted Johnstone's invitation to amplify his admissions of perjury before Manton and, Johnstone hoped, before Judge Seabury. Once in New York, Marshall's resolve left him. He refused to talk to anybody except his mother and insisted he be permitted to telephone her.

Whitman's office, meanwhile, had heard about Marshall's indiscretions and Assistant District Attorney Frederick Groehl was sent to Marshall's mother's house to find out where the dancer was. He arrived just as Marshall phoned. Groehl got on the phone, telling Marshall to keep his mouth shut. Groehl notified his office and detectives were sent to bring Marshall in. He immediately signed another affidavit stating that he was drunk when he signed the Philadelphia affidavit and did not know what he was saying; that his testimony in the Becker trial was the truth.

Manton took the first Marshall affidavit before Justice Thomas Weeks of the New York Supreme Court in a motion for a new trial. Whitman submitted the second Marshall affidavit in rebuttal and the hearing became a legal debate. Manton lost it.

Becker's appeal was still pending before the Court of Appeals. Manton argued the appeal in Albany on March 24. He seemed confident that the Court would find, as the previous Court had found, that the corroboration of the alleged conspiracy to murder Rosenthal was not credible. But it was a different court and the fact that Marshall was not involved in the conspiracy, even remotely, altered the relationship of the witnesses. The Court upheld Becker's conviction on May 26. Its ruling noted that Vallon, in both trials, had testified as to the presence of a "little colored boy" at the Harlem meeting. Marshall was in fact there. Vallon could not have known this unless he himself was there too. In other words, the informers and Marshall were corroborating each other.

In its ruling, the Court said:

"We desire that the views which led us to affirm this judgment shall be made unmistakably clear. Doubtless, a very strong argument can be made in favor of the defendant, based upon the inducement of the avowed accomplices to swear falsely, their opportunity to fabricate evidence, and the lack of conclusiveness in the corroboration. All of this, however, was a question for the jury in whose determination we are not justified in interfering unless it was plainly wrong. . . .

"It is not our duty to try the case again upon the printed record. We have not seen the witnesses. We are deprived of the aid furnished by their appearance, demeanor, facial expression and manner of testifying. These advantages the jury enjoyed, and there being sufficient evidence in quality and quantity to take the case to the jury, their verdict, in the absence of any of the statutory grounds for reversal, is conclusive even upon the Court of Appeals."

Manton submitted a motion to reargue the case but the Court denied it.

What avenues were left for Becker? He had less than two months in which to do anything. His execution had been set now for July 12.

The Tammany hierarchy, which had sunk a considerable amount of money in Becker's defense, pondered the wisdom of investing any more. Already there were rumors that Becker was trying to negotiate terms with Whitman, that he was offering to trade his life for information about higher-ups. He was willing to squeal on the system.

No sooner had this appeared in print than Becker denied it. "I haven't anything to tell," he said. Governor Whitman denied it too. "I will not bargain with a convicted murderer."

The possibility of such a calamity must have frightened the Tammany brass. Cockran was brought back into the case and so was John McIntyre. Together they mapped an assault on the Federal Courts and on the U. S. Supreme Court.

Helen Becker visited her husband once a week. He was openly dispirited and she came away from these visits with a sense of hopelessness.

Describing her suffering to a friend, Mrs. Becker said it was at its worst not in moments of tragedy, such as a guilty verdict or a rejection by the higher courts; her life became unbearable only when she was alone. "When I realize I am living in a house that I no longer own, or when people come to try and cheer me up; they only impress upon me that I am alone, that there is nothing they can really do to help."

Her fellow teachers underlined her agony by giving a tea in her honor; vaguely, without an explanation of what they were honoring her for. She bore the maddening inconsequentials of it for nearly an hour, then ran from the room in tears.

"Religion is no help to me," she said. "My only source of strength is my love for my husband and the knowledge that he is innocent and that his innocence must be proven."

The staggering challenge of this last necessity came alive as she said it and her voice began to crack. She twisted her tiny hands in her lap and bit her lip.

"There is nothing in the world but the love you give and the love someone gives to you. If I do not get my husband back, I will die."

Despair seized Becker, too. A few days after the Court of Appeals turned him down, he sent this letter to his wife:

> My heart's blood,
> Your dear letters came and with them a whiff of cheer. As I hope to see you today, I shall say nothing except to tell you my heart cries out for you, for your love and your caresses. There is no way in which I can tell you all you are and have been to me. You are simply the flower of my life, the guiding star of my hopes and my comfort in my anguish of soul. This I know, my spirit shall ever hover near you until we meet in the green pastures beside the still waters in the great beyond.
> Your lover,
> Charlie

He had no sooner written it than Manton arrived at the Sing Sing death house with an idea and Becker's spirits revived.

"I think we can force Whitman to recognize that it's unfair for you to have to submit a plea for clemency to him when he is responsible for your conviction. In other words, his is not the dispassionate point of view. I am going to publicly request that he appoint the lieutenant governor to review your case and to entertain your petition for executive clemency."

Issuing pleas to anybody still rubbed Becker's pride raw. But he was less than a month from death and Manton obtained his consent. A second restorative came two days later when a condemned convict named Joseph Murphy, who occupied a death house cell near Becker, sent word that he could help him. Becker asked Manton to interview the man. Murphy said that while he was in the Tombs awaiting trial, Rose, Vallon and Webber were confined in cells nearby, that he frequently overheard them talking to each other. On the day they were transferred to the West Side Prison, Murphy said, he heard Rose say, "We haven't got a chance in the world, unless we frame

Becker. And since they can't convict an innocent man, we'll all get out."

Manton asked Murphy to send this information to the Governor in a letter. Murphy complied. The day he received the letter, Whitman had Murphy brought to him in Albany, shackled and in chains. Murphy was taken into the Governor's private office with only one guard and the Governor's aide present. The outer office was filled with reporters. When Murphy emerged half an hour later, his face a blank, the reporters assailed Whitman with questions. The aide answered them all with a single statement.

"The Governor," he said, "shook him like a terrier shakes a rat."

Whitman not only dismissed Murphy's revelations as immaterial, he also summarily refused to entertain Manton's proposal that the lieutenant governor, or an independent commission, review the case.

Through Manton, Mrs. Becker arranged to meet Bald Jack Rose, to beg him not to stand by while Becker was executed.

They met, of all places, in a jewelry store at Seventh Avenue near 43d Street, a jewelry store operated by the infamous Sam Schepps. Mrs. Becker would not reveal the substance of their conversation. In any case, it was brief. Schepps, who was present, told reporters that Rose was downright rude. He listened to Mrs. Becker for a moment and then cut her off.

Afterward, Rose explained: "I'd like to help her, but there's nothing I can do. Becker's as guilty as hell."

Mrs. Becker's efforts to save her husband grew frenzied and futile. She began to circulate a petition among the city's politicians but the few signatures she got were obviously of no value. McIntyre proposed a plan whereby Rose, Webber, and Vallon could admit their conspiracy and still escape prosecution. He asked Judge Seabury about it.

"If these men will admit they lied to escape punishment themselves, if they will admit it now to save an innocent man

294

from execution, will you guarantee them immunity from further prosecution?"

Seabury thought it over for several days, and finally indicated to McIntyre that something could be worked out, unprecedented as the proposal was. It was no use, though. Rose indignantly refused even to discuss it. Webber said it was ridiculous, that they had not lied.

On July 11, Cockran filed a petition for a writ of error before the United States Supreme Court and Whitman postponed the execution to the week of July 26 to give Becker's attorneys sufficient time to prepare this appeal. At the same time, Whitman turned down a routine request by Manton that Becker's sentence be commuted to life imprisonment. He also explained why he refused Manton's previous request, that Whitman appoint a commission of retired jurors to review the case. Whitman said he could not and would not abdicate the exclusive authority of his office.

The Supreme Court was not in session and could not, therefore, rule on Cockran's writ of error before the scheduled date of execution. Most of the justices had left Washington for the summer and were scattered over the country. At last, Cockran found Justice Charles Evans Hughes vacationing in Rangeley, Maine. He caught a train for the resort town and submitted the appeal to Justice Hughes in person. In the petition, Cockran had argued that the immunity agreements between the district attorney's office and Rose, Webber and Vallon were unconstitutional. The accused in a capital offense cannot be exonerated, he contended, by turning state's evidence.

Justice Hughes took the petition under submission for two days and then declined to give a ruling. "There is no substantial federal question involved," he wrote.

In these lengthening days of travail, Becker had returned to Catholicism. Father James Curry, assistant Catholic chaplain at Sing Sing, was with him daily and the two men became close friends.

"It is impossible to look into Charles Becker's eyes and not know that he is innocent," the priest told the press.

Two weeks before his scheduled execution, Becker's pride gave way. He announced that he would personally appeal to Whitman for executive clemency. He was not crawling, however. He wanted to be spared from death so that he would have a chance to prove his innocence and to bring to justice the real criminals.

At the same time, Becker's silent and unseen supporters in and around the Tammany councils decided that enough was enough. They cast Becker adrift. Even if Becker did squeal, which was doubtful, they calculated that accusations hurled by a doomed man would be regarded as hysterical gestures aimed at survival. They also calculated that Whitman was committed to the extermination of Becker and would never admit he might have convicted the wrong man.

Their reckoning, acute as ever, was shy one consideration. Becker still had hope. On July 21, 1915, Becker dragged Tammany, albeit backwards, into the case. He delivered to Governor Whitman, with copies to the press, a 10,000-word narrative which he had spent more than a month laboriously composing. He had intended it as a posthumous disclosure, but now that he was alone, and hopeful, he decided to use it on his own immediate behalf. It was an impressive revelation, forceful and full of pride, detailing his entire career with the New York Police Department and sketching the role that had been played by Big Tim Sullivan, the late and lamented Tammany boss. It was accompanied by a letter, almost as long, which began by pointing out that Becker did not believe he was enjoying the same Constitutional privileges accorded other doomed men whose convictions were subject to review by an impartial governor. In his own case, Becker wrote, executive review "must be the work of a man whose present political eminence is built upon my conviction and whose political future must depend on my execution." He reiterated his claim of innocence and for the next several pages, Becker tediously related his relationship with Bald Jack Rose, explaining as to a child the tenuous role of the stool pigeon in the enforcement of law and order. It was his long and frequent association with Rose, Becker pointed out, that was most circumstantially damning, ". . . yet surely you must realize that this association was not merely consistent with my duty as a policeman, but it was a most important element in enabling me to discharge efficiently the peculiar tasks assigned me. . . ." In other words, Rose was a superb stoolie, who could press other, lesser stoolies into service and thus preserve his own hide. It was only natural, he said, that to further protect himself, Rose would claim to be Becker's collector.

Had Becker stuck to demonstrating his innocence in the Rosenthal murder, he might have written a persuasive letter. But he went too far. He tried to make himself appear naïve, too. He painted a self-portrait that no one, except perhaps his wife, would ever have recognized. The only ring of truth came when he told about Big Tim Sullivan.

> I called to see Senator Sullivan at his office in the Shanley Building on the invitation of his half-brother, Lawrence Mulligan . . . That meeting was my first with the man so widely known as "Big Tim." Your Excellency may have some difficulty now in realizing the value which I then placed on this invitation to meet Mr. Sullivan, although your experience as district attorney must have made you familiar with the extraordinary power he wielded. His influence in the Police Department, no matter who might be its head, was believed to be unbounded. A policeman who succeeded in enlisting his favor was considered sure of promotion. Mr. Sullivan was the author of the law against carrying concealed weapons, enforcement of which was among the peculiar duties of my squad.
>
> To be assured that my manner of enforcing this law had impressed the Senator so favorably that he wanted to thank me personally for it, was, perhaps, the most agreeable and hopeful news ever imparted to me since I was appointed to the force. Sullivan told me that he was interested in Rosenthal's house to the amount of $12,500. Sullivan's munificence was undoubtedly

297

one source of his popularity. Any gambler who had been raided, or who had otherwise experienced hard fortune, could nearly always borrow money from him. . . .

. . . I think it by no means impossible that Rosenthal may have believed the $1,500 put in his house by Rose was really money advanced by me. Rosenthal would hardly have allowed Rose for the $1,500 a half interest in the establishment which had cost him at least $12,500 to equip, according to Sullivan's statement, unless Rose was believed to have contributed something else in addition. . . . The fury displayed by Rosenthal after the raid did not seem to me at all extraordinary. He was known to have boasted that he never failed "to get" any member of the force who had molested him. The publication in the *World* I regarded as the culmination of his efforts. . . .

After I had obtained authority from the Police Commissioner to institute a suit for libel against the *World* I was so little concerned about the matter that I proceeded with my wife to spend the day at Brighton Beach. On my return about one o'clock in the morning, my private telephone rang, and a man describing himself as Mr. Applebaum, Senator Sullivan's private secretary, said the Senator wanted to see me. He said the matter was urgent and the Senator must see me tonight and added, "I will call for you in about thirty minutes in an automobile and take you down to meet him." Mr. Applebaum appeared, accompanied by Jack Rose, and said the Senator was waiting at the Circle Theater. All three of us went to Sixtieth Street, where Sullivan stepped out of a limousine and invited me to his private office. We went up two flights of stairs, and on entering his room, he asked me, "What about this Rosenthal affair?" I said, "There's nothing of it." He said, "It must not be allowed to go any further. Rosenthal has gone so far now, he can't be stopped. He must be got away."

"That," I said at once, "would be the very worst thing could happen to us. Everybody would say that either you or I had caused his disappearance, and naturally it would seem that, if we induced him to leave, it must be because he had something discreditable to reveal. . . ."

The Senator answered, "Where a fire of this kind is started, there is no knowing where it will reach. Rosenthal has always been very close to me politically and personally, and once inquiry starts they reach into election matters. And secret investigations of elections by grand juries have always been sources of great trouble.

". . . Whatever happens in this row between you two, I want you to promise me that you will never mention the fact that I spoke to you about letting Rosenthal open." This promise I gave. He expressed very warm appreciation of my attitude, and coming downstairs, just as we emerged from the building, he said: "I would give $5,000—yes, $25,000—to have prevented this thing or to stop it now if I could." I did not pay much attention to the remark, but rejoined Mr. Applebaum and Rose in the other auto and went home to bed. . . .

Before my arrest, but after I had been transferred from Headquarters to duty at the 65th Precinct, Mr. Applebaum called on me twice. Once we met in the Captain's private room in the station house, and a few days later I met him at the south end of Washington Bridge. Each time his object was to convey a request from Senator Sullivan that whatever might happen I would make no mention either of the Senator's request about allowing Rosenthal to open a gambling house or of my having met him at the Circle Theater the evening before the murder. I answered if these informers, who all professed to be devoted followers of Sullivan, refrained from mentioning his name he could count on my silence. That promise I have kept until now. . . .

26. Epitaph for a Governor

WHEN Becker's letter and its appended preachment of innocence reached Albany, Governor Whitman was already keenly aware of the moral dilemma he would soon face, a dilemma that was growing in both meaning and effect. *The New York Times* had expressed it the same week in commenting editorially upon proposals and efforts Becker and his attorneys were making in the last desperate effort to stave off electrocution. Said *The New York Times:*

"Should the innocence, or even the partial innocence, of Charles Becker be demonstrated by a John Doe or any other legal proceeding, the position of Governor Whitman will be most extraordinary.

"The Governor's entire political standing is based upon the convictions in the Rosenthal murder case. His uncompromising determination to send the culprits, and above all, Becker, to the electric chair is the very stuff of which his reputation as an unflinching public servant and antagonist of evil is made up. It was the second conviction of Becker that made him governor. It would be most painful for him and his admirers to discover now that he has been the victim of blind zeal and misinformed prejudice. We refuse to give credence to such a theory without overwhelming proof."

The New York Times was articulating public sentiment. Popular faith had been invested in Whitman. What he had done had the prevailing sanction. The people were no more willing to believe they had duped themselves than Whitman was willing to admit to excessive zeal arising from ambition.

Worse, if this were true, the career to which he had given his life would end abruptly. Whitman and the public shut it out of their minds. As *The New York Times* put it, "We refuse to give credence to such a theory without overwhelming proof."

Even with proof, would Whitman give it credence? Already, the Governor's mailbox was beginning to sag with letters urging him to save Becker. There were some who wrote urging him to stand by his principles, but these would always be in a minority because they asked him to do what he had already pledged himself to do.

From a political standpoint, it was a problem of assessing the public sentiment. From a personal standpoint, it was a question of being able to live with himself in the years after Becker was gone and forgotten. Leaders who unjustly executed their enemies were no novelty. Whitman could only wonder about their consciences.

Becker was the basis for Whitman's rise to power. If he pardoned him, or commuted the sentence, on what grounds? Surely he could not admit that there existed reasonable doubt as to Becker's guilt. For that matter, was there any doubt? Becker had been convicted on the testimony of criminals, but criminals were the only witnesses available in a case like this. All of them had lied, at some time over some point; Whitman knew this. But he could not with certainty separate the lies from the truth. Neither could the liars. In the underworld, truth is relative and it is the relativity of it which is believed. One man's truth is another man's lie.

Perhaps it was enough that Becker was evil, represented

evil, directed evil, profited by evil. It was not Becker that was being destroyed, it was evil. Becker was not accused of being evil; only of having arranged a stupid murder. But Becker *was* evil. As long as he existed, evil existed and murder was an inherent part of evil; organized, commercialized evil, at any rate. Did Governor Charles Seymour Whitman have a choice? Was not his decision made for him by the entire sum and substance of his life?

He rudely denied Becker's plea for clemency. The condemned man's wordy document he dismissed. He was not impressed by it.

"A condemned man cannot challenge the authority of the Governor," he said. "As far as Becker's conviction is concerned, there was never a criminal case more perfectly proven in the annals of crime. I have never had any doubt about Becker's guilt. If I had any now I would pardon him."

This rigidity was expected by Cockran, by Manton and, in truth, by Becker; but Becker's plea was not intended to sway Whitman, it was intended to sway the public, to raise and spread the tide of sentiment they knew was running in Becker's favor. However, Whitman had sampled the tide and found it woefully weak by his own measure. Moreover, he was committed. He had always been committed. And now there was more to it than just Becker. Whitman had broken Tammany's overt grip on crime, he had jammed indefinitely the gears of New York's time-tested political-criminal machine, he had proven that there are limits to which any man, whatever his power, can defy the law. Becker's death would seal the matter.

If Whitman entertained any private doubts about Becker's guilt, he never shared this doubt with anyone. Soon it would be over. It was already the 23d of July. In three days Becker would be dead.

But on July 25, Manton filed a petition before Justice John Ford of the New York County Supreme Court asking for a new trial on the grounds of newly discovered evidence. Appended to the petition were a dozen affidavits from witnesses whose allegations, on the face of it, contained substantial proof of Becker's innocence. Among them:

Harry Applebaum, confidential secretary to Big Tim Sullivan, who testified to the Circle Theater conference between Becker and the boss; he said it was Rose who proposed killing Rosenthal and Becker angrily denounced the idea. "That's the worst thing you could do," he quoted Becker as saying.

Harry Cohen, alias Moe Levy, the cab driver named as the Harlem meeting chauffeur. It never happened, Cohen said.

Louis Harris, gambler, who said he was having a beer in Dollar John's saloon the day Rosenthal's exposé broke in the *World;* that Webber came in and said to Dollar John, "If you back Rosenthal up we'll take care of you like we're gonna take care of him."

Isaac Cohen, a gambler and Tammany minion, who swore to the existence of a note in the amount of $12,500 which Big Tim had lent Rosenthal to open the Hesper Club.

Edward C. Ginty, a gambler, testified that a fund of $6,000 was raised to buy off Rosenthal and get him out of town. It was his belief that Rose gave $1,000 of it to the gunmen for the killing and pocketed the remainder.

Governor Whitman granted Becker a stay to July 30 to allow Judge Ford time to rule. On July 27, Charles Plitt, whose treacherous testimony in the second trial helped convict the man he once served as a press agent, paid a mysterious call on the Governor's office. Whitman admitted him and they talked for half an hour. When he came out, Plitt was ashen. He returned to New York and immediately contacted some reporter acquaintances. He who had abandoned Becker for the district attorney now wanted to abandon the ex-district attorney for Becker. He was not, however, merely a recanting perjurer. His testimony at the trial had been the truth. He was just sorry he had given it. His only motive was to extricate himself from the Tombs and the coils of a perjury indictment. In making his deal with Whitman, he said, the district attorney had promised him that if he was elected Governor he would pardon Becker; that his sole desire was to obtain a conviction to facilitate his election. What did the Governor say, the reporters wanted to know?

"He told me he didn't recall any such conversation with me." Plitt appeared dazed.

Impeached Governor William Sulzer, who had publicly voiced the belief that Becker was the victim of a gangbuster's momentous zeal, expanded on this theme.

"Several of Becker's friends came to see me shortly after his conviction and at their urging I made a thorough investigation of the case myself. It was my belief that Becker was innocent and it was my intention to pardon him if the Court of Appeals upheld the conviction. In the meantime, of course, I was removed from office and the documents I had assembled in the case I inadvertently left in my office when I vacated it. I am sure Governor Whitman is in possession of these documents which, in my opinion, constitute ample grounds for pardoning Becker."

Whitman said he did not know of the existence of any such documents, that they were not in his office now nor had they ever been.

On the morning of July 29, Judge Ford, after two sleepless nights, handed down his ruling. It said in part:

"Newly discovered evidence, according to the code must (1) be such that it will change the result if a new trial is granted, (2) have been discovered since the trial, (3) be such that it could not have been discovered before the trial by due diligence, (4) be material to the issue, (5) not be merely cumulative to the former issue, (6) not merely impeach or contradict former evidence."

Most of the evidence in the affidavits, the Judge said, was not admissible under the rules of evidence; the remainder did no more than contradict or impeach trial evidence, and in any case it all had been available and should have been introduced by Becker at his trial. Judge Ford understood Becker's pledge

304

to keep Big Tim's name out of the case, but the law did not provide for such pacts.

Therefore, said Judge Ford, "as I have studied the authorities and examined the affidavits the conviction has grown upon me that a new trial could not be granted without disregarding the law and usurping the functions of another department of government (the executive).

"The motion is denied."

Bald Jack Rose seemed vaguely outraged over the introduction of Big Tim Sullivan's name and memory, and the sinister influences it connoted.

"What's all this talk about Sullivan and the system? There ain't no system, no system but Becker's. I collected $10,000 a week for him and, outside of what he gave me, he kept the rest. He didn't share it with anybody. The only system in New York was Becker's system. Sullivan wasn't the boss, Becker was the boss."

Within moments after he had been notified of Ford's denial, Manton was on the phone to the Governor's office. He spoke to Major John Stanley Moore, the Governor's military secretary.

"Mrs. Becker would like to see the Governor," Manton said, simply.

"I'm afraid that won't be possible," Moore replied.

"Her husband will be executed in less than 24 hours," said Manton. "I do not believe the Governor's refusal to see her now will add to his stature as the chief executive of the state."

There was a long silence during which Moore apparently left the phone. Manton seemed puzzled. He kept calling "Hello" into the mouthpiece. He was about to hang up when Moore returned.

"The Governor will see Mrs. Becker in his office at 2 o'clock this afternoon," he said.

Manton did not accompany her. Instead, he sent his young associate, John B. Johnstone. They caught a late morning train and arrived in Albany shortly before 2 P.M. Mrs. Becker was dumb with grief and terror. She wore a white silk suit with black trimming. Her face was lined and ashen. She walked woodenly, as though with each step her life was ebbing.

Mrs. Becker and Johnstone arrived at the Governor's mansion to find that he had left nearly two hours earlier for Peekskill, down the Hudson, to review a military pageant.

"But he promised to see me," Mrs. Becker said, hollowly. To agony was now added frustration. The Governor's secretary could offer no explanation. He knew nothing, he said, about the matter. He suggested Mrs. Becker go to Peekskill, perhaps the Governor would see her there. He was sorry, he said.

It was nearly 6 P.M. before they reached Peekskill only to find that the Governor had gone to a hotel in Poughkeepsie to spend the night. They found him in the Nelson House and Major Moore met them at the door to the Governor's suite.

"The Governor expresses his sincerest apologies," Moore said, gravely. "When I spoke to you this morning I did not know that he had made previous commitments he was unable to postpone. He will see you now."

Johnstone helped Mrs. Becker to a seat in the corridor and went in alone. He remained an hour. When he came out, beckoning to Mrs. Becker, she could not stand. Johnstone and Moore helped her to her feet and she walked awkwardly, testing the floor before her.

Whitman stood in the middle of the room, nodding his head in a bow as Mrs. Becker entered. His hands were clasped behind his back. When he spoke his voice was soft and solemn. This was his last ordeal. If he could withstand it, he and his beliefs would have survived. Major Moore and Johnstone stood immediately behind Mrs. Becker, strangely alert and apprehensive. Mrs. Becker's arms hung by her sides, in one hand a small black purse. She looked at the Governor but did not seem to see him. He spoke first.

"I am ready, Mrs. Becker, to hear anything you have to say which you feel will help your husband." Is it possible that for an instant he pictured his own wife in such a role? When Mrs.

Becker did not respond immediately, he spoke again. There was urging, with a suggestion of sympathy.

"You may have the fullest confidence that anything you tell me will remain . . ."

Abruptly, Mrs. Becker found her voice. She seemed to have been summoning strength and when it came she spoke.

"I have come only to ask that you give us time to review Judge Ford's decision. It was only rendered this morning. I'm sure you realize my position . . ."

She paused, tried to clear her throat. Whitman waited, his face impassive. She opened her mouth but no sound came. She looked away. Her eyes filled with tears and without warning she fell to the floor on her knees sobbing, sobbing, sobbing.

Whitman moved toward her, then stopped. His eyes met Moore's. The Major shook his head slowly from side to side. Whitman quietly left the room. Johnstone and Moore waited. At last they helped Mrs. Becker to her feet. Her eyes were swollen almost shut. They helped her to a chair where for several minutes she sat crying quietly. It was over.

At the railroad station, Johnstone found that the next train due would not reach Ossining until early morning. He and Mrs. Becker took a cab. They pulled up to the gates of Sing Sing after a ride that neither could remember, at midnight. The fare was $18. Mrs. Becker was taken to the office of Warden Thomas Osborne. The warden, like his predecessor an opponent of capital punishment, had fled to New York leaving the prison in command of his deputy, Charles Johnson. In the death house, both Becker and the prison were preparing for death. The execution had been scheduled for 5:45 A.M. Becker sat huddled and withdrawn in his cell, now stripped of all but the bed. He wore the traditional coarse black garb. Beside him was Father James Curry, his head bent over a Missal from which he read, softly and in toneless Latin, the aged words of unction.

Johnson appeared unnoticed at the cell door.

"Mrs. Becker is here," he said.

Becker reared up. Father Curry saw the expression of terror and gently took Becker's hand, holding it. Becker looked at the priest in bewilderment. Johnson unlocked the cell door. At the sound Becker arose, not of his own volition, but drawn erect by a force he could not know. He must go, it seemed. He must die twice; now in the eyes of his wife, afterward in the eyes of justice. Johnson and Father Curry supported him, two guards trailing them, on the long walk across the prison yard.

There is, of course, no record of this last goodbye. Johnson was present but, out of friendship for Becker, he refused to say how, or even whether, this fragile, grief-drained woman, who would never understand why fate had scoured her life of all meaning, came to terms with the meticulous irrationality of the electric chair. For Becker, the burden was the greater; to prepare both himself and his wife for death. For his own despair, he would drift into the litany of the Church. He had nothing else to offer his wife. They were together an hour. Between then and the bright, warm July dawn, Becker sat on his bed, Father Curry at his side, and wrote letters of farewell. He wrote with a furious intensity of purpose, to consume as rapidly as possible, the remainder of his life.

Jack (Jacob Reich) Sullivan, whom he addressed as "My dear, loyal friend," he begged "to do all in your power to clear my name . . . and if there is ever anything you can do to help my loyal, brave, faithful, loving wife, I pray you to do so. No better woman ever lived. I shall now bid you a last loving and fond farewell. May God bless you and keep you and yours from all harm is my prayer." He signed it, "Your grateful friend."

To Father Curry, he bequeathed pathetically his gratitude "for a loyalty as a friend and spiritual adviser that few men can pride themselves as having known. I feel, though I may be mistaken, that I am a better man for knowing you. I am tired of the world and its injustice to me; my happy life is ruined." Of the priest, Becker also asked help for his wife. This letter he signed simply, "Your tired friend."

308

Becker also wrote his dying declaration. In it he swore again his innocence, and he beseeched God to pardon all those who had thus wronged him. "And now, on the brink of death, I declare to the world that I am proud to have been the husband of the purest, noblest woman that ever lived, Helen Becker. This acknowledgment is the only legacy I can leave her."

To Governor Whitman, Becker penned a woeful cry: "Not all the judges in this state, nor in this country, nor the Governor of this state, nor all of them combined, can destroy permanently the character of an innocent man."

At 5 A.M., Becker took Holy Communion and then was given the last rites of the Catholic Church. At 5:40 they came for him. He turned again to the priest. "I am sacrificed for my friends," he said.

Unhurried, unmoved, Father Curry proceeded with his final responsibilities.

"Do you leave this world, Charles Becker, bearing malice toward anyone?"

"I forgive them all," Becker cried out. "And to those I have wronged, I beg forgiveness."

The distance from his cell to the execution chamber was less than fifty feet, less than a minute's walking time, but how far is fifty feet and how long is a minute to a man for whom it remains the only barrier to death, to a man who has lived only so that he may die?

Father Curry, his voice firm and clear in recitation, walked by Becker's side, the doomed man intent on every word of which he understood none. He grasped at sounds. The priest left him at the chamber and joined Deputy Warden Johnson in the little room adjoining which held the thirty witnesses, several of them newspapermen. Father Curry and Johnson made no move to stem their tears, nor to wipe them away. They watched through the small glass panels as Becker was strapped into the tall, black chair, but only for a moment. They turned away.

Inside the chamber, on a thick rubber mat, stood Father

309

William Cashin, the chaplain, and Dr. Charles Farr, the prison physician, a stethoscope swaying from his ears. Their eyes were dry of tears but their faces were blank with horror. Tears, however, washed the eyes of Frank O'Toole, the guard who now was fixing the electrodes and the straps to Becker's legs, his chest, and his head over which O'Toole gently lowered the black hood. Becker's hands moved. There was a crackle in his throat. O'Toole, who had turned to leave, stopped and waited. Becker was trying to speak. O'Toole waited. There was a stir of uneasiness among the witnesses. Johnson glanced through the glass. What was the delay? At last Becker spoke, husky, raw, distant; the words hurried, pushed together.

"Thank you, Frank, for the favors you have shown me and Mrs. Becker." O'Toole reached down, gripped Becker's hand quickly and left the chamber, wiping at his eyes.

Johnson and the priest were staring at each other, waiting. Nothing happened. There was a scuffle in the chamber. Johnson turned to look. O'Toole had returned. The strap around Becker's chest had been placed over his arms instead of under them. O'Toole fumbled interminably. Becker's hands twitched and clutched at the arms of the chair. Father Curry began to pray. Father Cashin had closed his eyes and was praying too. From the chamber came another prayer, uttered by the empty, rasping voice of death.

"Jesus, Mary and Joseph . . ."

Dr. Farr signaled with his hand and the first surge of current severed Becker's voice as it threw him against the straps. His head dropped but it was still moving, nodding convulsively. Dr. Farr stepped forward, ripped open Becker's shirt and applied the stethoscope. The heart still beat. Dr. Farr stepped back onto the mat and signaled again. Another charge of current. The leather straps creaked with the pressure of Becker's big body. For ten seconds. "God!" swore Johnson softly. The satanic whine of the dynamo stopped and Dr. Farr stepped forward again. He listened again. He signaled again. Becker was still alive. The doctor had prescribed another measure of 2500 volts. Sweat congealed on the faces of the witnesses. A few began to look away. The others stared on, hypnotized by the spectacle. The whine stopped at last. The witnesses scurried to leave. Few of them heard Dr. Farr announce that Charles Becker was dead.

In a Bronx funeral parlor, a brass plate three inches long and two inches wide lay on the mortician's desk. It was to have been placed on the head of Becker's coffin, but the mortician had checked with the police. The brass plate would not be used. Etched boldly on it were the words, CHARLES A. BECKER, MURDERED JULY 30, 1915, BY GOVERNOR WHITMAN.

Becker was pronounced dead at 5:53 A.M.

In Albany, Governor Whitman, who had been tossing fretfully in his bed, finally fell into a deep sleep.

In New York, various clocks and watches registered the time and signaled the end of various all-night vigils.

In the Tammany clubrooms on East 14th Street, Boss Charles F. Murphy and a group of subordinates sat staring in silence at a large clock on the wall. They waited until 6 A.M. when Murphy arose from his chair and reached for his hat. "I guess it's over," he said.

And there is a story that in Jack's restaurant off Broadway, another group sat waiting, less patiently, perhaps. Their eyes were focused on a large gold watch resting in the middle of the bright white tablecloth. The watch belonged to Arnold Rothstein, the gambler. It was never wrong. At exactly 5:45 A.M., Rothstein picked up the watch, snapped shut its cover and dropped it deftly into his pocket. He touched the man next to him, Nicky Arnstein, and together they stood, stretched and moved leisurely away from the table.

"Well," Rothstein announced tonelessly, "that's it."

The others followed and, as at all these gatherings around Manhattan, they put on their hats and walked out into the dawn of a new day and a new era; an era which Charlie Becker had conceived and which he had been forced, before its birth, to deliver into the custody of others. The System would go on.

Epilogue

BECKER'S EXECUTION festered in the public conscience for several years and the question of his guilt remained among the most durable of barroom arguments. Mrs. Becker undertook several abortive campaigns to clear her husband's name and at one point announced she intended to sue Governor Whitman. She never did. In addition to Becker's legacy of love for his wife, he also left her several thousand dollars in debts which, over the years, she paid out of her meager teacher's salary. She never remarried, although she had several proposals. "I prefer to remain a widow," she said, "in memory of a man who was put to death by the great State of New York for a crime he did not commit."

The memory of Becker lingered, too, in Whitman's shadow and his stock among the voters of New York dropped steadily. To Franklin P. Adams, the reason was not so much Becker as Whitman himself. "His ambition has been a fetter to his greatness," he wrote. In the end, talk of Whitman for President waned in the state's Republican councils. Whitman served two creditable terms as Governor but when he tried for his third term in 1918, a Tammany man defeated him; the Tammany

313

man was Alfred E. Smith, whom the voters found human if not energetically moralistic. As Tammany Boss Dick Croker used to say, "maybe the people can't stand corruption, but they can't stand reform either."

Whitman not only failed to make the Presidency, he was unable to break again into any public office, even that of district attorney. He returned to private practice, served a term as president of the American Bar Association and helped form the anti-Tammany fusion forces which elected La Guardia in 1933. Two years later, Whitman was appointed to the New York Port Authority where he served with inconspicuous distinction for ten years. He died in 1947 in his rooms at the University Club on West 54th Street at the age of seventy-eight.

Bald Jack Rose, tiring of unsuccessful authorship and bored with evangelism, moved to Long Island and went into the catering business. His name, however, remained on Broadway in the form of a cocktail, the formula for which, unfortunately, perished during prohibition. The other informers who, like Rose, had doomed Becker to save themselves, also wandered into socially respectable occupations and, in general, prospered. However, they had many disagreements among themselves over the years and became bitter enemies.

The case branded Tammany with a mark of supreme corruption which time failed to erase altogether. The Tiger recovered only enough of its power to become New York's perennial motive for reform.

Bibliography

The Rosenthal–Becker case, as it came to be known, retained a singular fascination for the newspapers of New York for slightly more than three years and some aspect of it was discussed or reported almost daily, frequently on the front pages. There were a dozen daily newspapers competing spiritedly with each other in New York at the time and this may help to explain the contradictory coverage given the case. I relied primarily on *The New York Times,* the *Tribune* and the *World* whose accounts of the Becker–Whitman struggle agreed more consistently in fact. Public attitudes toward the case are preserved in the memories of a few surviving New Yorkers and in the editorials which abounded in such magazines of the period as *Collier's, Literary Digest, Outlook, Nation, New Republic, Harper's Weekly, McClure's, Century* and *Forum.* This entire interval in American history, from the turn of the century to World War I, is a somewhat neglected one but I have included here a list of books which concern themselves with this era and its dominant personalities and, to some extent, the case itself.

Asbury, Herbert—*The Gangs of New York,* New York, Garden City Publishing Co., 1928; *Sucker's Progress,* New York, Dodd Mead & Co., 1938.

Crane, Milton—*The Sins of New York*, New York, Boni & Gaer, 1947.

Katcher, Leo—*The Big Bankroll*, New York, Harper & Bros., 1958.

Lynch, Denis—*Boss Tweed*, New York, Boni & Liveright, 1927.

Parkhurst, Charles—*Our Fight With Tammany*, New York, Scribner's, 1895.

Pink, Louis—*Gaynor—The Tammany Mayor Who Swallowed the Tiger*, New York, The International Press, 1931.

Smith, Mortimer—*William Jay Gaynor*, Chicago, H. Regnery & Co., 1951.

Steffans, Lincoln—*Autobiography*, New York, Harcourt Brace & Co., 1931.

Stoddard, Theodore—*Master of Manhattan*, New York, Longmans, Green & Co., 1931.

Sullivan, Mark—*Our Times*, New York, Scribner's, 1927.

Tebbel, John—*The Life and Good Times of William Randolph Hearst*, New York, E. P. Dutton & Co., 1952.

Thompson, Craig—*Gang Rule in New York*, New York, The Dial Press, 1940.

Tully, Andrew—*Era of Elegance*, New York, Funk & Wagnalls, 1947.

Werner, M. R.—*Tammany Hall*, Garden City, N.Y., Doubleday, Doran & Co., 1928; *It Happened in New York*, New York, Coward-McCann Inc., 1957.